NO COMPROMISE.

The Life Story of Keith Green

NO COMPROMISE.

The Life Story of Keith Green

by **Melody Green** and David Hazard

Foreword by Winkie Pratney
Memories of Keith by Leonard Ravenhill

A SPARROW PRESS BOOK
THE SPARROW CORPORATION
CHATSWORTH, CA
1989

Table of Contents

Dedicated to
Rachel Hope   Rebekah Joy   Dawn Michele
In loving memory of
Keith Green
one of a kind who served One of a kind
and
Bethany Grace and Josiah David

Once upon a time, in a generation steeped in much emptiness and spiritual darkness, a boy was born who was given a great gift. Deeply talented, trained as a musician, he had a unique ability (some would later say genius) to take spiritual truth and put it in the language and vocabulary of the common people of his time.

His biographical writings (now available for others to see) record the intensity of his struggles, his early odyssey into pathways that promised so much but sadly led nowhere. These records chronicle the search of a young man seemingly out of step with his age—who was not afraid to risk everything for what he had found to be real and right. He was nothing if he was not intense—and in that intensity, he questioned everything and everyone that seemed to hold a key to life and reality. And once he found that Answer (as we know now he did), nothing could turn him from it.

That commitment given, he began a lifelong crusade to see his world likewise transformed. No one who knew him would deny that he offended many. He often especially shocked established religious people in his youthful zeal to bring compassion, honesty, and reality back to the Church. Perhaps the truest practical test of a real prophet is this; "Does he make me uncomfortable?" If he does, he probably is. If he doesn't, he probably isn't. After all, you never read in the Bible of a popular prophet except the false ones who always went around telling people the things they wanted to hear.

He was blunt, he was funny, he was tactless, and sometimes even crude. He steadfastly refused to accept the spiritual status quo. He quietly mocked hypocrisy with laughter while he laid bare his own struggles and fears with tears. Many of his songs are simply sermons set to music—prophetic pieces in harmony that set standards for a generation. He was controversial. He was criticized. He was cut off by some and almost canonized by others—but he was impossible to ignore. His life and his work literally affected millions around the world. Although gone from us now, he impacted his generation like a spiritual H-bomb, and the reverberations of his life, courage, and commitment will still be felt for generations to come.

Most people today who have never before had the opportunity to read his writings and journals know him only by his music. (After all, not everyone can write a song that will still be sung five centuries after his death!) We remember him today as the man who launched the Reformation; the musician with the hunger to know God and to make Him known by faith; the man called Martin Luther.

And this, of course, is not his story. But in another century, another culture, and in another country, with not as much time to accomplish a task, on a smaller scale, it might have been. Keith loved Jesus. He did what he could in the few intense years I was privileged to know him. If you have never had the opportunity to share in the life of someone like him who LIVED for Jesus, you will catch a glimpse of that love in this, his story. He was my friend. I miss him. Thanks, Mel, for this "inside track."

Winkie Pratney
May 1989

"One Day You're Up . . ."

At the Bla Bla Cafe.

NYTHING CAN HAPPEN ON THE STREETS OF HOLLYWOOD. I'D seen some pretty wild things, but never anything so bizarre as what I saw one night on Ventura Boulevard.

As Keith and I walked out of The Bla Bla Cafe, a blast of hot night air hit us in the face. It was after 2 a.m., but the street was still awake with activity. Four drag queens swept by us, followed by a couple in disco outfits, all headed inside for a late-night breakfast. Next door, the watchdogs at Bruno's Corvette Repairs were pacing inside their chain-linked fence, barking at everything that moved—including us. Keith had played three sets tonight, and we were headed for home, exhausted. I was glad to see "Victor", our VW van with its hippie-style, Indian print curtains, parked at the curb.

Keith had been performing at The Bla—as it was affectionately known to its regulars—for almost a year. It was a small showcase nightclub in the San Fernando Valley, just down the road from Hollywood. The Bla spotlighted showbiz hopefuls and was frequented by talent scouts from big record companies. Keith was one of those hopefuls. But tonight, he'd given it his all one more time—and now we were leaving, still *un*discovered.

As Keith walked around the front of the van, I opened the passenger door. That was when we spotted a figure, looming toward us out of the dark. It was Harmony.

Harmony looked like a gruff mountain-man with his brown scraggly hair and beard. Here we were in 1974, but this guy struck us as someone caught in a '60s time warp. He was calm and easy. All he talked about was peace, love and living off the land. He wasn't a close friend, but he and Keith had gotten stoned together once.

"Hey—how's it goin'?" Keith called. He shut his door again and stepped back on the sidewalk.

Sleepily, I leaned my head back, knowing I was in for a wait. Inevitably, most of our conversations drifted toward spiritual experiences these days. Keith and I had tried a lot of things—a *lot* of things. Recently, we'd been looking into Jesus Christ. We weren't Christians. Church was a dead institution to us. But Jesus *did* seem to be a spiritual Master of some sort, and we had a degree of respect for his life and teachings.

Sure enough, Keith and Harmony immediately began talking about the supernatural. It was just a typical conversation—for people who were into drugs and the mystical. Which was a lot of the people we knew.

"I've been reading about Jesus lately," Keith was saying. "He was a pretty radical person."

Harmony's eyes seemed to brighten—then, slowly, a strange look came over his face. His eyes got misty and distant. Very calmly, he said, "I *am* Jesus Christ."

Keith reacted like he'd been stung by a scorpion. Without missing a beat, he shot back, "Beware of the false prophets who come to you in sheep's clothing, but inwardly are ravenous wolves!" I recognized the quote as something Jesus had said. What happened next was really hard to believe.

Harmony's eyes grew wide. Then they narrowed to slits, furrows creased across his forehead, and his bushy eyebrows knit together. A sneer came over his usually mild face, and his upper lip curled back, exposing yellow smoke-stained teeth. Leaning toward Keith, his teeth bared, he let out a growl that started in the throat, like that of a wolf, and ended with the horrible hissing sound of a snake.

It happened in only seconds. Harmony's face relaxed. But his eyes looked confused. Embarrassed. The hiss seemed to hang in the still night air.

My skin was still tingling from the shock. Keith had obviously been rocked by it, too. He looked from Harmony to me with wide eyes. This *was* Hollywood—but things like this only happened in the movies. I wondered what Keith was thinking.

It was like someone or something took control of Harmony momentarily, using him for its own purposes. Then just as quickly, it discarded him—leaving him to pick up the pieces in confused embarrassment. Dazed, Harmony mumbled something. But Keith quickly excused himself, jumped into Victor and shoved the key in the ignition.

As we drove home over the dark streets, we kept looking at each other in disbelief. Keith was more animated than usual. He kept saying, "Did he *really* do that? I can't believe it!"

We talked about nothing else until we crawled into bed and fell asleep, sometime after 3:30 a.m.

The weird experience with Harmony did have one major effect on us. It brought some things into sharp focus. Namely, that there was, indeed, a very real spiritual realm—a realm full of power and possibly even danger. We were just coming to a deeper realization that there must be spiritual forces beyond our knowing. Had we heard a voice from that other side, speaking through Harmony? Or was it just the "voice" of the age? After all, a lot of musicians, artists and writers—the "beautiful" people—were saying things like, "You are your own god. There is no right or wrong."

But we wondered: Is there a dark side and a light side to spiritual energy?

Keith and I had both been caught up in a search to find our "spiritual identities" for some time. We were looking for truth— whatever it was—and our search for light had taken us both on many strange paths, from Buddhism to stuff like astral projection and, of course, drugs. We were both convinced "the truth" was hidden out there somewhere like a pearl in the ocean, and that when we found it, it would fill an empty spot in our hearts. That it would make life really worth living. Until then every day held the potential of being the day of the great revelation.

At the time of our weird encounter with Harmony however, we'd been slipping a bit, losing hope, and even dabbling with drugs again—which we'd sworn off, but kept falling back into.

Our spiritual ambitions never kept us out of the fog for long. In fact, the constant lure of those other "voices" had pretty well convinced us there *was* a dark and a light side. After Harmony, Keith, with his usual all-or-nothing manner, was determined to know how to tell the difference. Although we never forgot the incident outside The Bla, there were more pressing matters. Like Keith's all-consuming dream.

In particular, our whole life revolved around Keith's drive to make it big in the music business. Now that he was performing at The Bla, we lived with the constant hunger that the "right" person would walk in one night and "discover" *Keith Green*.

The Bla was just down Ventura Boulevard from The Queen Mary, and Keith's audience was always seasoned with gays and straights alike. Neither camp seemed to mind the other. To be honest, it was often difficult to tell who belonged where. The biggest standouts were the drag queens, sweeping in wearing satin dresses, jangly jewels and high-styled wigs with only their exaggerated feminine gestures and five o'clock shadows shining through heavy layers of make-up to betray their true gender.

Keith's family, and my mom, lived here in southern California. But The Bla was like a second home to us. The people, family. Even though Keith's last set ended at 1 a.m., we often stayed until Albie, the owner, closed the doors three hours later. Keith and Albie would lift a table onto the empty stage and we'd get a foursome together, shuffling the cards for a lot of laughs and a hot game of Bid-Whist. Sometimes a gang from The Bla got together on Sunday afternoons to play softball.

Albie, who was in his forties, took pride in running a successful club and in rubbing shoulders with the "almost-elite" of Hollywood's underside. He doted like a mother hen over his performers, and expected the audience to give each act full attention. Albie had also become a friend and mentor to Keith. That's why his sudden ultimatum threw Keith for such a loop.

It came one Wednesday night after Keith's third set. People-wise, the turnout had been disappointing. Wednesday wasn't the greatest night, of course, but it was a start. Albie's eyes were kind, his manner fatherly as usual when he came up to our table. Then he lowered the boom.

"I'm sorry Keith, but you've got two weeks to pack 'em in—or I'll have to replace you with another act."

"You're kidding," Keith said in surprise. I felt a stab of rejection, too.

"I'm not. If you want your own night," Albie said, "you gotta

—
4

draw more people. I've got a club to run. Salaries to pay. I'm sorry, Keith, but I just can't afford to keep losing money on you."

We couldn't believe our ears. Keith went home that night deeply depressed. Even the Quaalude he took to soothe his bruised feelings couldn't touch the real hurt—the whispers of failure. It seemed to me that the worst part about performing was having to sell yourself. Being so vulnerable. When you don't measure up, nothing eases the sickening feeling that maybe it's not just your "act" that isn't good enough. Maybe it's you.

After Albie's ultimatum Keith sprang into immediate action. He was never one to take a challenge lying down. Starting on Thursday, he spent all week phoning everyone and anyone he knew. He almost begged them to come, telling them about all his new songs, how he wanted to see them—and how he was going to lose his job unless the place was packed. I felt embarrassed for him—and even worse when he insisted I call my friends as well! But we were in a terrible bind.

Keith had already pitched himself to every major record label in town. That resulted in some nibbles. One company had flown us to New York. Nothing materialized. Keith had even tried to sing on a Grand Funk "sound alike" record, but didn't sound enough alike. And there were some more nibbles—but not bites. Money was tight and getting tighter.

We'd already sold my red Triumph sports car and my prized Martin D-35 guitar. My savings account had breathed its last. So to supplement our small income from The Bla—sometimes less than $15—Keith clenched his teeth and played proms, parties and banquets. It was the bottom of the barrel for any serious artist, but the word for us in 1974 was *survival*. And now the threat of getting fired from The Bla Bla—a small potatoes club as Hollywood nightspots go—would be the final humiliation.

The following Wednesday, we walked into The Bla about 8:30 p.m., feeling quiet apprehension. I looked around and was struck with how empty this place could look.

The Bla was dark and narrow inside, with a small stage to the right as you walked in the front door. The bar, which was too small for anyone to sit at, ran across the back, right in front of the tiny, one-man kitchen. The most consistent thing about the decor was its inconsistency. Absolutely nothing matched. Between the stage and the bar was a collection of banged-up wooden tables. On the walls, huge dragonflies in vivid yellows and oranges hung beside oversized photos autographed by "sorta knowns." When packed, The Bla could hold about sixty-five people, seated on chrome-

and-vinyl chairs—the kind you'd find around a formica table in someone's kitchen in the 1950s. Right now those chairs were mostly empty.

Only a few patrons sat in quiet conversation as Keith nervously eyed the stage. Albie was getting a check ready at one of the tables. The cook and the two waiters, Eddie and "Mr. Sally", were at the back bar, the only others in the whole place. Albie caught Keith's eye. Neither one said anything. But it was a knowing glance—tonight was it.

Keith and I sat silently in the back of the skinny little club, watching each other watch the door. We certainly looked like West Coast musicians, if nothing else. Married for only eight months, we made quite a pair. Me, in my Indian print skirt, embroidered gauze blouse and long straight hair. And Keith, wearing blue jeans and a new flowered cowboy shirt. His long curly ponytail had recently been left on the hair stylist's floor. What remained had been layered into a new California style called The Shag—short for shaggy. Even freshly cut, his hair still hung well below his shoulders. I silently admired his new professional image. Less hippie . . . but still very hip.

Slowly, in twos and threes, people started arriving. One cigarette after another was lit, and spirals of blue smoke curled gracefully to the ceiling. As the chairs filled, the noise level began to rise. Chairs scraped against the cement floor. Loud laughter punctuated conversations. Eddie, the head waiter, clipped his orders to the revolving wheel and the smell and sizzle of burgers drifted from the tiny kitchen.

Still there weren't enough people and we knew it. "Mr. Sally" stepped over to our table to take my order, wearing his usual get-up—a custom-made T-shirt with a portrait of him in a bouffant hairdo with "Mr. Sally" scrawled across the front in fancy white script and a few well-placed rhinestones. I wasn't very hungry, so I ordered Guac-And-Papa's—fried potato slices with a bowl of guacamole. Would any of our friends bother to show up? Keith's first hour-long set started at 9 p.m. We had only ten minutes to go.

Keith's right leg was bouncing nervously. He was all raw energy and ready to start. More tense minutes ticked by.

"Do I look O.K.?" he asked, poking at his hair.

"You look great, honey," I assured him.

I loved the way Keith looked. His clear blue eyes and fair skin gave him a pure, almost childlike air. And now that he'd shaved off his beard, the fact that he was just twenty years old was very plain.

"It's 8:58," Keith said, breaking into my thoughts. "Where *is* everybody?" He was all wound up and ready to pop.

I tried to calm him down a bit.

"They'll be here in a few minutes," I responded, trying to conceal my own fears. "We've got a little more time. . . ."

"There is no more time. This is it." Keith shoved back his chair, with disappointment written all over him. Yet I sensed his determination. He was a fighter, and even though the odds were against him I knew Keith would give it his all.

Albie had started to pace in the back as Keith made his way to the stage and sat at the battered upright piano. He squinted into the single spotlight and, leaning toward the microphone, spoke in mock military fashion.

"Ladies and gentlemen . . . and *others*. I'd like to interrupt your rambling conversation for some music."

Keith started doodling on the piano, but few people in the scant crowd paid attention. Keith fidgeted in his seat while his fingers wandered over the keys for a few moments. I could tell he was trying to figure out what to play. He finally launched into "Life Goes On"—a song he'd just written with his new friend Randy Stonehill:

> *Marvin was a connoisseur of twenty-cent wine.*
> *You could see him bummin' nickels down on Sunset and Vine.*
> *One day his wealthy uncle passed away in Bel Air.*
> *And now he's sippin' from a vintage year.*
> *Marvin's sippin' from a vintage year!*

Then the chorus:

> *Life goes on and the world goes 'round.*
> *One day you're up, the next day you're down.*
> *Don't count on good luck, there's nothing to say except,*
> *"Thank you, Lord, for another day!"*

The funny lyrics and funky rhythm grabbed everyone's attention. Keith pounded the keys in a way that sent terror into the heart of every piano teacher he ever had. I often held my breath hoping he wouldn't miss a note, but even when he did it didn't matter. It wasn't perfection that drew you to Keith's music, or to him for that matter. It was heart.

A few more tables were filling up. And to my relief, some were clapping along as Keith rolled into the second verse:

There was a famous senator that everyone knew.
One day a sly reporter found a girl in his room.
The re-election survey said that he'd make a kill—
But now he's washing dishes down at Joe's Bar and Grill.
He makes his famous speeches now at Joe's Bar and Grill!

The chorus came around again and people began to sing
with enthusiasm, imitating Keith's comical gestures. Keith sang,
"One day you're up"—pointing to the ceiling. Then plunged his
thumb toward the floor as he shook his head and sang, "Next day
you're down. . . ." The night was coming alive.

Eddie danced his orders down the narrow aisles, balancing
tray-loads of shish-ka-bobs, burgers, and beer above his head. Mr.
Sally ran a fork across the soda fountain grates, and I kept
rhythm by playing my water glass with a spoon. More tables filled
as Keith played his second and third numbers. I had yet to see
any of our friends—but then a movement at the door caught my
eye. It was our Jewish friend, Michelle Brandes, whom I
recognized even in the dim light. A birth defect had left her with
a pronounced limp. She made her way slowly through the smoky
haze and sat beside me.

Still, I was paying far more attention to the door than to
Keith. He kicked into Joni Mitchell's song, "Free Man In Paris,"
and I could tell he was starting to relax a little. Since I was
wondering where all our friends were, I felt especially tuned into
the message of the song.

"Free Man In Paris" tells the story of a record company exec
on vacation in Paris who was tired of cranking out hit artists—
"Stoking the starmaker machinery behind the popular song."
Another part says, "I was a free man in Paris, I felt unfettered and
alive. Nobody calling me up for favors, nobody's future to decide."

Keith had become all too familiar with the "starmaker
machinery"—the record companies, producers, publishers and
agents—and all the fighting over "who gets what" of various
royalty rights. When an artist becomes a hit, he's a "hot property"
and then everybody "loves him" as they clamor for their piece of
the pie. Until then though, you just look for connections and wait
for your "big break". And the gears of the machinery are oiled
with the tears of countless hopeful artists who never get their
break. I loved Joni Mitchell's music, and this song was one of my
favorites. But it made me shudder.

Keith's fear of not succeeding was overshadowed only by the
fear of blowing it—of getting involved with the wrong people out
of desperation.

As I glanced around the smoky room I thought, "Someone could be here right now who could help Keith in a big way." But then, there were some people whose help we definitely didn't want.

Like the guy last September. He heard Keith at The Bla and just flipped. Keith later met with him in his fancy Hollywood office, and the guy was bubbling over with "I-can-make-you-a-star" noises. Here was a voice promising the success and stardom Keith wanted. But, as Keith confided to his daily journal, a log he kept for years, there was—as usual—a string attached:

He's very rich and he has a big name in the business. He's also incredibly gay and I felt him vibing on me. Even though he could do a lot for me—bread and contact wise—I gave a "nay" to working with him.

And that wasn't the first time a record company executive tried to "hit" on Keith. Then there had been the movie score. A popular director, but a pretty sleazy movie even by our standards. The more Keith got into it, the more he wanted out. Things soured on the money end, too. Keith had finished the music for two reels when he quit the project. In his journal he said it fell through "due to cheapness and underhanded tactics on their part, and lack of true desire on mine." That was another problem—Keith's high standards.

As Michelle and I watched Keith now, I couldn't help but think that maybe he would have been "discovered" already if he'd just been a bit more *flexible*. But for Keith, some things were set in concrete. Keith's dad had been his manager for years and had instilled very high standards in him. If something didn't *feel* right to Keith, he wasn't going to do it, and that was that. His high principles were admirable, but secretly I was afraid he might be just a little too picky for his own good.

As Keith continued on with the next few songs, he squinted through the glaring stage light keeping a check on the crowd. A few more people filtered in. Several faithful friends made a two-hour drive in from the desert in Lancaster. Keith's parents came to cheer him on. Another friend, Karen Bender, had even brought her daughter, Dawn, who had the longest braids I'd ever seen on a little kid. I was disappointed that Todd, Keith's best friend, wasn't able to come, but our poker-playing buddies from Marina Del Rey showed and so did a few industry friends.

Keith played for another twenty minutes before taking his first break. He finished to an enthusiastic round of applause and joyfully jumped off the stage, his blue eyes sparkling with the victory of the moment.

A full house!

As he walked over to the table, sweat glistening on his face, excitement made his usually springy steps even springier. Not only were we high on the moment, but our friend Harriet had come bearing "gifts".

Harriet shoved a shoe box toward Keith.

"Shoes?"

"Open it."

Keith lifted the lid. His eyes brightened. "Brownies!"

"My own special recipe," Harriet winked. "Homegrown, if you know what I mean."

"You put *grass* in them?"

"The best."

"Eddie! Hey, Eddie! Bring me a large milk."

Keith grabbed a handful of the marijuana-laced goodies and passed the box to some select friends in a ritual of "sharing the wealth"—patterned after Indians passing the peace-pipe. We made the rounds, telling everyone we were glad they came.

As the brownies hit bottom things began to look even more "up". The strain left Keith's eyes, and he was obviously soaring with the moment.

Albie walked up smiling broadly. He slapped Keith on the back and said, "You did it, kid. A great night! I'm happy for you."

Keith's face was one big grin. "Yeah? So when do I get Saturdays?"

Albie chuckled and shook his head. The question didn't demand an answer—not immediately. But Keith already had his eyes on the future, on something far beyond a big night of his own at The Bla Bla Cafe.

When Keith started his second set, the haze, clinking glasses and melodic piano all merged as my mind started to drift. I stared at the funny dragonflies on the wall—savoring the feeling of success.

Somehow, though, my thoughts were pulled to our future and what might lie ahead. I just knew Keith was supposed to be up in front of a lot of people—people who were being moved by his music and what he had to say. But the problem was, it wasn't clear even to Keith exactly *what* he had to say. He just felt he had a message to offer the world—something from his spiritual search. An important message. But what?

By the time Keith finished his third set that evening a decided victory was won. It was one of Keith's best nights yet.

Driving home I was still hyped from the excitement of the evening—and Harriet's tasty brownies. My mind was hung up on a million questions.

Was this the beginning of a big break for Keith? Was he finally on a roll?

And why did someone like Keith, who was loaded with talent, need to resort to begging his friends to come hear him play? It seemed like such a contradiction, but then again there were lots of contradictions in our lives.

In areas like honesty and integrity it seemed Keith had the highest standards of anyone I'd ever met. We didn't cheat on our taxes—but sometimes we'd take illegal drugs. Was there a difference?

And even if Keith made it in music, would we make it as a couple? As much as we liked to talk about living in harmony with the universe and each other, we sure had our share of arguments. Big arguments.

It was hard to live with so many unanswered questions, and not just regarding Keith's career. Some of the other battles we were fighting were on an entirely different front—one that was even more vague and elusive. It was as if something was tugging at us, pulling us out into uncharted waters. Something that would change us forever.

In fact, we had no idea we were on the verge of a breakthrough much bigger than we ever imagined.

All I knew right at the moment was that this man I married sure had a lot of complex facets to his personality. In the days following our victory at The Bla, my mind wandered over the many strands that wove together inside him. I thought about the sensitive inner man, who was determined to find spiritual answers. Yet there was another side of him—the little boy who always wanted to be in show business. That side explained so much about who Keith was now. But did it offer any clues about where we were going?

Captivating one year old.

Late Sixties teen.

"Run To The End Of The Highway"

KEITH GREEN EXCLUSIVELY ON DECCA RECORDS

11 years old.

KEITH CONTINUED PLAYING AT THE BLA, WAITING FOR "THE discovery".

In the meantime, though, we made a discovery of our own. We could write songs together. Keith made room for me inside his "creative bubble", as he called it, and I was thrilled. But sometimes it had its drawbacks.

One day I worked several hours on a song lyric, then I found Keith in the living room and proudly handed him the words all neatly recopied on a fresh piece of paper. Keith read it silently. I knew he would tell me exactly what he thought, so I was holding my breath.

"Mel," Keith said finally, "these rhymes are really trite."

"Trite? What do you mean?"

"They're expected. Like moon, June, spoon . . ."

"I didn't even use those words."

"I know, but you need to be more creative."

"Well, forget the words I used. What about the message?"

"You're not saying anything new. Anybody could write a song like this."

"Do you realize how long I worked on those? Are you telling me there isn't anything worth saving?" I was starting to get angry now—and hurt too. Blinking back the gathering tears I took the sheet of paper, wadded it up and threw it in the trash.

"Don't you want me to tell you the truth?" Keith asked.

"Of course I do," I said, pouting a bit.

"Look. I know you can do better. You just need to keep writing. Keep trying and don't give up."

I calmed down some. It was hard to admit, but I knew he was right. It really wasn't a very good song. I had a musical background—of sorts—but nothing like Keith's musical genius. I was glad he wanted me to do my best, but why couldn't he say the same thing in a different way? Walking back to the trash, I retrieved the crumpled lyric. I wished this tension that suddenly rose between us over trivial things would go away—but I knew it sprang from something deeper than petty disagreements.

Keith had been on edge for several months. Sometimes we had great days. Others we'd just as soon forget. Keith had a strong sense of calling on his life, a spiritual destiny, and he knew it wasn't being fulfilled. This was frustrating for him. Coupled with the fact that we were still adjusting to our first year of marriage, it amounted to some anxiety between us.

Married on Christmas Day 1973, we were now only three months away from celebrating our first anniversary. Sometimes I found it hard to believe I was actually married and living in a rented house in the suburbs—with a backyard full of fruit trees. We had plenty of time and space to write music. But for Keith, it seemed like there was no time. He was always in motion, always searching for something. Where had this drive and energy come from?

It didn't make life any easier that the promise of a "deal" always lingered out there. We were constantly running all over town to meet with someone in the business. Besides partying and playing poker with a wide assortment of friends, Keith and I kept writing songs together. We usually worked really well as a team and we'd spend hours transposing concepts and ideas into word pictures and rhymes. Most of the time we worked hard, but when it got too intense, one of us would suggest a stupid rhyme or make a joke to release the tension. Once we wrote a little jingle to help our friends remember our phone number—349-2510. We sang it with a blues feel: "Three four nine, a quarter and a dime, let's get together and buy some wine! Oh baby, uh uh huh, oh baby!"

What we really wanted was to write a "hit song" and get it recorded by a big-name recording artist. A lot of famous singer/songwriters got their big break that way. Keith kept making appointments to play his songs at major publishing companies hoping they'd "run" the song to a popular artist. They'd also tell us who was looking for new album material and we'd go back home and try to write songs in their style. We wrote songs for people like Cher, Olivia Newton-John and Helen Reddy. We wrote them, but they never got recorded.

One of the publishers Keith went to all the time was CBS in downtown Hollywood. Keith always brought our dog, Libre, up the elevator and right into the executive offices. He was never lacking in nerve, and before the CBS people knew what was happening Libre was laying quietly under a desk or a coffee table while Keith assured them she was housebroken. In spite of the clumps of hair Libre left on their shag carpeting, CBS really liked Keith's music. In fact they liked it so much that they had just asked Keith to go on salary for $250 a week as a staff writer.

As usual, Keith immediately wanted to discuss the proposed contract with his dad. Keith and his family were close, and he was always phoning his parents or running over to their house. So we jumped into Victor and made the twenty-minute drive across the San Fernando Valley to Canoga Park. As usual, Keith's folks were glad to see us. Keith joined his dad at the dining room table where they spread out the bulky contract for close inspection. This was not the first time they'd poured over a contract together, and Keith's father was already eyeing some of the drawbacks of this agreement.

"The normal thing, since you're unknown, would be for them to take one hundred percent of your publishing rights—but you can't let them have that, Keith. If you do, you'll be sorry one day," his father began.

"I know. But do you think they'll go along with that?"

"It doesn't hurt to ask."

Keith's mom was in the kitchen, making a pot of her wonderful chicken soup. Overhearing their conversation she poked her head out. "Honey, maybe you ought to go down to CBS with Keith and make sure he gets a fair deal."

"I will if I need to. Now let's take a look at all the fine print. . . ."

I wandered from the kitchen, where I'd made myself a cup of tea, and settled on the couch in the den. I liked visiting Keith's parents. They were always so supportive of Keith. They had long ago recognized his talent and did anything they could to help him. Even if Keith and his parents didn't see everything eye-to-eye, they had an obvious love for each other. And they'd welcomed me into the family with open arms.

Now Keith and his dad were deep into discussing different points of the CBS contract and I figured they'd be awhile. Looking across the room, I spotted one of Keith's baby pictures. He was not only a beautiful little boy, but his genius had appeared early.

Keith once told me he couldn't remember a time when his life was devoid of music or the potential for great success. When you were with him you had the feeling there were triplets, eighth notes and drum rolls pumping through his veins. He was definitely not nine-to-five office material. He wanted something more out of life.

Keith was third generation show business. His grandfather on his mother's side was a successful composer, screenplay writer and a pioneer in the music industry. He worked for Warner Brothers and wrote for the singer Eddie Cantor. He'd also had the keen eye to put the three Ritz Brothers together as an act. He also owned Jaguar Records, one of the first rhythm 'n' blues record companies, and had once signed the legendary Hank Williams as an artist.

The same love of music was passed on to Keith's mother. From where I sat now, in the den, I could see her as she swept the floor and watered her many plants. She was a pretty woman, with short blonde hair and an infectious laugh. Right out of high school she started singing popular music with the big bands. She was even offered a contract to sing with Benny Goodman, but turned it down to marry Keith's dad when he was still a handsome baseball rookie on the N.Y. Giants farm team.

When Keith was born, it didn't take long for the distinctive characteristics of this unusual child to emerge. His mom had often told me that, as soon as Keith was up off all fours, he walked as if he had springs in his feet. Not the average heel-to-toe lift-off. Keith slapped his whole foot to the ground all at once, then power-launched his body forward from the ball of his foot. Though he was now over six feet tall Keith never outgrew that springy walk. To this day he walked fast and with purpose. I always had to rush to keep up with him because Keith was always in a hurry—as if he was rushing to pack every moment with the most it could possibly hold.

Keith's mom, who had studied voice for five years at Carnegie Hall, said that by the time Keith was nine months old he could hum "Rock A Bye Baby" on perfect pitch. His grandfather gave him a small record player he could work by himself, so he'd play his gold plastic 78 RPM kiddie records for hours on end, happily singing and bouncing along with the tunes. When he was learning to walk, he'd plop his diapered bottom down right on top of it, leaving his mom to replace many broken needles. But her patience bore lasting fruit. With his "Gerber Baby" good looks at the age of two-and-a-half, Keith won a kiddie talent show by singing, "Love and Marriage"—and his young career was under way. By the time Keith was three he could sing harmony to his mom's alto—and to everyone's amazement he was also strumming a ukulele.

It was the Green's move to Canoga Park, a suburb in the San Fernando Valley, in 1957, that opened new doors of possibility. Keith's talent continued to blossom under the watchful eyes of his parents—and so did his precocious nature. Unlike his older sister, Keith was into everything and on his first day in kindergarten he was benched by the principal for misbehavior. In fact, wherever Keith went, it seemed he found something to worry his mother about.

The first time he was in a department store he found the control switch for the escalator and pushed it, which brought the escalator to a screaming halt. This caused no small stir. Next he found the Coke machine and shoved his hand up the hole where the bottles came down. Naturally, his hand got stuck and he needed to be rescued, amidst his tearful screams. As he grew, however, his talent for getting attention—and for generating income—carried him far beyond normal limits for a kid his age.

By the time Keith was five he could play anything he heard on his ukulele. And at the age of seven, his parents bought him his first piano. They found Keith a teacher who liked both classical and pop music, and it was at her suggestion that Keith began to take acting lessons, too. Keith was seven when he did his first television commercial.

Keith's eighth year, 1962, was an exciting one—and the year he began developing a "stage presence". He made his live theater debut playing a little Italian street urchin in Arthur Laurent's romantic comedy, "The Time of The Cuckoo". *The Los Angeles Times* reviewed Keith's performance at the outdoor Chatsworth Summer Theater and said, "Roguish-looking, eight-year-old Keith

Green gave a winning portrayal . . . alternately amusing and pathetic." Another review said Keith "stole the show".

Keith also wrote his first song that year. His grandfather had taught him three rock and roll chords and that was all it took. Keith quickly became a prolific writer. One day he stayed home from school because he was sick, and he wrote the words and music to three songs.

That year, Keith brought the house down at the famous Troubadour nightclub in Hollywood—later called Rocky's. The Troubadour had one evening they called "Hoot Night". They only allowed folk singers—rock and rollers were not allowed. So Keith learned two folk songs on the guitar. On "Hoot Night", when he finished his first song, the audience gave him a standing ovation. He played an encore and they screamed and yelled and wouldn't let him leave the stage again. Keith told everyone the only other songs he knew were rock 'n' roll. They shouted for him to play one anyway, and he launched into the Buddy Holly tune, "Peggy Sue". That won him a third standing ovation!

Two years later, at ten, Keith moved indoors to legitimate theater. He played Kurt Von Trapp opposite Janet Blair's Maria in a 1964 production of "The Sound of Music" in the San Fernando Valley. The local newspaper remarked about Keith's talented performance.

Unfortunately, Keith got a different sort of attention from his sixth-grade classmates. Since Keith's curls had now aged to brown, he needed some help from Lady Clairol to revive his once-golden hair for the part of Kurt Von Trapp. And once the production was finished, Keith needed to keep his hair blond for awhile to maintain a more "youthful" appearance. One day as Keith walked down the school hallway he noticed a few of his friends standing off to the side snickering. As soon as he passed by one of them called out behind his back, "Proxy locks! You big sissy!"

Eventually, Keith was able to let his hair grow out, but as the black roots inched their way upward they were not only a source of embarrassment—they were a painful reminder. They made it evident to everyone, especially Keith, that he was *different* somehow. As much as he enjoyed being different, he also had the longings of any boy about to hit puberty. He wanted to fit in and be accepted by his classmates as part of the crowd. But that was not going to happen.

In January 1965, upon the release of Keith's first 45 record produced by his grandfather and Jay Colonna, *Teen Scene Magazine* called Keith, "the youngest new face on the Hollywood scene." This first solo release was called, "Cheese and Crackers"

—

backed with "I Want To Hurt You". A photo of Keith with a big smile appeared in *Teen Scene* with an address and the line, "We know he'd love to hear from his present and future fans".

It was about this time that Keith's father started to represent him as an artist. After years of exposure to the business of "show biz", he became quite skilled when it came to dealing with record companies and legal contracts. He was also extremely honest when it came to business—or anything else for that matter. With his dad taking a bigger role in his career, things started to take off. One executive at Capital Records wanted to sign Keith to a recording contract but could not get it approved by his superiors because they felt Keith was too young. No one as young as Keith— including The Osmonds or the Jackson Five—was recording yet.

His dad moved on to Decca Records, where Keith was signed to a five-year recording contract. *The Los Angeles Times* watched with interest, and their music reviewer wrote, "Keith's first disc will be released in March, and one of the many songs he's written has been published. The name of the song is, 'The Way I Used To Be', which at Keith Green's age doesn't leave much leeway. He's only 11. Absolutely nothing else can be heard when, with amazing gusto, the husky blond boy starts slamming away at the piano and singing all out in an alto that promises to become a strong baritone." He quoted Keith, who said, "I've written about 40 songs and they're still coming. I'll never run out!"

Upon the publishing of Keith's first song, at the age of eleven, he became the youngest member of ASCAP—The American Society of Composers, Authors, and Publishers. They flew Keith to New York to honor him along with the songwriter who was the oldest member. Keith's youthful success made him somewhat unique in the music world. He was also flown to New York to sing on two national network television shows, and from there landed appearances in a television special with Sammy Davis Jr. and was on "The Jack Benny Show", "The Joey Bishop Show", and "Walt Disney's Wonderful World Of Color". He also did a program with Steve Allen who later asked him his secret of success. Keith replied in all seriousness, "I started when I was very young!"

Around this time, Keith also played his guitar and sang on a local morning television show. When he and his dad got home there was an important message waiting. They were to phone a certain extension at Metro-Goldwyn-Mayer Studios. They phoned right away, and the mysterious caller turned out to be none other than Colonel Parker, Elvis Presley's long-time manager. Keith's dad listened, astonished, as Colonel Parker said, "Your boy's got a great talent. If I wasn't tied up full-time with Elvis, I'd take Keith on. But you call me if you ever need any help."

In March 1966, *Time* magazine even pointed to Keith as a budding young star in a music article which looked at "harnessing the lucrative potential of the almost untouched pre-teen pocketbook". They talked about the new merchandising angles aimed at four-to-twelve-year-olds. One of the up-and-coming young talents they expected to shake dollars from the pre-teen piggy banks was Keith. Keith must have read with growing excitement, as *Time* reported, "Decca Records has a pre-pubescent dreamboat named Keith Green. . . . He has already written 50 rock 'n' roll songs, which he croons in a voice trembling with conviction, 'Youuu are the girlll / I am the boyyy / Yes, it seems we're in looove'."

With such strong support and encouragement from his family—and their combined talents all focused on Keith—it's no wonder Keith accomplished so much at such a young age. Keith himself was not only loaded with performing genius, he had the high energy and stubborn determination it would take to succeed. With everything lining up the way it was, Keith and his family just knew his career was about to take off. Like a rocket on a launching pad, all systems were go. But then, strangely, things didn't quite fall into place.

Keith's record release from Decca made it into the top ten in Hawaii. However, the major national breakthrough that was hoped for did not materialize. A short time later, Donny Osmond came on the scene capturing the pre-teen and teenage listeners that Decca Records had envisioned for Keith. Keith's dreams suddenly came crashing down. Success was nearly his—but somehow it had passed him by. . . .

I heard Keith and his father laughing in the other room as they shoved their chairs away from the table noisily. They'd often joke about the outrageous things companies tried to write into their contracts. I wondered if CBS was any different. Looking at my watch, I realized they'd been talking for over an hour. As they walked into the family room they were smiling and slapping each other on the back. Whatever questions they had about the CBS contract they must have worked them through.

On the drive home Keith told me more details about what CBS was offering him. It was a great deal. Besides the $250 a week, there were no office hours. He just needed to give them eighteen acceptable songs in a twelve-month period. Even better than that, they were hiring him mainly to write commercial melodies, not lyrics. They didn't feel his lyrics were commercial enough because they had too much "spiritual" content for their tastes—which was fine with Keith.

"This is incredibly perfect," Keith said, beaming. "I don't have to sell out my ideals to commercialism. Music is music."

"That's really great," I replied.

"This new job is really a responsibility and a privilege," he continued. "I need to be careful to stay honest."

"Of course. They're giving you a lot of money."

"Yeah—that's why I'm going to ask CBS to sign you, too."

"What?" I shot back. "Why would you ask them to sign me?"

"Because I don't want to be tempted to cheat."

"What do you mean?"

Keith explained that, since we were starting to write a lot of songs together, if CBS only signed *him*, they wouldn't own any of my share in a song Keith and I co-wrote. This would obviously benefit us financially. It would have been one hundred percent legal and ethical for us to get more publishing when we wrote a song together, but Keith didn't want to be tempted by money.

"I don't want you to write with me for the wrong reasons," he said. "I'd rather make less money and have a clear conscience. I don't want to struggle trying to figure out my motives every time we write together."

"But I'm not as good as you are," I protested. "Why would they want to pay me anything?"

"I'm not going to ask them to pay you anything. We'll still get just $250 a week. I only want your name added onto the contract."

When he suggested his idea to CBS a few days later, they were astonished. It was an unusual request, but it meant they were getting two writers for the price of one. It also meant they would own any acceptable songs I might write by myself as part of our yearly eighteen song quota—which at that point seemed highly unlikely. They accepted Keith's offer and we both became staff writers for CBS.

As much as Keith was caught up in the world of music, there was still another part of him—a side that ran much deeper. Keith was caught up in what seemed to be a lifelong spiritual search. The incident that happened with Harmony a short time before, outside The Bla Bla Cafe, had been a real turning point for him. Keith shocked himself when he quoted the words of Jesus into the wolf-like face of Harmony. On one hand it felt a little odd to quote a Bible verse, since our spiritual life seemed to be so stunted. Yet Harmony's response went a long way toward impressing Keith that some kind of power had forced Harmony out of his weird state the moment Keith had spoken those words.

One night Todd, who was Keith's best friend and almost a permanent fixture in our house, came over for dinner. He and Keith had known each other for years and they'd even kept a journal together at one time. They were such good friends that sometimes I got a little jealous of their deep relationship. And it didn't help matters when Keith, who was so used to talking with his buddy about everything, occasionally forgot who he was talking to and called me Todd. But Todd *was* a great guy and I usually enjoyed having him around. Just now he and Keith were immersed in a debate about some scripture in the Bible, and I slipped out of the living room to start making the salad. As I listened to them from the kitchen, I was impressed by Keith's unquenchable thirst for the things of the spirit. It was one of the things I loved about him. . . .

Spiritual roots ran deep in Keith's family. Keith's grandfather had been a Christian Scientist for sixty years. His mom was raised in Christian Science and when Keith's parents married, his dad followed suit. As Keith grew up he saw many physical healings. And he often saw his parents study the Bible, or Mary Baker Eddy's *Science and Health*. Keith and his father formed a publishing company named after one of the names of God, "I Am that I Am. . . ." I Am Music became the cradle for all of Keith's early songs.

Keith was raised in a good, moral atmosphere, and he was basically a good kid. What it was exactly that brought on the sudden changes as he entered his teens, no one knew. But when Keith hit puberty, it hit back. Maybe it was the disappointment of having his dream with Decca Records suddenly vanish into thin air, or maybe he was just sucked into the 1960s revolutionary spirit of southern California. Keith grew dissatisfied with himself and the life he was living. Growing up in an atmosphere of moral purity, free of alcohol and drugs, had a wonderfully preserving effect on Keith during his early years. Not being exposed to those things at home kept him from developing destructive habits—for a while anyway.

When Keith graduated from junior high and entered high school he came at it from a whole different universe than most other kids. While most of his friends were trying to figure out what they wanted to be when they grew up, Keith started the tenth grade as an "almost-was". He *almost* made it, but didn't. Underneath lay the dull pain of failure. Never being a quitter, Keith's bouncy step kept him in a forward momentum, winning talent contests, writing songs, and waiting—it seemed, forever, for that magic door to open and lay the world at his feet. There were, however, some dangerous curves ahead.

By the time Keith was fifteen he was growing more and more restless, and his relationships at home grew stormier. He was getting more argumentative, harder to understand, and less tolerant. Keith felt like his parents didn't understand him at all. From his point of view, they suddenly looked old-fashioned and "totally uncool". The California "scene" was promising something more to life than Keith was experiencing, and he wasted no time pursuing it. He already had more money in the pockets of his blue jeans than ten kids his age and decided to use it to finance every parent's worst fear.

In July of 1969, four days after the holiday fireworks, Keith withdrew his bank savings, tucked his coin collection in his backpack and financed a get-a-way with two older friends.

On the road Keith started keeping a record of his daily thoughts and activities in a notebook. This journal would become a lifelong friend and he confided his innermost feelings to its pages. In fact, it captured so much of Keith's heart and who he was that, once we became serious, Keith sat me down and, with great excitement, read *all* of his journals to me out loud.

When he did that, I couldn't believe how he kept track of things in such detail. He'd often stop to fill in details, too. I felt honored to have him let me into his private inner world like that. His entries were always interesting, and at times even embarrassing—because he held nothing back, not even his relationships with other girls, or his innermost dreams, fears and failures. But that was Keith's all-or-nothing nature. He wanted me to know absolutely everything about him—the good, and the not so good. He needed to know I accepted him for who he was without any illusions.

So I heard them all—from *beginning* to *end*—starting with the first entry, written in a car the first time he ran away at fifteen:

The Beginning
JULY 8, 1969

Sorry about the messy writing. We're driving. Hi there. My name is Keith Green. I'm splitting Canoga Park. Our final goal is Canada! We've been planning to leave for two months. We have luggage, organ and amplifier, $175.39 and my coin collection worth about $100.00. I hope to get some jobs along the coast of California singing and playing. We're going to go as

far from L.A. as we can. I feel really sorry about my parents. I love them. They're goin' to feel bad.—Later.

Their "trip to Canada" took them only as far north as San Francisco. There they met a young Eskimo girl and they all rented a cheap hotel room to live in. The guys got backbreaking jobs, unloading crates of tires from railroad boxcars. It was a time of first experiments. Keith also wrote:

That girl I met in 'Frisco was named Carolyn. . . . She really kind of dug me. She didn't know how old I was. When she found out, she was really surprised. We had it all figured out. We were [all] gonna get an apartment and Carolyn [was] gonna cook and clean. Then we all started getting crabby. I told Carolyn to get lost. I wanted to get rid of her. The rat I was.

[One of my friends] started talking about his probation hassles and I started thinking about home. . . . We decided to go back.

The great runaway lasted a total of four days. Keith called home, and his dad flew up and rented a real limousine from the airport to pick him up in. Then they flew back to L.A. together. On that trip Keith had his first taste of manual labor, which he hated—and his first taste of life on the road, which he loved.

In the next few years Keith would run away from home two more times. One time, in fact, his parents hoped to teach him a lesson, and they allowed him to be thrown in jail as a runaway. He spent his time there writing songs. Having no paper, he scratched out words on the cell wall with the heel of his shoe.

When Keith entered his junior year in Canoga Park's El Camino Real High School in September 1970, his life had become a blur of friends, parties, music and trying to stay one step ahead of the principal. Playing the class clown from a back-corner desk, Keith's wild antics and lack of attention in class gave him problems with his teachers, but never with his grades. Keith had a nearly photographic memory—his mind stored facts and figures like a filing cabinet. He could just reach in and pull out the desired information at will. El Camino had two hang-outs—the upper lawn and the lower lawn. Between classes, everyone who dabbled in drugs and thrived on loud music hung out on the upper lawn. It was there that Todd and Keith first met.

One afternoon, Todd saw Keith obviously "hitting" on a girl he knew. She didn't seem interested but went along with the game of brotherly love and hippie-hugs. Keith pursued girls like someone hunting deer in a game park. He stopped his pursuit that day just long enough to sell Todd a marijuana joint for $1. From that day on they became, in their words, "doper brothers".

Besides the dope, Todd and Keith found there were two more important things that bound them together. One was their love of music, the other was their hunger for spiritual things. Todd and Keith both played guitar and they would frequently "jam" on the upper lawn together. Todd was quiet and thoughtful, which complemented Keith's extravagant emotions. Todd's lean good looks, warm green eyes, and long straight brown hair appealed to the ladies. But his shyness was a handicap. No matter, Keith took care of that. When they were out, instead of just finding a girl for himself, he hunted for pairs, usually giving Todd second choice. But their bond of friendship was ultimately founded on something less tangible than girls, drugs or music.

Keith was like a magnet. It seemed like whatever he was into, he had a way of drawing others into his orbit, like a big planet with a huge gravity field. Keith was like this with his spiritual search. He and Todd would sit and talk for hours on end— watching the sunrise and wondering about life, the universe, and God. There had to be more to life than what they were experiencing with their five senses. Everywhere they looked they saw people drowning in mediocrity, traditions, and the boring daily grind. Keith had no intention of winding up like that. There were new things to taste and experience. Why be narrow-minded when the world was full of beautiful things and beautiful people? Everyone was saying "if it feels good, do it"—and they did.

Couples everywhere were starting to live together openly. Now it was the "in" thing to do. It was "prehistoric" to think a marriage license could hold a relationship together. Who needed a piece of paper if you really loved somebody? And if you really *did* love someone, you wouldn't want to tie that person down. Stephen Stills' hit song summed it up: "If you can't be with the one you love, love the one you're with!"

Everywhere Keith looked people were basically saying forget "the system"—women had burned their bras and men had burned their draft cards. Someone even burned the American flag. Nothing was sacred. Everything was up for grabs. And no one over 30 could be trusted. The true power to bring about peace would not, could not come through brute force—but by embracing the world and each other in brotherly love. What was needed was a Peaceful Revolution. The perfect example was when a demon-strator at an anti-war rally walked up to one of the National

Guards and put a flower down his gun barrel. Flower-power was born.

It seemed like seekers everywhere were united in a common theology that dressed itself in bare feet, Indian beads, headbands, wood stoves, incense, eastern music, and organic gardens that sprouted green beans and homegrown marijuana. Keith joined in the search.

That search led him to Box Canyon, a desolate place in the mountains on the fringe of Los Angeles County. Box Canyon became a popular place to film western movies—and became equally *un*popular when it became known as the hide-out of the infamous Charles Manson and his hippie "family".

Keith started doing Saturday night concerts in Box Canyon at a place called The Fountain of the World, a mansion-like building that resembled a small medieval monastery. A huge white sign out front bore the cryptic letters F L K W—standing for Faith, Love, Knowledge and Wisdom. Over the main entrance was a sign, "He Who Enters Here Walks On Holy Ground". A large stone stairway led down inside the building which was constructed in dark stonework and stained glass. Inside were lots of tables and chairs and a small stage. This organic-looking church was the perfect place for the sandaled, beaded and bearded to hang out amid the smoke of incense and pot. Keith and Todd were right at home. What impressed Keith most about The Fountain was its founder, "Brother Jeremiah". Brother Jeremiah wore sandals, a saffron-colored robe and frequently performed skits with spiritual significance. He also inspired Keith to uphold some word of truth in the songs he wrote—and to be more careful about the content of the ones he chose to play from his "top-40" repertoire. Keith's concerts began to draw quite a crowd.

Keith had been raised as a Christian Scientist, but "organized religion" started to feel "dead" to him. What he saw in Brother Jeremiah seemed fresh and alive. It was at The Fountain of the World that Keith's questions about life began to pile up on each other. Behind all the heady spiritual talk, people were still people. Why *couldn't* everyone live in harmony? Where *was* the love and the unity? It seemed like everyone had given up on high ideals and, instead, they were looking through the fragmented prism-colors of windowpane LSD. Keith's friends were finding their answers over the radio and in the rosy glow of the hash-pipe. Maybe the secret of life would be revealed by getting back to Mother Nature—back to life as it was before modern man polluted the world with machines, smog and greed.

One person Keith was especially impressed with was a guy

who called himself "Cougar". Cougar lived close to The Fountain and Keith frequently went to his house to party and talk. Cougar had rejected materialism and the conventional way of life and, at eighteen, he seemed to have all the answers. Keith thought everything about Cougar was cool—where he lived, what he said and how he said it. Cougar wasn't just preaching brotherhood, he was living it. This, coupled with Brother Jeremiah's influence, seemed to open up a world of mystical truth for Keith.

In the summer of 1970, the second time Keith ran away from home, he felt he made an extraordinary breakthrough into the spiritual realm. Keith got as far north as Seattle this time. While he was there, he "tripped" on LSD. Parts of the trip were frightening—but Keith felt like he saw things clearly for the first time. In fact, he was so excited that he called Todd from Seattle to tell him, "I found God!" When Keith returned home, all he wanted to talk about was his spiritual experience.

"Todd, you wouldn't believe it. It was like I was *one* with everything around me."

"But how do you know you found God? Did you *see* him?" Todd asked skeptically.

"No, but I felt him. He was warm and pure. It might seem crazy but I know he was really with me."

"Did you hear his voice?"

Keith hesitated. "Not out loud. But I heard his words clearly in my mind."

That made Todd eager for a similar experience. A short time later, they took their first psychedelic trip together in Keith's backyard. Lying on lounge chairs looking up into the starry, night sky, Keith read to Todd out of his "Life Notebook and Journey Guide". Keith's notebook now began to fill up with his philosophy of simplistic naturalism—borrowing from the ideals of the hippie movement, his drug trips, and his understanding of Christian Science.

As Keith and Todd continued sorting through the various things they believed in, they came up with their own philosophy. They gave it the mystical name "New Dawn" which they borrowed from a line in a David Crosby song—"the darkest hour is just before the dawn". To them "New Dawn" referred to the time when all mankind would live together in peace and brotherly love. It also included the eastern idea of karma—that you have to pay for past sins in your next reincarnated life. If you blew it on earth, you always had another chance in your next life to do better.

With this new philosophy and his zealous idealism, it was natural for Keith to "evangelize" his friends. He was that way with everything. For instance, if Keith fixed his sandwich a certain way in a restaurant, he would tell everyone at his table, "You *gotta* try this, man. You'll love it!" Imagine his determination when it came to trying to lead others to where he'd been spiritually.

Keith got into the habit of gathering several friends together—usually at someone's house while their parents were gone. Then they'd all drop LSD together and sit in a circle on the floor, holding hands while Keith proceeded to "take them to the light". As they started to come on to the "acid", Keith would begin describing the visions he saw out loud. In his mind's eye he could see a great, blue-green sky, arching over a vast, empty plain. Moving rapidly across the sky were multi-colored clouds, churning and tumbling together. The clouds changed shapes constantly, the last image merging into the next. Keith called out the different images as they came—an eagle, a lion, an Indian doing a rain dance. As the sky filled with shadows, it was like entering a long dark tunnel. But straight ahead, in the middle, was a pinprick of light. As they raced toward it through the billowing blackness, the light ahead grew bigger and more brilliant. Keith's voice grew louder with excitement as he described the quickly approaching blaze of light, flecked with radiant prisms. Suddenly they'd burst through the blinding light together, releasing their hands, and falling into a heap on the floor—exhausted but exhilarated.

But even these "spiritual exercises", as Keith called them, raised questions in his mind. What was this light at the end of the tunnel? Was it God? If it was God, what was he really like?

Keith and Todd spent lots of time together, that fall of 1970, trading their journal back and forth. Their philosophy started to take shape:

Diary of God's Children

OCTOBER 25, 1970, 4 p.m.

Me and my brother Todd are musicians and songwriters and children of God. (As everyone is.) We feel we have been placed together for a reason—to help the Peaceful Revolutionary movement!

But for all his ideals, Keith's life was filled with contradictions. He wanted to purify his body and became a vegetarian—but on the other hand he bought peyote from friends in Oregon. Keith rationalized taking drugs to trigger his spiritual experiences, even as he teased Todd about taking vitamins to enhance his health.

OCTOBER 28, 1970, 9:30 a.m.

Our dream is to have a big musical family, sort of like a communal living type thing. We'd like to grow our own fruits

and vegetables. So I told Todd if he wants to start getting into the commune living type life, to stop taking vitamins, because we can't grow them.

If being careful about what they ate was a step toward purity, they were well on their way. Keith and Todd were not as careful, however, in relating to the girls they were meeting. Keith convinced Todd that the best romances were the ones with no strings attached. Which seemed like a pretty good deal to two teenaged guys. Still, Keith confided in his journal that " . . . sex is not important to the Brotherhood Movement". But even though his mind told him it wasn't important, his body was sending different signals.

In the first week of November 1970, Keith ran away from home a third time. To him, it was the first step in launching this peaceful Brotherhood Movement.

Keith hitchhiked up to Seattle to chase down his dream of a musical family. His hopes centered on Timothy, a guy he'd met the first time he ran away. Timothy was the leader of a rock band in Seattle and Keith hoped they could start a musical group together, one that would bring a message of peace to the world. Keith felt he and Timothy were brothers in the spirit, and that the message of true brotherly love would be spread for the good of mankind through the music they'd make. Keith believed intensely that Timothy was the one who was supposed to start this band with him.

NOVEMBER 10, 1970, 9 p.m.

We're 30 miles south of Portland. This is my 24th ride and probably my last. I paid this guy $6 for gas. He's taking me to Tim . . . the time is right for us to come together. I miss brother Todd. He's so much a part of it all. Now that me and Tim are coming together, oh, the music!! We will write together, play together, not only be one, but express oneness. . . . A better day has come!

When Keith found Timothy, in a tavern where his band was playing, he was really excited because the new songs Timothy had written reflected the brotherhood philosophy. However, Keith had shown up unannounced and was surprised to learn that the band was about to go to Idaho for three weeks. But that didn't throw him. He decided to go to Bellingham until Timothy returned. Still optimistic, he felt a strong sense of destiny about this time away from home. Three nights after leaving home he wrote, "I'm up here for a reason and I haven't found out what it is".

While he was waiting for Timothy to return, Keith spent most of his time making new friends, playing his music, and wondering why he was in Seattle. After about a week, Keith decided to take an LSD trip which was somewhat of a departure from his latest belief that organic, or natural drugs were superior to those made in a test tube. What was striking about this acid trip was that Keith thought he saw God. He was so excited about it, he wrote in his journal while he was tripping, which was in it itself quite a feat. As the LSD took effect the words on the journal pages grew into large, uneven scrawls:

NOVEMBER 20, 1970, 11 a.m.

It's snowing!!!!!!

I'm tripping!!!!!!!!

It's toooo beautiful for words. . . . It's going to be a long, long, long, cold dark age before the dawn.

God walked with me. Into the sun and out of the snow. He said, "Look at the snow, in it are crystals of brotherhood holding softly but tightly together. For in them you will see the secret to hold through the dark ages ahead. . . ."

He left me with a warm, loving, but assured embrace that light is ahead and said "Keep Faith".

Later that day, he also wrote,

That trip really was something. I feel different from the guy that took it. I feel like I went to another change. Good feelings. But one thing is for sure. The Dark Age started today. Got to get together with Todd and Tim soon.

Unlike the other times Keith ran away, this time he decided he'd keep in touch with his parents. They started by sending letters back and forth through a friend in Los Angeles so Keith could keep his exact location a secret. His parents were grateful for the contact and didn't call the police.

NOVEMBER 23, 1970, 11:30 a.m.

I've been away from home now for two weeks. I hope my people [family] are taking it all pretty well. After a few months they'll have to. Anyway after they get used to me being gone, they will really be better off, for it. They will see. It's right for me to be here. . . .

Keith felt he was learning a lot about himself, and a lot about life. But being out on his own had its ups and downs. He was ecstatic about receiving a "3-minute standing ovation" at a coffee house he played in. But he was also forced to buy boots at the Salvation Army because his shoes had holes in them and his toes were getting "wet, cold, and frozen" in the snow. He didn't have a car and didn't know where he was going to sleep from one night to the next.

As each snowy, rainy day of the Pacific Northwest slowly passed, everywhere Keith turned people were gearing up for the Christmas holidays. Twinkling lights and wreaths were starting to decorate store windows and homes. People all around him were making holiday plans with family and friends. The Christmas season was a difficult time for Keith to be alone. The one thing keeping him going was his hope that when Timothy returned they'd put together a spiritual band with a spiritual message. He hung onto that dream waiting for the three weeks to pass.

Even beyond wanting to work with Timothy, Keith was on his own personal pilgrimage—watching, listening, and hoping. He was also asking many questions. Was there really a way to tell right from wrong? And how could he be sure he was going to spend his life doing what he was called to do? He felt like he was just stumbling in the dark.

At the beginning of December, Keith talked three guys he knew into going to a Sunday morning Christian Science church service. Four nights later he went again. The services underscored what he'd surmised from his own studies—that there's no literal hell, and that only certain parts of the Bible are the "inspired" Word of God.

Afterward, he and his friends somehow ended up at a Christian coffee house. The evening exploded into a heated debate.

DECEMBER 10, 1970, 12:45 a.m.

. . . We went to a "Jesus Freak" coffee house and they tried the trip on me about believing the whole Bible, word for word, even the part that says God kills my brother and I just don't believe that. Not my wonderful Father!

I'm still trusting my bro' Jesus Christ and Father God, who are one together, and one with me, and we're one with everyone. But it's easier to say, that the universe and everything in it is one! Peace through unity.

Keith was irritated by being confronted with the fundamental Christian belief that, although God created us, a redemptive process was needed to enter into a relationship with the Creator. That thought was new to Keith. He didn't like it. Keith believed that if he could only have "perfect thoughts" he would experience God's perfection in body, mind, and spirit.

The other thing that really bothered him was the belief that the whole Bible was the inspired Word of God. Keith believed there were certain "inspired parts" of the Bible—but everyone knew it was written by men, and men make mistakes. Anyway, didn't the Bible say that God was a loving Father, full of mercy and peace? So how could a loving Father punish any of his children? These "Jesus Freaks", as Keith called them, had challenged his thinking, but failed to convince him.

As Timothy's return grew closer, Keith's anticipation ran high.
DECEMBER 25, 1970, Christmas day

I am at Tim's farm. Tim isn't here. He probably won't be here till late today.

I also called home! They are trying very hard, but they still don't understand. Sometimes I don't understand it either! But my Father knows.

Well, it's X-mas day and I feel like giving! I want to play! I am going to crash! Brother Tim; there is a reason! Good night all. X-mas comes and goes, but feelings last.

Unfortunately when Tim finally did arrive, after all the waiting, the much hoped for musical dream did not materialize.

By the end of the first week in January 1971, Keith knew his time in Washington was coming to a close. He made some New Year's resolutions—to "put down dope" and also to keep sex "in check". He returned home on January 9th because he missed Todd, and the "settled, stable feeling of home".

Throughout the spring and summer of that year Keith aggressively pursued a new dream—a record deal. He hung out with Todd and, in fact, they became inseparable as they focused on their dream of putting a band together to play music that would lead people to higher levels in their spiritual search.

They wrote songs about all their beliefs, and with guitars in hand, sang them everywhere to anyone who would listen. However, they didn't expect to have a chance to sing for their all-time favorite woman singer/songwriter—who was also one of the most popular and talented women in music at the time.

On the first day of May, Keith wrote, "Drum roll . . . we played for Joni Mitchell." Joni, a top-selling recording artist, was one of Keith's musical idols. She lived in a rustic area of the Hollywood Hills, and Keith had taken the trouble to find out exactly which house she lived in. On this day, Keith and Todd hitchhiked to a friend's house and on the way noticed Joni's gate was open. They got their friend and his guitar and the three of them walked back to Joni's.

Keith, of course, had the nerve to knock on her door. There was no answer, so they decided to serenade her house with a song they'd just written. As they sang the last note, the door opened— and there stood Joni Mitchell. To their amazement, she invited them inside.

Keith sat at her piano and sang her all the songs he was writing for his album. He even asked her to write the liner notes, and Todd nearly died of embarrassment. Keith also wrote, "She gave us organic apple juice. It was all such a beautiful dream. . . . I wish it never ended. I left a piece of my soul with her."

Probably one of the most surprising things about the afternoon was that, although Joni was at the peak of success, she had some unanswered spiritual questions, too. On one hand, Keith already believed the truth was something much deeper than position or possessions. But he was also disappointed. He had such an immense level of love and respect for Joni he figured if she didn't have the answers, who did? He later wrote, "She seems troubled with an inner-conflict. I love her. God help her and us all. You are our only salvation. I feel so discontented today. I feel unfulfilled. Searching for something to quench my thirst for fulfillment."

In September 1971, the long-sought recording contract finally became a reality.

Keith's first album, with Amos Records, would be called "Revelations". The bulk of the songs centered on his philosophy of peace and hope through the unity of mankind. In mid-'72, when Timothy came down from Seattle to play on the album, it seemed like the dream of a "brotherhood band" was about to happen. And then—just like Keith's hope of becoming a pre-teen idol— this dream came crashing in, too.

On June 1, 1972, Timothy wrote a "guest entry" in Keith's journal:

[Keith] seems to be dwelling so intensely on all the confusion . . . and personal grief . . . he seems to have too much going on inside to realize why I came here. I pray for what is right. Why are we here? Why are we all here?

Shortly, their dream of working together came to an end. When Keith realized the vision was dead, he laid it to rest this time with a tinge of sadness, knowing it would never be.

Though the hoped-for musical family with Timothy did not

happen, Keith and Todd continued to hold on a little longer to their dreams. They quit playing for "drunken dances" because no one was paying attention to the message of the music. And they continued their search for a meaningful relationship with God. They were both accepted into the Rosicrucian Order—a mystical occult group espousing ideas like astral projection. After doing some of the studies, they couldn't agree with all of the teachings and dropped out of the order—and Keith scratched one more thing off his list of possibilities.

That same summer of 1972 Keith heard about an event in Colorado called The World Family Gathering, that was supposed to usher in the New Age. In July, Keith drove all the way to Rocky Mountain National Park hoping that in such a beautiful setting, with thousands of other seekers, he'd find the answers he was looking for. But there was no sense of family at this "family gathering". Instead people were rowdy, getting high on everything imaginable, and often out of control and violating each others rights. It ended up being a rather mindless, prolonged party—not the spiritual event Keith had hoped for.

When Keith returned to California he had one more thing to scratch off his list. In fact, it seemed like he'd been scratching a lot of things off his "list of potential truths" lately. Over the past several months he'd been on a reading marathon examining the works of Hess, Jung, Heinlein, Castaneda, Gibran, Baba Ram Dass—and the Bible. Keith was finding interesting food for thought, but nothing was totally satisfying. He'd had his tarot cards read, his astrology chart done, and even gone to a lecture on the mystery of the pyramids. The World Family Gathering was a bust, Joni Mitchell didn't have all the answers, the "Revelations" album was not taking off, the musical dream with Timothy died, and he'd burned all his Rosicrucian Order notes to "symbolically and physically cast off the chains of wrong belief".

Even Keith's old friend Cougar ended up letting him down. It was Cougar who first inspired Keith with his brotherhood philosophy, but now he was totally devoid of all "brotherhood" beliefs. Not only that, he'd become part of "the establishment". Keith wrote, "Cougar got frustrated with me and lost faith in brotherhood, and started acting like a 9:00 to 5:00 freak." Keith couldn't get over the fact that his "teacher" had sold-out to materialism and no longer believed in any of the things he once preached with such passion. Keith felt ripped off. Not only that, but if Cougar had given up, maybe the truth was impossible to find. Maybe there was nothing beyond this life.

And then a startling event shook Keith at a deep level. Keith's nineteenth birthday was near the end of October, and he planned a special way to celebrate the end of a season in his life. He planned to take one final mescaline trip with a close friend of his named Bill, a record company executive in his late thirties or early forties. Keith, who had been trying to quit drugs, felt this trip would be his very last.

On the evening of October 21st, Keith drove to Bill's house in the Hollywood Hills to kick-off his "farewell to drugs" trip. Psychedelic drugs are portioned out in small amounts called "hits" or "tabs", and usually taking between a quarter of a tab and a whole tab is plenty to get you where you want to go. But on this night, perhaps because Keith wanted to go out with a bang, he dropped three hits.

He was in for one of the most terrifying experiences of his whole life. When they were in the heaviest part of their trip, Bill started playing with Keith's mind. One of the frightening things about taking psychedelic drugs, is that most of the time it's impossible to tell the difference between fantasy and reality. You see and hear things that are not really there, and actual reality is either obscured or terribly distorted. The worst thing that can happen is to have someone you really trust mess with your mind when you're in that vulnerable and confusing state.

As Keith and his friend sat in their car on a high cliff overlooking the Pacific Ocean, Bill told him he'd made an appointment that night to meet with people from another planet. It sounded crazy, but after three hits of mescaline anything could be true. It was a dark night and the moon looked pure white.

"Come off it," Keith said. "You're not serious."

"I am. I've made contact and they should be here soon."

"Come on, don't mess with me. . . ."

"It's true. They're meeting us in a few minutes. And they want to take you back with them in their spacecraft."

They talked back and forth like that for quite some time, and Keith started to panic. What if it was true? In all his readings, he'd heard stories about people who'd met aliens. His heart was pounding so hard it felt like it might burst from his chest. The negative energy was real, and very frightening. Dark forces were reaching for him. Occult powers seemed to be pushing him close to the edge of a black and empty place. He fought with all his might to keep from falling in.

When the trip was over Keith did some heavy soul-searching. He had a very strong sense that all of the eastern/mystical/occult paths he'd been walking might actually be leading him in the wrong direction. The spiritual darkness he'd felt that night was an unfriendly presence that he never wanted to experience again. But even as he cut all these things loose, he still had no certainty of where to turn. A few days later he wrote:

OCTOBER 28, 1972

Towers of happiness built on the sand of confusion usually tumble down. I'm digging deep, I'm digging deep, gotta find that solid rock foundation. I'm digging deep, I'm washing with water and cleansing in soil. When I reach a solid self, if there is [one], then I'll build a cabin of home in my heart. And maybe share it with another solid soul.

As the end of 1972 drew near, Keith had scratched so many things off his spiritual search list he barely had one left. He had narrowed things down quite a bit, and spent a lot of time reading "them two books—the Bible and *Science and Health*". For a few weeks he thought he'd get totally into Christian Science. He went to the local Reading Room, and had a deep conversation with his grandfather. Just when he thought he'd take the plunge, he suddenly changed his mind. He wrote, "I dig the teachings, but the organized machine scares me."

Even though Keith was turned off by the idea of an organized group, there did seem to be one common thread running through all the teachings Keith had studied. That thread was the person of Jesus Christ. Everybody seemed to say that, at the very least, Jesus was a "good guy". Some said he was the Son of God, others said he was a prophet, others said he was an ascended spiritual master—even Buddha thought Jesus was okay. Everyone said something different, but it was all positive. And to top it off, Jesus even said good things about himself. He said he was the *only* way to God.

Keith had been running scared since the mescaline trip he took on his birthday. He doubted everybody and everything. But Jesus himself seemed like a safe bet. So Keith decided to deal with Jesus directly—not through any man, and not through any organization. He wouldn't even call himself a Christian because he didn't want to be one. He thought they were rejects. Losers. Besides, Christians were so straight, it seemed that in order to be one you needed to have a barber in the family and sleep in a suit and tie. Keith was not ready for that, but he was ready to deal with Jesus one on one. And that's exactly what he did.

Keith opened his heart to Jesus without really knowing who he was or what it might lead to. He only knew he had a deep need and prayed a simple prayer.

Jesus, you are hereby officially welcomed into me. Now only action will reveal your effect on me.

Keith had taken a step toward Jesus in a small, but definite way. The next day he had a long talk with Todd. "Todd and I reached an agreement finally today. Christ is the common denominator to all our trips so far." Keith closed out the year with a hopeful heart, feeling he'd stepped onto the right path. But he was still uncertain about where it might lead. On New Year's Eve he wrote:

Gotta Find A Home
My roots dangle. Un-nourished, I refuse to root here! Gotta find a home and get it settled and peaceful. Gotta find a place inside where I can rest between crisis. . . .
Please Jesus! I know you more each day and recognize the signs you show me. The immaculate birth makes you special above all men and strengthens all the links to the Christian trip—keep the signs coming. I'd almost given myself up for lost. . . . Bless you. Beloved clean brother on highest.

Keith was doing all he knew how to do in trying to get closer to God. He would often fast for one or two days a week—and he was trying to make sure he prayed every day. Still, Keith was groping. "God is a concept. . . . Everything is getting numb. I am so numb. I need to feel again. I am almost dead." Keith was working on finishing the words to a song he was writing called "Manchilde". The second verse was for Timothy:

> *Oh, I am a Manchilde*
> *Lost between the tame and wild*
> *I'm tired though the journey's just beginning*
>
> *A road I traveled led to you*
> *And we've been through a lot it's true*
> *For being such close friends it wasn't all that smooth*
>
> *I just wanna thank you because you're you*
> *And there's nothing I wouldn't do for you*
> *If I could only stop thinking of me. . . .*

A short time later, perhaps to show God that he really meant business, Keith decided he wanted to start wearing a cross. He wrote, "Gotta find a cross to wear. I've already got one to bear."

One afternoon he went into a little secondhand shop and he saw something that caught his eye. The man behind the counter lifted a small, silver cross out of the glass case and handed it to Keith. He held it in the palm of his hand. It wasn't much bigger than a dime and it looked really old.

"Man, this thing looks ancient," Keith said.

"It's over 150 years old," said the shopkeeper.

"Are you kidding me?"

"No. It was worn by a monk in an Ecuadoran monastery."

Keith turned it slowly over in his hand. The man *said* it was silver, but it looked more like old brass. It was obviously handmade—uneven and rough around the edges. Keith could barely see a faint raised outline of Jesus lying on this beautiful old cross. The shopkeeper explained that was because the monk had rubbed it and rubbed it every time he prayed. It was almost rubbed flat at the top. The cross had a certain mystique to it, a sense of spiritual history. Obviously, somebody who really loved Jesus had worn it. Maybe, Keith hoped, that same intensity of devotion might rub off on him.

"How much is it?"

"Ten dollars."

Keith had $14 of poker winnings in his pocket from the night before. It was just enough to buy the cross and have a few dollars left over. He paid the man and left the store with a determination to make an even deeper commitment. It seemed like everybody had someone they were following, a guru or a spiritual teacher of some kind. Keith decided that he would be comfortable making Jesus his spiritual master.

Keith got into his car, slipped the cross around his neck and started driving. As he drove he found himself praying to a God he didn't know. It wasn't a tidy little religious prayer—like the cross it was rough and uneven—a prayer of desperation. Keith knew he'd reached the bottom of his list. Everything was scratched off but Jesus. If Jesus didn't come through he didn't know what he'd do.

But before he could get any words out, gathering tears started spilling down his cheeks and running into his beard. His chest started heaving with deep uncontrollable sobs. He drove through the blinding tears as an overwhelming urgency filled his heart.

In between broken sobs, he choked out a prayer. "Oh Jesus, Jesus . . . if you're really real . . . if you are who you say you are— please prove it to me. I need you. I need something. . . . Show me the way. Prove that you're real, and I'll serve you forever. . . ."

I popped my head out of the kitchen to see if Keith and Todd were winding up their extended spiritual rap yet. It had gone on all evening—through supper, a card game, and now the dishes were done too.

I slipped off to go to bed figuring they'd be up half the night talking. It seemed to me there was lots of spiritual talk these days, but few real, lasting changes.

Just as I was drifting off to sleep, an old feeling overtook me in a wave. A sense of hopelessness. Of going nowhere.

Or was this feeling something else? Was some kind of "new dawn" experience heading Keith's way after all? Maybe everything in his life before now, the fall of 1974, was only a prelude.

But Keith was always so far ahead of me. Would I be ready when it came?

Me and Keith. 1974

"You're On My List Of Things To Do!"

Melody in Tokyo with The Sweetie Seven. 1968

OUR DAYS BEFORE CHRISTMAS IN 1974 WE HAD A BIG GOING away party at The Bla Bla Cafe. We were going to Canada for several weeks where Keith would play piano in a band and didn't know when we'd return to The Bla. It was a great night. Besides the fact that so many of our friends were there, two industry people came and they gave Keith a lot of encouragement. Marv Mattis, who signed Keith to CBS, was there. He saw a lot of depth in Keith's new songs and told him, "Keep writing from that place". Also, a guy from Helen Reddy's management team came to see Keith—for the *second* time—and expressed an interest in developing his career. Keith came away from that night excited about what might happen next.

This would be our first Christmas in the little house we'd recently rented in the suburbs of Woodland Hills. It had three bedrooms, so Keith's upright piano had a nice room all to itself! Our last house exploded from a gas leak. We hoped life in this house on Dolorosa Street would be a little less eventful.

Besides that, our first anniversary was coming up on Christmas Day—and I wanted to do something special for Keith. I wondered what would make him the happiest and decided to buy him a Bible. When I first met Keith in early 1973, he was just beginning to pray to this man, Jesus. He had told me, "Jesus is my master". He was wearing the antique Ecuadoran cross around his neck. It wasn't exactly a bold statement of faith—it was more like holding up a candle of hope against the darkness. Since Christmas was supposed to be Jesus' birthday, and since—apart from music—trying to decide who Jesus was, was all Keith talked about, a Bible seemed like the perfect surprise.

The only Bible I'd ever owned was a Gideon Bible I took from a hotel room once. I'd never *bought* one. I wasn't sure where to start. Then I remembered there was a Berean Bookstore right next to a vegetarian restaurant Keith and I liked. I made up some excuse to get out of the house and drove there.

As soon as I walked into the bookstore I felt a twinge of awkwardness. It was really quiet—not like the hippie bookstores I was used to at all. I wondered if I needed to whisper. Then I saw a man behind the counter and thought I'd ask him to show me where the Bibles were. He had *very* short black hair, perfectly combed—and he was wearing a navy blue suit. I had on my 1940s burgundy velvet thriftstore coat and my beat-up leather boots. I didn't know if anyone like me had ever even been in this store before. But the man had kind brown eyes, and I relaxed a little.

"May I help you with something?"

"Uh, yes. I want to buy a Bible," I said.

"What kind of Bible are you interested in?"

"Oh . . . ," I started feeling dumb. "Well, what kind are there?"

He led me to the shelf and I couldn't believe my eyes. There were so many different kinds of Bibles! He started pulling them down one by one and showing them to me. There were several different translations—some used common everyday language and others were filled with Thee's and Thou's. Then there were different grades of covers ranging from genuine leather to paperback, and different grades of paper, too. Some had large print, others small. Some even had all the words of Jesus printed in red. As we went through the Bibles, the stack of "possibles" in my arms grew.

"This one has study notes," he was saying. "And this one has a concordance."

"What's a concordance?"

"You can find a scripture you want by looking up a single word in it."

"Oh."

"And this one has colored maps of Paul's missionary journeys."

I didn't know who Paul was, but rather than admit it, I just nodded and said, brightly, "Great!" But I was beginning to worry about how much one of these Bibles was going to cost.

"Can you tell me the prices of some of these?"

With the clerk's patient help, I finally picked out a small, King James, red-letter edition with a genuine, chocolate-brown leather cover that was waxed to a shine. It had a concordance and maps—and the pages were edged with shiny gold which looked beautiful when it was closed. It was, indeed, a very holy-looking book.

I took it home, where I got out my pen and india ink and inscribed the "presented to" page with: "Keith, my beloved husband, in celebration of the Birth of Christ and our first year of Marriage. With much love, May God always Bless you." Then I wrapped the box and hid it.

On Christmas Eve, I excitedly waited for the right moment to give Keith his Bible. But first we needed to do some more packing for our trip to Canada the next night. Unfortunately, within minutes the peaceful atmosphere changed and we were having one of our all too familiar disagreements. This time it was a "packing fight".

Keith said something I didn't like, and I shot something back. We were both being unreasonable, and we both reacted. Keith picked up one of the shirts I was packing for him and threw it at me. When it hit, I saw red. I got so angry I grabbed a pair of scissors and threw them—all the way across the room. Now we were on a roll. I was even more upset because I'd wanted to bless Keith with the Bible and now the whole evening was getting ruined.

We kept arguing and I got so angry that, without thinking, I pulled off my wedding ring and threw it straight at Keith. Hard. As soon as it hit him, I realized what I'd done. Keith just stared. I felt terrible. Some way to celebrate our first anniversary.

Afterward, we were both really sorry—and embarrassed—for everything we'd said and done.

Late that evening, I brought out the gift box I'd been hiding and handed it to Keith, expectantly. Keith was sitting on the rug by the antique pine cabinet we'd just nabbed at a garage sale. He unwrapped the box, opened the Bible, and read the inscription. His eyes were shining with happiness. Before we went to bed, we sat there together on the floor because Keith, of course, wanted to read out loud to me from the new Bible.

At bedtime, Keith made a simple note in his journal:

We had the largest fight in months. . . . After the storm died Mel gave me a new beautiful Bible.

As we prepared to meet 1975 I found myself wondering why two people who loved each other and wanted to live good lives just couldn't seem to do it. Keith could get me upset. He sparked those feelings in a lot of people—you either loved him or got mad at him. Sometimes both. There weren't many grays in Keith's world. There was black or white, good or bad. In many ways he was exactly what I needed, but I was also finding that some of the things I really liked about him—such as his intensity and conviction—could often be a bit difficult to live with. Like the time right after he'd first moved into my apartment with me.

When Keith moved *in,* he started moving some of my things *out.* Because he'd made Jesus his master, some of the books on my shelf made him really uneasy. Especially the ones having to do with astrology and the occult. He wanted me to get rid of them and I wasn't exactly happy or willing. Some of them were very expensive hardcover books. I thought Keith had a lot of nerve moving into *my* apartment, and then insisting that I throw my books away. Even though I hadn't found the answers I was looking for after all my years of reading them, I wasn't convinced they were totally wrong either. But Keith was so persistent I reluctantly gave in and threw them away. Besides, deep in my heart I knew he meant it for my good. It seemed like Keith was always challenging me about something. Mostly he challenged me to know who I was.

Even though Keith could drive you to the brink, there was something about being with him that made me face tough questions about myself—made me comb back through my life and try to figure out what I believed and why I believed it. He seemed to have a compass, but I was more unsure of my direction. At the time I met Keith, even though I was twenty-six years old, I really wasn't sure *who* I was. Unlike Keith's close-knit family which was always pulling together to help him build his career, whenever I thought of my family I was left with kind of a hollow feeling. It

44

was Keith's influence on me—after a difficult, painful past—that was pushing me further away from the dangerous places where I'd been wandering. . . .

I was born in a place many people would die to live in—Hollywood, California. Actually, we lived just off the boardwalk at Venice beach—but the hospital was in Hollywood and it was a nice name to drop when anyone asked where I was born. My mother was one of seven children born to Jewish immigrants who had escaped on the last ship from Odessa, Russia, before the worst of the Czarist persecution. My mom, Helen, and her younger sister were the only children born in America. They settled in San Francisco where my grandfather, who had been a rabbi in Russia, opened a kosher poultry store. But Grandma and Grandpa Sosnovsky died before I was born. It was a shock when Mom married my father—because he wasn't Jewish.

My dad, Charles Steiner, was of German descent and his parents were devout Methodists. His dad was a doctor and his mother visited the sick and needy in the church. Even so, my father never went to church. What I do remember about my dad was seeing him sit at his workbench in our tiny living room, winding pure silk thread around the bamboo fishing rods he made by hand. He also tied beautiful fishing flies. I would quietly walk up and look at all the bright colored feathers, spools of silk, sinkers and barbed hooks. One look from my dad kept me from touching anything, but I loved to watch. My dad loved working with his hands—even if he had a hard time making a go of it financially.

Because money was tight, we lived in a tiny one-bedroom apartment on Brooks Avenue and "Speedway", which was a narrow alley that ran parallel to the beach about 100 feet behind the buildings sitting on the boardwalk. With no front yard but this little alley, the long stretch of sand between the boardwalk and the ocean was my only place to play. Maybe that's why I loved going to visit my grandmother. She lived alone in a little house in Redondo Beach—but she had a *yard*, with a flower garden and a large fig tree. I guess it made such an impression on me because my world was one of cement sidewalks and alleyways. I grew up with dreams of living in a nicer house, in a nicer place.

My parents managed to save up a little nest egg while my dad was in the Navy. When he got home my mom wanted to use the money for a down payment on a house. But Dad wanted to start a business. My dad won out and the savings were used to start a small business instead.

Dad, however, was not really a very good businessman. He

gave away as much as he sold and money problems got worse. It resulted in some loud "discussions" between him and my mom—and even more strain when the business folded. Mom wanted nothing more than to stay home and raise me in a loving environment, but after I started school she reluctantly took a secretarial job to pay the bills.

When I was six I would go off to kindergarten wearing the key to our front door on a string around my neck so I could let myself in after school. That same year we moved one block further east on Brooks Avenue. It wasn't the house of my dreams, but it was a nicer and larger upstairs duplex. Two great things happened then. I got my own bedroom—and I met Mrs. Hilliard.

Mrs. Hilliard lived two houses down, and it was like having my very own grandmother right next door. This was great, since my grandmother had become old and confused and was now in a nursing home. Mrs. Hilliard had one of the only front yards on the block. It was very small, but it was filled with flowers. My favorites were the red and yellow snapdragons. I spent hours at her house and I was especially interested in Mrs. Hilliard's birds—several, beautiful, blue and white parakeets and a yellow canary, too. My mom wasn't big on pets, but she let Mrs. Hilliard give me a parakeet that I trained to sit on my finger.

Mostly, I loved just being *with* Mrs. Hilliard, inside her house. Everything was tidy and spotless, even the knickknacks always stayed in the same place. She had pretty carpets, and her dining room chairs had upholstered seats. But I never sat on those because we spent all our time together in her kitchen. After school I'd rush over and sit on a tall stool and watch her cook dinner. I'd make up songs and sing them to her. We talked a lot, too. Somehow I knew that she loved me. I really loved her, too. That's why I couldn't understand why she did what she did.

One day when I knocked on her door, it took her longer than usual to answer. I fidgeted with the buckle of my sandal while I waited. When she didn't come I figured she was at the store or something and skipped back home.

But the next day the same thing happened. Mrs. Hilliard didn't answer my knock. For days, in fact, I felt an unexplained sadness every time I looked at her silent house.

Finally I asked my mom if she knew where Mrs. Hilliard was. She hesitated. "Mrs. Hilliard moved away, honey. She won't be coming back".

I noticed that Mom wouldn't look at me, and I stood there, confused. Mrs. Hilliard was my friend. She wouldn't just leave without saying goodbye. Tears came to my eyes and a crushing pain filled my chest. Why didn't she tell me? I thought she loved me—but maybe I was wrong. Maybe I wasn't as important to her as I thought. Mrs. Hilliard never answered her door again.

Years later, I found out that Mrs. Hilliard had actually died, but my parents had wanted to spare me the pain of knowing the truth. Of course they meant well, but knowing what really happened would have explained her leaving me so suddenly. Then maybe I wouldn't have been left with such a lingering sense of loss and abandonment.

Even *that* young, I started to hunger for something I couldn't even define. I wondered about how I ended up living on earth, and if there was life on other planets. I'd lie in bed at night and stretch out one arm toward the ceiling. Then I'd move my wrist back and forth, staring at it in amazement for the longest time and thinking, "This is *my* arm, I can move it any way I want to. This is *my* body—but how did *I* get inside of it?" God had something to do with it. But who was he? My parents never talked much about God—since they had an interfaith marriage, they decided not to push me in any direction. They told me I could choose what religion I wanted to be when I grew up. So I did what came naturally. I examined my options.

There was a little Jewish synagogue right next door to us. When I was about eight years old I decided I'd go to their Sabbath School. I learned a little about Moses and the Old Testament. We drew pictures of Noah's Ark and things like that and taped them onto the wall. Although I didn't go for very long, I really enjoyed it. I always had a warm feeling when we talked about God, but he somehow seemed just out of reach.

Next I set my sights on the church across the street from us. I found myself wondering what kind of things they believed in there—the Twenty-First Church of Christian Science. From my second-story window, I liked to watch everyone come out of church—the crowds were extra big on holidays like Christmas. And everyone got really dressed up on Easter Sunday. The little girls wore frilly pastel-colored dresses and white patent leather shoes with matching pocketbooks. It seemed like those little girls were always holding hands with two happy parents, and that everyone was smiling and laughing. To me, Easter was the Easter Bunny, colored egg hunts, yellow marshmallow chickens and chocolate rabbits—but why people wanted to go to *church* on Easter was a mystery to me.

One Saturday, I announced to my parents that I'd be getting up the next morning and going to church. All by myself, I got dressed and bravely walked across the street. I went alone since my mom was Jewish and, I guess, my dad wasn't interested. The church had really high ceilings and it wasn't very crowded. I sat toward the back and just listened. Someone was up front talking for a while and then some people in the congregation stood up and talked a little. At the end of the service, I walked slowly back across the street, disappointed. I was hoping to feel different, but instead I didn't feel anything.

Because everyone at school could say, "I'm Catholic," "I'm Jewish," or "I'm Baptist," at first I thought it was fun to be two things. So I'd say, "I'm Jewish *and* Protestant. I'm both!" But after a while it seemed like being two things was the same as being nothing. I wanted to be *something,* so I made a choice. I decided to be Jewish. But other than the sense of awe and respect I felt on the few occasions I went to Temple with my mother, I had no sense of having a real connection with God.

Even though I decided to be Jewish, we always celebrated Christmas at my house. We'd get a big tree and I'd leave cookies and milk out for Santa Claus. One year was extra special to me because I'd saved up my money to buy my dad a really nice wallet for a present. The only problem was, someone else had the same idea.

There was a boy in the neighborhood whom my dad had taken under his wing. My dad was an avid fisherman, and I begged him for years to take me with him. His reply was always the same: "When you get older, Melody." But when I got older he started taking this boy, who was the same age I was, instead. I couldn't believe it—the very Christmas I bought my dad the expensive wallet, this boy gave him a wallet he made himself. My dad told me he didn't want to hurt this boy's feelings, so his wallet went into my dad's pocket—and mine went into his dresser drawer. He never used it. He never took me fishing, either.

In the next few years I was caught in a tension between two worlds—my young-girl's world of singing, tap-dancing lessons, experimenting with my hair and make-up—and the shaky adult world at home. As I got more and more interested in boys, I hoped I'd have better luck than my parents. My mom still worked hard at a full-time job, and my dad worked on and off. When my dad was home he spent most of his time secluded in the basement—his craftsmanship now expanded to making rifles. He hand-carved the stock, tooled and blued the barrels, and engraved the metal part above the trigger. It seemed just as well that he spent so much time downstairs, because whenever he was upstairs the arguments grew louder. I started shutting out their world.

The year I turned twelve my parents decided to get a divorce.

However painful it was for them, for me it was a relief. I was glad it was over. My mother and I moved to a one-bedroom apartment in Santa Monica, where I started a new life at a new school, with some new friends I'd met at the bus stop. My new friends weren't as innocent as the ones I'd left behind in Venice—and I immediately decided to keep pace if I was going to "fit in".

Almost overnight, I was a different kid. I was already taller than my mom's petite 5'2", and I decided I was too big to give in to her tearful pleas. I wanted to do my own thing and so I did. Before my mom knew what hit her, I was smoking, drinking, and had a sixteen-year-old boyfriend with a car. Eddie was Bolivian and he had beautiful, olive skin and dark brown eyes. His family came to America when the Communists moved into the government where his father had been an official. I was in love—and at the age of twelve I started a steady relationship with Eddie that lasted four years before we broke up.

But one experience with Eddie would later linger in my mind. One day we went to church together. It was raining as we walked into the cathedral. I'd never been in a Catholic church before so I didn't know how to cross myself, or when to kneel, and the priest spoke in Latin during the Mass, so I couldn't understand anything. But as I looked around at the high arched ceilings, the statues, the candles, and the big cross in front with Jesus hanging on it—I had an overwhelming sense that I was in the presence of God. The air was charged with a beautiful energy that settled over me. I'd never felt this way before, and I soaked up every minute like a dry sponge.

About a year after my parents' divorce, my dad had a stroke. He was only forty-nine. A WWII vet, he ended up in the Veterans' Hospital in West Los Angeles, paralyzed on the left side. My mom and I went to visit him once a week. I don't know what was worse about that hospital, the awful green walls or the sickening, unclean smell that hit you in the face as soon as you walked in. And there was my dad—slumped slightly to one side in his wheelchair, his light brown hair turning gray, a two-day stubble of beard, and a bit of saliva trickling down the weak corner of his mouth. He could talk fairly well, but his words were slurred. We'd bring him spending money, a bag of assorted candy bars and several packs of Chesterfield unfiltered cigarettes. With his good right hand he'd reach out and take the brown paper bag and sit it on his lap.

We'd make small talk on those visits, but there really wasn't much to say. Dad would always pay a lot of attention to his paralyzed leg, adjusting his foot on the little wheelchair platform so it wouldn't drag on the floor. But mostly he would cry. The tears would well up in his eyes and he'd just hang his head over his chest and weep uncontrollably. When he could talk again, he'd beg my mom to take him home and take care of him even though they were divorced. But it seemed like our dream of having a home together had been paralyzed years ago. With tears still streaming down his face he'd beg us, "You can have my Social Security checks. Please take me home with you."

My years in high school were one big blur of parties and skipping school. My mother was less and less able to keep me in line. I totally resisted all of her suggestions—which is what I considered her guidance to be. My mom eventually remarried and, after a while, stopped visiting my dad. From then on I went to see him alone or with a boyfriend.

When I graduated from high school in 1964 I got an office job and moved into my own apartment. A couple of years later, I enrolled in the Los Angeles Trade Technical College so I could study design and go into the fashion industry.

Once my dad knew I had a place of my own, he began begging *me* to take him in and take care of him. Every time he asked, I'd feel a battle raging in my heart. I'd always say, "No Dad. I can't." The truth was, I *wouldn't*. And I felt so guilty. Maybe he wasn't the best dad in the world—but he was still my father and I loved him. On the other hand, I didn't know him and he didn't know me. We'd shared a house for twelve years, but he was like a total stranger. I was so torn by his tearful pleas and the tug to live my own life that my visits became more sporadic over the coming months. I felt too guilty and too hurt to keep telling him, "No".

One evening, during this time, I got an invitation to a party at a very posh home in the Hollywood Hills. When my friend and I arrived at this gorgeous home, we were surprised to see a huge pile of shoes at the front door—but we just shrugged, took off our shoes and went in. Instead of the wild Hollywood party I expected, there was a room full of people sitting around calmly with all the lights on. At one end of the living room a man was standing up, talking—and behind him was some type of oriental shrine with a scroll hanging in it. I wanted to leave, but there was no way to slip out gracefully. Just then, a nicely-dressed man across the room stood up and was given a moment to speak.

"When I came here last month, I thought all the chanting stuff they talked about was crazy. But my company was failing and I had nothing to lose, so I gave it a try. Now we're miraculously back in the black. Chanting has saved my business!"

Immediately, a really pretty lady right in front of me jumped to her feet. She was almost in tears. "I'd given up on my marriage. My husband had already left and was going to file for divorce. But I started chanting and within weeks he totally changed his mind. Now we're back together."

With that, everyone burst into spontaneous applause and cheers. I couldn't help but join in. It was a touching story, even though I didn't understand what was going on.

The evening went on like that, with more interesting testimonies, and even some rousing "pep-rally" type of songs, which we stood up and sang together. When the man at the front dismissed the meeting, I went to get some punch at the dining room table. There a young girl introduced herself to me.

"Hi. I'm Morgana. Did you enjoy the meeting?"

"Well," I hesitated, "it was interesting. But what's it all about?"

"Oh, this is *Nishren Sho Shu*. It's Buddhist and it's really cool. I've been doing it for five months."

"What do you do? I mean, what's this chanting they were talking about?"

She smiled. "It's really simple. Here let me show you." She led me over to the shrine at the front of the living room. It was made out of shiny black lacquered wood about three feet tall and maybe a foot-and-a-half wide. It looked kind of like a deep-set TV cabinet—but instead of having a TV in it, there was an open scroll hanging on its back wall. The scroll was made out of white paper, about six inches across and eight inches long. On it were Japanese characters in elegant black brush strokes. There were also small drawers in the front of the shrine.

"What are the drawers for?" I asked.

"That's where you keep your incense, your prayer book, and your *Gongyo* beads."

"*Gongyo* beads?"

"That's what the chanting's called. You do *Gongyo* at least once a day and rub the beads in your hand. They're made out of sandalwood. Smell them," she said as she picked up the beads laying on the shrine and handed them to me.

They *did* smell good. . . . But the rest of this smelled a little fishy to me. I knew I needed something—only I wasn't sure this was what I wanted.

Morgana explained, "You just chant a simple prayer to this scroll, called a *Gohonzon*, and you can get anything you want—physical, material, or spiritual. That's all there is to it, and it really works," she said brightly.

"Are you serious?"

"Yeah. And besides that, chanting is going to usher in world peace."

"How's it going to do that?"

"Easy. As soon as one-third of the world is chanting we'll have peace."

"Why just a third?"

"One-third will be against it, and the other third will be neutral. But when you add up those who are neutral and those who are chanting, you'll have more good energy than bad."

Who wasn't *for* world peace? I know I was. And it sure sounded good—this idea of releasing as much good energy into the universe as possible. I thought for a moment and asked, "How many people in the world are chanting?"

"I'm not sure, but one-third of Japan is already chanting. It's really a cool thing, they're already experiencing peace over there," she said wistfully.

Morgana looked at me and smiled, "You should try chanting for a few weeks. If it doesn't work, you haven't lost anything, right?"

She opened up the small *Gongyo* prayer book and showed me how to do it. It was all in Japanese, but under each character was the phonetic pronunciation of the words. It looked easy enough, and Morgana said it only took about twenty minutes a day. All I had to do was chant out loud while concentrating on something I wanted. The same chant worked for everything—whatever you desired.

Well, I had at least one desire just then. His name was Mark. I'd met him the previous summer, and I really liked him. At the moment, he was in the Army, and I hadn't heard from him in a while. I'd been hoping for a letter from him—maybe I could chant for one. It seemed a little strange, but I decided I'd give it a try. All the folks I'd met at the Hollywood Hills party seemed very nice—so why not?

I went out and bought everything I needed—a scroll, beads, incense, a prayer book, and an inexpensive version of the shrine. I set it all up in my bedroom so I could have my own place to chant like everyone else. From the people I met at the party, I soon learned that *Nishren Sho Shu* was a national organization, with a leadership structure that went all the way from home group leaders and a U.S. Director to President Ikeda, the International Director, who lived in Japan. Very quickly, I was drawn into it all.

The organization was putting together a singing group to represent all the American women who were chanting. This group would be featured at some concerts in the States, but they would also perform in Japan. I'd been taking guitar lessons for some time and going to a songwriting class—and I loved to sing. So I decided to audition. If nothing else, it seemed like a great chance to travel.

Much to my surprise I passed the audition and got a spot with six other girls. We were called, of all things, "The Sweetie Seven". We started learning some Beatles and Simon and Garfunkel songs in preparation for a program at the Santa Monica Civic Auditorium. We were also going to travel to Japan for what was called *Tozon*. Going on *Tozon* was to this group what going to Israel was for Christians and Jews. Although I was chanting regularly, I realized right away that I was not as serious in my faith as the other girls in "The Sweetie Seven". They'd been involved for several years and were known for their strong commitment. But the exciting idea of a trip to Asia, along with the opportunity to sing, kept me rehearsing half the night for weeks and driving almost an hour each way to do it. Even if I was a novice, I could go along for the ride. I was open, even *hoping* I might find some spiritual reality along the way.

As the trip to Japan got closer, the excitement grew. Most of the talk centered around the possibility of meeting President Ikeda. One night, as we took a short break from rehearsal, one of the girls said, "I've heard that President Ikeda is enlightened".

Another girl added, "I was told that if I was lucky enough to just see him drive by in a car, I could be instantly enlightened—just by catching a glimpse of him."

I sat there wondering what it might feel like to be enlightened. It sounded like pretty wild stuff—but then again I'd been chanting and things were starting to happen. To my complete amazement, I'd already gotten that letter I wanted from Mark. Now there was the hope of enlightenment. . . .

As soon as the plane touched down in Tokyo, I was riveted to my window, amazed that I was on the other side of the world. Outside, I was hit by the dense August humidity of Asia, by the sounds of a language I didn't know, and lots of people with jet-black hair and dark eyes. We were all so excited that as soon as we got into our chartered bus we burst into a song. Immediately, though, one of the leaders shushed us. "Oh, no . . . don't sing that song now." I wondered why, but didn't think too much about it at the time.

An hour later, we were driving through downtown Tokyo and someone started to chant. We all joined in loudly, half expecting the people on the sidewalks to chime in, too. After all, this was the "holy land"! But right away our leader said, "Maybe you should wait until we get to the countryside. You know, some people might not like what you're doing."

I was curious. I thought, *What do you mean? I thought these people were all into this.*

I had expected to feel an immediate oneness of spirit with the Japanese people. That our arrival—as the American counterpart of this world peace movement—would somehow be a big event. But as I watched from the window of the bus, I saw skyscrapers, rickshaws, blue-jeaned teenagers and old ladies in kimonos—but nobody was chanting and there wasn't a welcoming committee in sight.

For the next few days, everywhere I went, I was hoping to get a glimpse of this President Ikeda—never imagining what would happen next.

"The Sweetie Seven" sang five songs for a gathering of about 20,000 *Nishren Sho Shu* devotees in a large arena in Tokyo. Their thunderous applause at the end was absolutely electrifying. Buzzing with energy—plus the No-Doz I took to fight jet lag—I ran back to the dressing room with the others, where we quickly changed into our marching band uniforms to join the drill team in their floor exercises. There were about one hundred and fifty of us marching together, and once again the crowd cheered us on when we were finished. We all filed off the arena floor and headed for the door. I happened to be one of the last ones out.

And then I heard a commotion behind me in the auditorium. As I turned I saw a Japanese man standing at the railing all the way across the arena. He had on a suit and he was waving. The crowd was going wild and some people were screaming. The girl next to me said, "It's President Ikeda!" Then she took off running toward him, and so did I.

I was one of the first ones to get to President Ikeda and I pressed myself against the stadium wall, stretching my arm as far as it would go, trying to touch him. He put his hand over the railing to make a speech and the palm of his hand closed over my little finger! For the next few minutes he addressed the crowd in Japanese—and the whole time his hand still rested on top of my pinkie. All around me people were pressing against me to get closer. To try and touch him. But there I was, the luckiest one of all.

Strong emotions rose in me and tears started flowing. I cried through the whole speech. There were tearstained faces everywhere I looked.

But something inside of me was almost standing back watching the whole scene. The hysteria. The tears. Why? What was I caught up in anyway? President Ikeda finished his message and his escorts whisked him out of the arena. People all around me were still sobbing. I just stood there thinking, *I not only saw him, he touched me. But nothing happened. I don't think I got enlightened.*

Two more incidents before I left Japan slowly dampened my enthusiasm. First, we traveled to a Buddhist Temple called *Taisegigi,* near the foot of Mount Fuji. The holy of holies was there—the original *Gohonzon,* over six feet high and carved in stone. We all got a turn to see it and they told us to take a list of everything we wanted into the shrine, so we wouldn't forget anything. As my group settled down for our twenty-minute stay, many around me started crying and chanting. I felt a little mercenary for bringing my list of "wants" here. Something just didn't feel right. All I knew was that I felt as cold as the stone I was staring at.

Shortly before we were to leave Japan, my group leader woke me in the middle of the night. "Be quiet. Come with me." I got up off my straw sleeping mat and was led down a winding path by strangers with flashlights.

"The Sweetie Seven" had been summoned by President Ikeda. When we arrived at his house we stood there in a daze as he spoke to us through an interpreter. He gave us gifts—silk purses and sandalwood beads. We were only there about ten minutes, but it was enough. I kept thinking, *If he's so enlightened, why can't he speak English? And why did we have to sneak out?* It was then I decided to drop out of this group when I got home.

And that's exactly what I did. They continued to phone me for about a year, encouraging me to keep chanting. The U.S. Director even wanted to talk to me in person. But I couldn't go back. I knew they didn't have the answers I was looking for.

Leaving the group left a big hole in my life because I'd invested so much time and energy. As I started to think about adjusting to a more normal lifestyle, I remembered friends I hadn't seen in quite awhile. I also thought of my father.

I'd been so busy with the Buddhists, it had been about six months since I'd made one of my routine visits to see my dad. He was still begging me to get him out of the hospital the last time I'd seen him. Even though I didn't see any way I could take care of him, I hoped there was still a chance for us to build a deeper relationship. So, one Sunday after returning from Japan, I decided to go visit him.

On the way to the hospital I stopped and bought him the candy and cigarettes he liked. When I got to the hospital and went to his room, though, he wasn't there. Figuring they'd moved him, I went to the nursing station. I gave the nurse his name, but she gave me a blank stare and asked, "*Who* is it you want?"

"Charles Steiner," I repeated.

"We don't have anyone by that name here."

I insisted I was in the right place.

"When was the last time you saw your father?" she asked me.

My eyes avoided hers. "About six months . . . Uh, I've been traveling."

"Six months? I haven't been here that long. Let me get someone else for you."

When a second nurse walked up, she looked right at me and asked, "Who are you?"

"I came to see Charles Steiner. I'm Melody, his daughter."

Without much hesitation she said, "Honey, he's dead. He died several months ago. Didn't you know?"

I was stunned. Grabbing the bag of candy and cigarettes, I ran out to my car in disbelief. I was angry. Sad. I felt like the stone I'd seen in the Japanese temple. I slammed my car into gear and raced to my mom's place. Why had she kept this from me? Why didn't she *tell* me and spare me this painful, humiliating moment?

I burst through the living room door and cornered my mom.

"Why didn't you tell me Daddy was dead!" I cried.

She just stared at me. Now she was the one who was stunned. "Dead? Charlie's *dead*? I didn't know. . . . I didn't know."

Now my mother was upset. Could I blame her after my bold accusation?

As we started to inquire about my father, the hospital told us he died from pneumonia. But a friend who worked there pulled his records and told us the details surrounding his death. It seems the nurses had been taking my father's cigarettes away from him because he was coughing so badly. Also, since he could only use one hand, he was constantly burning himself. He must have gone into the bathroom with some cigarettes to sneak a smoke. He evidently caught himself on fire and was burned seriously before anyone could come to his rescue. During his recovery, pneumonia set in as a complication to the burns, and he died. We were never notified when he was burned—or when his life was threatened by pneumonia. My dad died pretty much as he lived. Alone.

I was left to wonder why so much of what I *really* wanted in life had been taken away from me. I never had the family or the home I wanted, Mrs. Hilliard had slipped from my life, and the Buddhist experience was a flop. Now my father was dead. I knew we didn't have the greatest relationship but at least I had a father—or somebody I could *call* my father. Now there was no chance for a relationship. I was told they buried him somewhere in the veterans' cemetery near the hospital. Whenever I drove by all I could do was stare at the straight rows of white crosses—acres and acres of them. My dad was somewhere out there beneath a simple white cross.

I never did visit his grave.

For the next few years I bounced around like a rubber ball. Graduating from L.A. Trade Technical College in 1969, I did land several jobs in the fashion industry. And between jobs, I'd usually run my unemployment benefits dry—which only reflected how I was feeling inside. Dry. I continued my spiritual search, going from astrology, to yoga, to getting a mantra and meditating, to studying an obscure occult science.

The only thing left that held out any promise of happiness and a future were the letters from Mark. I found I was able to pour my heart out to him—but he was still in the Army. The loneliness I felt left me open to all kinds of influences.

One of the girls I'd gone to design college with came over to my apartment one spring evening. We decided to drop some acid. I was playing the Beatles *Abbey Road* album on my stereo, but as we came onto the LSD the music started sounding all jumbled together. The acid hit us hard. As I stared at the lit candle on the coffee table it was like watching time-lapse photography as I "saw" it melt down, then grow back to its original size and melt down again. The walls seemed to be closing in on us, too. Everything was spinning and moving so fast I thought I might flip out. We needed more space, so we decided to get outside for some fresh air even though it was after midnight.

Walking down the side streets of Santa Monica, I was wishing I could come down, but the acid had just hit—and it was stronger than I expected. I felt like I was being turned inside out.

Then the strangest thing happened. We were standing at the bottom of a hill and as I looked up into the black, midnight sky I saw a huge glowing cross hanging in the heavens. I blinked, but it didn't go away. It was a fiery, radiant gold. And it was beautiful. I stared at it in awe, and felt a peace wash into my heart. Everything around me became calm and still. Hoping to hold onto the moment I was afraid to even move. Something deep inside me was responding, saying, *I need this peace so bad. I don't ever want to lose it.*

I glanced at my friend and noticed that she now had a long, flowing shawl draped over her head. To my surprise, so did I. We had on long dresses too, that were gently blowing in the evening breeze. As I stared up at the cross all the turmoil stopped and it was like I was in another place, at another time, standing at the foot of this cross . . . a place I never wanted to leave.

But of course, my friend wasn't seeing the same thing, and in a moment she started talking about something. I tried to stop her—but it was too late. The scene of us at the cross dissolved before my eyes. I caught my breath in disappointment, but try as I might I couldn't get the image back. Gone were the shawls, the long dresses, and the beautiful glowing cross. My peace was gone as well. I felt like something precious had just been torn from my hands. I was again caught up in the agitation of the trip. We wandered the streets for a few more hours before we returned to my apartment.

It was daylight before the acid wore off and I could get some sleep. But I didn't forget the cross, or the peace. Later on, when I woke up, I went back to the spot where it all happened. In the place of the cross there was only a tall telephone pole with a cross-beam. That must have been what my hallucination hung itself upon.

But the peace that came with it was what puzzled me. I knew Jesus died on a cross, but I'd never thought of looking to him for any answers. Jews didn't believe in Jesus. And anyway, could you really have a valid spiritual experience on drugs? I didn't think these questions had answers so I hid that experience in my heart and tried to move forward with life.

Eventually Mark got discharged from the Army, and we made plans to move in together. After four years of being apart we were like total strangers, but our excitement about each other overshadowed everything else. For me it was a dream come true. I finally had somebody I could call my own. Mark soon enrolled in college, and I landed a job in Canoga Park at a videotape production studio called Matrix Image. Now I had every reason to be happy—I had a good relationship with Mark and a good job. And yet I found myself deeply dissatisfied with everything around me—and looking for ways to forget the growing emptiness I was feeling. Even Mark couldn't fill the void.

I was at a real low point in my life and getting numb was more attractive than ever. Almost every day at lunch, I'd go out with the receptionist next door and drink margaritas. Only in her mid-twenties, she already had a drinking problem—and I wasn't doing much better. During work, I'd also go into the ladies' room frequently and smoke some marijuana or hash just to get through the afternoon. I'd even decided to sell some dope, which was really a first. I knew I was getting into a dangerous place.

Inwardly, I was giving up. For all my ideals, and all my searching for the truth, I was coming up empty.

Then the bottom dropped out.

One evening after dinner, Mark and I were having a casual conversation, when he suddenly got quiet. Then he said, "Babe, I want to tell you about something really beautiful that just happened to me."

"What?" I asked, smiling.

"Well, Marie and I got together."

"Got together . . . What do you mean?"

"You know, we made love. It was inevitable. I believe it was meant to be."

I felt like someone had just kicked me in the stomach. Marie was married to Mark's best friend. Was I really supposed to be happy?

"Where was her husband? Does he know?"

"He was there, babe. He saw it coming and just left us alone. He came in and woke us up in the morning. He's such a beautiful brother."

I didn't *want* to get upset. But even though I'd read the book *Open Marriage*, it was hard to get my mind open *that* far. I didn't know how to compute this in my emotions. As much as I tried to deny it, I felt betrayed. I sure wasn't perfect, but at least I'd been faithful. I let it go and we didn't talk about it again. But something inside of me was dying.

A short time later I walked into our living room just as Mark was kissing one of *my* best friends. This time I was so upset I took a few Quaaludes, and the next morning I phoned in sick.

So nothing was sacred after all. Reality was getting too hard to deal with. I didn't want to feel pain again. Mark and I didn't break up, but that bond of loyalty was broken. Somehow I always knew I was living out of a sense of loss—a sense of wanting something that would last. This only highlighted it. It just seemed a lot better to be numb—and I was getting more numb all the time.

The day I met Keith Green, the last thing I wanted was a serious relationship. In fact, all I could think of was getting *out* of the relationship with Mark.

Near the end of January 1973, Keith showed up at Matrix Image, along with his dad, his grandfather and a friend. Rumor had it that video would be the next big thing. They were looking into the possibility of combining Keith's music with some of the new video effects we were producing.

As I gave them a tour, Keith seemed to stay right on my

—

59

heels, asking questions and telling me more about himself than I really cared to know. But I soon found out you couldn't ignore Keith for long—especially if he wanted to get your attention.

About a week after the tour, I was sitting at my desk when the phone rang.

"Matrix Image. May I help you?" When I answered, a voice on the other end of the line said cheerfully, "Hi, I miss you."

"Who is this?" I said coolly.

"It's me—Keith. You know, I was in last week."

"Oh, yes I remember," I said. And I thought, *How can he say he misses me? He barely knows me.*

"I was calling to see if your boss listened to the music tape I left him."

"I don't know but I can check on it."

"O.K. Great. Have *you* listened to it yet?"

"No . . . not yet," I said, feeling a bit on the spot. "But I will soon."

"Great. Hey, do you wanna meet me for lunch today?"

I stalled him, my mind racing for an excuse. But Keith was cheerfully persistent. When I hung up I was a bit surprised at myself for saying I'd go. Although I was hurt about Mark, I still really cared about him. And I definitely didn't feel ready to jump into another relationship. I needed some space.

But this Keith Green—his directness threw me a bit. Most guys played it cool. Keith was aggressive, not a game-player.

I changed my mind several times before lunch time arrived, but met Keith as planned. He'd made sandwiches, and we went to Chatsworth Park for a picnic. He brought his guitar along and as we sat cross-legged on the grass he played me a song he'd just finished. It was a really beautiful tune, but more than the music, I immediately heard Keith's heart—or maybe I should say his heart cry. As he sang for me there in the park, he voiced some of the same questions I'd been struggling with, but said them in a way I never would have thought of saying them—like, "Is death the answer, or just a door? Does anyone know?"

I'd already told Keith I wrote songs too, but once I heard how good he was I felt a twinge of regret as he passed me his guitar and asked me to play him one. I sang a few of my songs for him and, to my relief he seemed to like them. Then he said, "I've got some other songs I want to play for you but I need a piano."

We drove to Pierce College, where Keith was taking some classes, and found an empty practice room with a piano. As he started playing, it was obvious he was in his element. He played easily and powerfully. He threw himself into each song with energy and emotion, sweat starting to show on his forehead. And his voice . . . his voice was soul-stirring. I stood there speechless. To say I was impressed would be an understatement.

I had never heard anyone, anywhere, like Keith Green. As I listened to him I thought, *This guy is incredible. I can't believe he's not making records.* But it wasn't just his music—it was all of him. The energy. The sincerity. The sheer power of his performance.

I was already going to be late getting back from lunch. Keith walked me to my car and gave me a small hug. I drove back to work thinking that this lunch had turned out to be very interesting.

It also hit me that I had just gone out with someone else while I was still in a relationship with Mark. That was really out of character for me—no matter that Mark had been with other girls.

Keith kept calling me at work, so I decided to listen to the tape of songs he'd left for my boss. I was especially taken up by one beautiful love song. It had a soaring, haunting melody line. But the words haunted me more. Most love songs out then were about "revolving door" relationships—here today, gone tomorrow. This song was different. And it was clear that this Keith Green was different as well.

About three weeks later, during another lunchtime get-together, Keith walked me to my car as I got ready to head back to work. We stood there for a moment and Keith looked at me intently. My car door was open and I was just about to get in when he stepped closer and warmly kissed me. I didn't resist. I liked the way he kissed and I kissed him back.

As I drove back to work I wondered what I was getting myself into.

Keith immediately wrote some free verse about our first kiss in his journal and later gave me a copy, which in part read:

> *With our electricity and music*
> *Through me*
> *We can amplify the beautiful song of us*
> *After all, you are a Melody*
> *And I am a minstrel*
> *And we are becoming a fact — US.*

In short order, things began to shift around in my little world. Mark decided to go to New York and finish the last semester of a college career he'd left dangling to go into the Army. He was planning to come back to California six months later. I was keeping my mouth shut about Keith.

True to form, Keith wrote a rather humorous song about the situation. He called it, "You're On My List Of Things To Do!" No one had ever written a song for me before, and I was really flattered when Keith sang it to me. The first verse said:

Well I met you at the office
Then you know it grew
And then there was your boyfriend
But then he never knew
That you liked me
And you hate it
Cause you don't know what to do
But honey, you're on my list of things to do!

Keith was anxiously counting the days until Mark left. A few weeks later in mid-April, I waved goodbye to him as he drove out of the Matrix Image parking lot on his way back east. Telling people things they might not want to hear was difficult for me, so I let him leave without saying anything about my growing feelings for Keith. Keith had been pushing to see me right away, but I needed some breathing room. So I actually managed to hold him off—for a week.

On Easter Sunday, Keith was to pick me up to go to the Renaissance Fair in Ventura County—even though I warned him I wanted to take everything slowly. I'd just regained my freedom and my heart didn't feel ready to make another commitment.

When Easter Sunday arrived, so did Keith—a few *hours* before the time we'd agreed on! His early knock woke me up and I stumbled to the door in a daze. I couldn't believe it when I opened up and found him standing there in a woven, Indian-print shirt.

"I was so excited I just couldn't wait any longer," he said sheepishly. I sighed and let him come in while I went off to get ready. What girl in her right mind could stay mad after an explanation like that?

At the Fair, Keith and I walked around for hours, buying organic food and looking at everyone in their medieval outfits. There were wandering minstrels, jugglers, palm readers, and artisans selling every kind of homemade item you could think of. The smell of burning incense and food cooking all mingled together in a pleasant way, and you could smell the perfumed oils—strawberry, sandalwood, patchouli—floating on the breeze. A lot of people had taken psychedelic drugs and some of them looked very wiped-out. Keith told me his last drug trip was on his nineteenth birthday last October when he took mescaline. It had been such an intense experience, he said, that he hadn't taken any drugs since. I was still a lot more involved in the drug scene, but I hadn't done any tripping for a while.

We sat on the grass in the warm sun and talked. Just talked— all afternoon. There was something about Keith that was different from anyone I'd ever known. He was a true seeker. A deep thinker. And even though he was quite serious about life, he had a wild sense of humor that I really enjoyed.

The difference in our ages did bother me a bit—but at least Keith's life experience and perspective on things helped close the seven-and-a-half year gap between us. He was young, and full of potential and hope for the future—but at the same time he said he often felt "old and senile" at nineteen. At just twenty-six, I knew what he meant.

Within a week, Mark phoned me long-distance. Keith was there, and I took the phone into the bathroom to talk privately. I half expected Keith to get mad and leave, acting like he didn't care, but not Keith.

He was afraid I might get back together with Mark and he stayed right there in the living room—fuming and pacing the floor. I was on the spot. It was killing me to think I was going to hurt Mark.

When I told him about Keith, he started crying. He wanted to turn around and drive right back to California, saying he was willing to make our relationship more permanent. But it was too late. I told him not to come back for me. We spent over an hour on the phone and I cried, too. I felt so torn. I felt like the most terrible person in the world at that moment. But the phone call ended my relationship with Mark.

Within a month, Keith moved into my apartment.

"Love With Me"

Officially engaged on Keith's twentieth birthday. 1973

W HEN KEITH MOVED INTO MY APARTMENT IN MAY OF 1974 IT was the biggest "moving in" I'd ever experienced. Keith's whole approach to life was unique. Actually, he was a ball of contradictions.

On the outside he looked like everyone else our age—but underneath it all he seemed out-of-step with the times. His ideas—even his whole character—seemed to be in opposition to the values that were so popular. It was like he'd been airlifted in from some other time and place.

One thing I particularly liked—besides the freshness Keith brought into my life—was the feeling of security I had when we were together. He seemed to like taking care of me. He questioned everything about everything, which challenged me to stretch my thinking. And when Keith was *into* something, he wanted everybody to get into it, too.

One really beautiful May morning, we woke up and Keith convinced me I should play hooky from work. It wasn't hard. Keith wanted to take a long drive, so he picked the route—the back roads of Simi Valley that eventually led up the coast to Santa Barbara. On our way, we came upon a little antique store and stopped. Inside, Keith spotted a large, silver Jerusalem cross with a turquoise stone in the center.

"Wow, look at this great cross, Mel. Let's get it for you."

I felt awkward. "It's really pretty but . . . I've never worn a cross in my life."

"Oh, come on, we've been looking into Jesus."

"I know but I'm . . . I'm still Jewish."

I had been open to Jesus only because of Keith's enthusiasm about him, and I liked what I saw in Keith. But wearing a cross? That was a different story. What would my mother think? Something inside me totally rejected that idea. On the other hand, I did like what I was learning about Jesus. I thought about it for a minute. "Well. . . ." At least nobody was hanging on it.

"Honey, it's beautiful. Come on, please let me get it for you," Keith insisted.

It seemed like Keith really wanted me to have a cross so I could be wearing one like he was.

"Well, alright. I guess it would be okay".

A grin spread across Keith's face. He quickly pulled out his wallet and plunked down the money. The cross didn't have a chain on it so I slipped it into my pocket. I knew Keith really wanted to share his faith with me and, after all, I was hungry for something, too. If Jesus held the answers I was open, even though it was a bit alien to me.

Later on as we drove, I took the cross out of my pocket and turned it over. On the back, it said, "Jerusalem". At least it was from Israel, which was a point of consolation for this Jewish girl.

It was quickly becoming clear that if I was going to be involved with this guy I was going to be carried along with him on his spiritual journey, too. But for now I was just falling in love.

As I found out more about Keith over the next few months I saw that he was someone who was capable of making deep commitments. I thought this was interesting, considering everyone around us had such a "hang-loose, whatever will be will be" attitude. Keith wasn't that way. When he cared about a person it was more than just pretty words, he wanted to show it.

For instance, Keith liked to spend a lot of time with Dawn, the ten-year-old daughter of his friend, Karen Bender. Dawn was a beautiful child, with long thick hair and freckles sprinkled lightly across her turned-up nose. Dawn seemed a bit more withdrawn than a kid her age should have been. She didn't smile a lot, but when she did it was like a burst of sunshine. Keith really loved her, and as I got to know her she won my heart as well. Her mom was divorced and worked long hours, so one weekend Keith decided to bring Dawn home with us so we could have some extra time together. We took her swimming, to an amusement park, and to the movies. We had a great time, but by the end of the weekend we realized being "parents" was a bigger job than we thought. Still we tried to get together with both Dawn and Karen as often as we could.

In fact, it was at a rather wild party at Karen's house one night late in the summer that Keith and I wandered off to talk about where we were in our relationship. We ended up in Dawn's bedroom, sitting on her bed. As we talked Keith totally surprised me.

"Mel, I've been wondering if it's really right for us to be living together."

I couldn't believe it. No one else we knew would even be raising this question.

"What do you mean 'really right'? We love each other don't we?"

"Yeah, but that's just the point. If we really love each other maybe we should have a deeper commitment."

I found myself staring at the frayed squares of the granny quilt on Dawn's bed, wondering where this conversation was going to lead. I'd never heard anyone talk like this before and I was getting a little nervous.

"What I'm trying to say", Keith continued, "is maybe we should be thinking about getting married. I'm not sure we should be living together without being married."

"Married?"

"Of course we'd need to get engaged first. So maybe we could get 'engaged to be engaged'."

"Keith, what does that mean?"

"It would be kind of a trial period. That way if things don't work out we won't have to break our engagement."

I'd never heard of anything like it. This was crazy—and a little wonderful. But, I was learning that Keith never did things the way everyone else did.

"I don't know, Keith . . . ."

"It'll be great. Who else do you know who ever got 'engaged to be engaged'?"

I thought about it for a moment. The idea had its merits. Since my disastrous relationship with Mark I still wasn't ready for a *real* commitment, even after several months of living with Keith.

"Well, you might have a good idea. That way we'd have time to decide what we really want to do."

"Mel, I want you to know that if we *do* end up getting married, I believe it's a lifetime commitment. I don't believe in divorce."

As Keith continued talking my mind started to reel. To me divorce seemed like too big a possibility to ever rule out. I really didn't know *any* happily married couples and wasn't even sure about the whole idea of marriage. Part of me was overwhelmed that someone as wonderful and talented as Keith wanted to marry me. But what if things didn't work out? It seemed much safer to leave a door open somewhere.

"Some of the things you're saying really scare me," I finally replied.

But Keith was insistent.

"Melody I *love* you, and I believe you love me. Let's not be afraid of this. If we get married I always want to be there for you, and I want to know you'll be there for me, too."

He continued to press his point. Finally, we did decide to be "engaged to be engaged". We also made plans to get "officially" engaged on Keith's twentieth birthday in October. It seemed like a safe enough position since it gave us a few months to weigh the whole matter. True to form I was most comfortable keeping my options open.

On October 21st, we had a birthday party for Keith and, as planned, we became officially engaged. Our house was full of friends and little Dawn was among them. She gave Keith a piece of driftwood for a present and we all clowned around, taking pictures and eating the cake I'd baked.

We set our wedding date for December 25th—Christmas day, in honor of Jesus—at the Little Brown Church on Coldwater Canyon Boulevard.

On the night we got engaged, we also started trying to live with another major decision we'd made. Several months before, Keith had come to the conclusion that if he didn't truly love someone then having a sexual relationship with them was wrong. A few days before we'd even met, Keith confided this decision to his journal.

I've been questioning the righteousness of sex in my heart. I know for a fact that sex without love is dead wrong. Now my use of the word "love" has a changeable definition. I know it has changed extremely the past four years. (Or has it? Have I become more cynical and does it take "love" longer to break through and reach me?) At any rate, love has been a different, deeper thing for me. Anyway, sex with love rings true in me. If it is wrong out of marriage . . . let it be shown to me.

The big question we'd been talking about recently centered on the last sentence of Keith's entry. What if you really *did* love someone, but you weren't married to them? What then? Most of our friends were barreling down the road in the opposite direction—trying to figure out how many people they could sleep with and how fast. And here we were, wondering how to make right choices. But this question was really important to Keith, and we talked about it a lot.

"I'm thinking that maybe we should go celibate until we get married," Keith said one day, to my shock.

"I've read some things in the Bible, and I'm beginning to think that sex outside of marriage is wrong."

"But we're living in the same house, sleeping in the same bed," I protested.

"Yeah, but we can do it."

"Keith, this is even *crazier* than getting 'engaged to be engaged'."

"Well, it worked didn't it?"

"And *how long* would you want to do this for?"

"Until we get married."

"Keith, I'm not that much against the idea of it, but how in the world do you expect it to work?"

"Well, I really think it's the right thing to do. Let's give it a try."

So we made a decision to go celibate on Keith's birthday. But, as I suspected, it was easier said than done.

In early December, Keith came to me with a mysterious look on his face. He took me by the hand and said, "Come here, I want you to listen to something." Then he led me over to the piano. "Stand there where I can see you."

He sat down and just started singing. . . .

> *You wanna love with me*
> *Love with me, then.*
> *I only ask*
> *That you still be my friend.*

For there are many
Where friendship's unknown.
They live together,
But really alone.

And the days
Go their ways
In silence—
Tense hours of woe.
We do not mean to have it so. . . .

As I listened to him sing I got so caught up in the soaring melody that it took me a minute to realize the song was a surprise. It was for me! My throat tightened up and I found myself starting to blink back a few tears. As Keith sang he closed his eyes, then peeked at me to see how I was reacting. I couldn't say a word.

The song was all about commitment. About a love that wouldn't change its mind, even during the hard times. It was Keith's way of saying that he knew he wasn't perfect, but he would give me a love that would keep growing and never give up. . . .

I know that sometimes
I'm harder to love.
I thrash out blindly
Like nothing's thought of.

But I will love you,
And love you, I do!
It's not complete yet,
But you know we're not through.

And the days
Go their ways
In blessings—
Moments of truth.
We truly dare not waste our youth.

You wanna love with me,
Love with me, then.

It was a bit overwhelming to have a song written for me, especially one as beautiful as "Love With Me".

The beauty of that moment helped offset the terrible arguments we were having, stemming from what I was beginning to think was a silly rule—Keith's idea about staying celibate until we got married. That fall was a very difficult time for us. We thought we had the right idea, but it wasn't easy to live up to our own convictions.

Fortunately, our wedding day arrived quickly. We woke up early on Christmas morning and dressed in our favorite Goodwill finds. I wore a green turtleneck sweater and a long, yellow cotton skirt, and Keith wore his Levi's and a nubby beige sweater. I'd never pictured myself walking down the aisle in a white dress, but it did feel odd to climb out of bed, help each other pick out clothes and drive off to go get married.

Keith and I were both nervously quiet as we drove down to the Little Brown Church. When we arrived, the dim lighting made the old wooden pews look warm and inviting as we stood in front and said our vows before the minister. It was a quick and simple ceremony, and within minutes we were married—and Keith made sure it was "in the name of Jesus". Todd was our only witness.

Afterward we drove off to visit Keith's folks. Keith's parents were surprised to see us so early in the day—with our crazy late-night schedule we never showed up anywhere before noon. We hung around with silly grins, waiting for them to guess what we'd done. Besides Todd, only my mom knew ahead of time—but we wouldn't let her come to the wedding since Keith's family didn't know about it. Keith kept waving his left hand around hoping they'd notice his ring. But they didn't. After a few hours, his mom finally ventured a smiling guess, "Did you two get married?" They were surprised, but it wasn't unexpected. Keith and I had become inseparable.

As word got out, their house filled with friends and relatives, including my mom. Some goodies were pulled together, and the day turned into a real party. We were on the receiving end of lots of hugs and kisses. And as I looked across the room at Keith he seemed really happy. He looked like he was sure we'd made the right decision. I hoped he was right.

Since we were already living together, going off to some romantic spot for a honeymoon didn't seem real important. We were pretty broke. We'd even had to sleep in "Victor" for two nights as we drove home from a recent trip to Seattle because we couldn't afford a motel. But Keith, never lacking for good ideas when it came to making money, got us a new job.

Three days after our wedding we started working at the local Pizza Man, so we spent our "honeymoon" racing pizzas around the San Fernando Valley. And I do mean racing. We got paid for each delivery so speed was of the utmost importance—and speed was right up Keith's alley.

Besides racing boxes of hot pizzas around, "Victor von Van" played another important role in keeping our cash-flow flowing. Keith figured we could turn our love for thrift-store shopping into a business by using "Victor" as a traveling boutique—hippie-style of course. We bought used clothing that still had resale value. Then we'd park "Victor" on the streets of Hollywood and hang the clothing all around the outside. We even set up a mirror inside "Victor" so our customers could climb inside to try things on.

Overall, we had a lot of fun, especially because we could do it together. And it helped us pay our rent in a *non*-nine-to-five way while we waited for Keith's big break.

We didn't have a lot of money, but it didn't matter. There wasn't anything more we wanted out of life—nothing that money could buy anyway. The things we were hungry for couldn't have been bought with a million dollars.

It seemed like all of southern California was on one big spiritual search just like we were. Not only were we interested in this Jesus Christ—whoever he was. It seemed like Jesus was getting pretty popular, too. On the West Coast there was talk about a Jesus Movement. Lots of people were being baptized right in the Pacific Ocean. At the same time there were several movies out with Christian themes. We saw *Brother Sun, Sister Moon* which was about the life of Saint Francis of Assisi. He was a young man of high ideals who gave up all his worldly possessions to take care of the poor and needy—even the lepers. He led a life of poverty, putting God first. We also saw *Godspell*. It was about the life of Jesus, acted out by lots of people our age. Then there was *Jesus Christ, Superstar*. We saw that twice when it hit the movie theaters and constantly listened to the soundtrack that climbed to the top of the charts.

Then, of all things, Keith met Teddy Neely, who played Jesus in the film version of *Jesus Christ, Superstar*. In fact we had him over for dinner and I kept looking at him thinking, *I can't believe it. I'm making hamburgers for Jesus!* I really didn't think Teddy was some kind of mystic, but just getting to know him after seeing him play Jesus, with his long straight hair and flowing muslin robes, really impacted me.

Teddy was full of stories about some things that happened while filming in Israel. It seemed there was some real supernatural activity during the crucifixion scene. Keith and I were all ears. That crucifixion scene, in particular, really touched me. It didn't look like Jesus did anything to deserve what happened to him. Jesus and the things he stood for were becoming more real and easier to relate to all the time.

We really loved the movies we were seeing with spiritual overtones—actually they were more inspiring than some of the people we'd met who said they were Christians. We specifically did *not* want to become like some of the "Jesus Freaks" we were encountering.

Shortly after Keith moved in with me he'd been asked to do a series of concerts in the Pacific Northwest. I'd been laid off from work, so I went with him. While we were in Seattle, Keith introduced me to a girl who said she was a Christian. She was the first "Jesus Freak" I'd ever met. Kathy was someone Keith had met when he'd first run away several years before. Something about Kathy made us totally uncomfortable. You couldn't have a normal conversation with her. She'd say things like, "Oh, we're out of milk, praise God," or "It's a beautiful day, praise the Lord." Every other sentence was punctuated with some religious exclamation. It gave me the creeps. We *never* wanted to walk around uttering mindless phrases like she did. We were content just to call ourselves followers of Jesus and leave it at that. We didn't want to become alienated from the human race!

My own reluctance ran even deeper. I wanted to know the truth, but because of my Jewish roots it was hard to believe I might find it in Jesus. Even though I'd gotten more out of reading small sections of his teachings in the Bible than I'd gotten from all the other mystical books I'd read put together, I was still uncomfortable when I thought of *following* him.

In fact, one night before we got married Keith and I had a pretty big disagreement at The Bla Bla Cafe—about our wedding rings. Keith wanted to get small crosses engraved on them. I dug in my heels. We took a heated walk outside The Bla between sets to work it out. Wearing a Jerusalem cross around my neck occasionally was one thing, but engraving a cross on a ring I'd wear every day for the rest of my life was something else. But Keith felt having crosses on our rings would be symbolic of our decision to make Jesus our master, and a constant reminder that we were married in his name. I was torn, but I really did want to honor Jesus in our marriage. Letting Keith's faith pull me along, I finally agreed. As we drove home from The Bla that night I found myself thinking back to my early childhood. As much as I struggled, it was slowly sinking in that God just might be really real.

When I was a little girl I once came down with pneumonia and was delirious with fever. When the doctor came, he became alarmed. He told my mom I was too sick to move to the hospital, and gave me a shot. Before he left, he said that if my fever didn't break by about four in the morning, I wouldn't survive the night.

My mom never left my side. Through the haze of fever I

watched her putting cool, wet washcloths on my forehead—and heard her desperate prayers. I felt bathed in her love—and in another kind of love that I seemed to be floating in. Was it just the fever?

When the doctor returned at 6 a.m., I woke up and ran to the door. He was shocked to see me. He ordered me back to bed and told my mom it was a miracle I made it through the night. He'd brought a death certificate with him in his black bag.

Since then, I knew that "someone somewhere" answered my mother's prayers. Could it be that God had reached out to me before I even started seeking him?

There were other influences in our lives, too. Shortly after Keith and I were married, we began to get closer to some people who were also into music—only it was *Christian* music. Recently, we'd even acquired a new "roommate" who was sleeping on our fold-out couch—Keith's friend Randy Stonehill. Keith had met Randy one night about a year-and-a-half before at The Bla. Since then they'd had a blast writing and singing together occasionally. Randy had even recorded a whole album of rock 'n' roll Christian songs—an idea that was really new to us.

Now besides being involved in music together, Keith and Randy had their share of fairly "energized" spiritual debates. The thing that always upset Keith was the fact that Randy didn't think Keith was quite "there" as a Christian. Except for our question— "Was Jesus really God?"—Keith couldn't see any major differences in their beliefs. But Randy didn't see how Keith thought he could be a Christian without settling the "God question", as we called it.

"Keith, you can't *be* a Christian if you don't believe Jesus is God," Randy would say.

"But I believe Jesus is God's son. I believe in what he says. I want to live my life by his teachings. Doesn't *that* make me a Christian?"

"You're just not getting it," Randy said, shaking his head.

'Round and 'round the question would go.

They developed a deep but rocky friendship, revolving around their mutual love of music and their crazy personalities. So it was inevitable that they'd end up doing some concerts together.

The Salt Company was a Christian club in Hollywood. And the summer before we were married, Randy had invited Keith to do some songs with him there. It was their first performance together and they were great! Their high energy levels made the air around them pulsate. They were also hilariously funny and kept the crowd in stitches between, and even during, some of their songs.

As a result of Keith's friendship with Randy, a few more Christian concerts were opening up. Keith was invited to play at California Lutheran College and then we made plans to go to northern California with Randy who had been invited up there to do a few concerts. We thought we were going so Keith could do a "guest set" at Randy's concerts. We had no way of knowing we were about to meet someone who would have a lasting impact on our whole lives.

The first night of our trip, Keith and Randy played at a small, sparsely-attended Christian coffee house in Fresno. The following day, we drove out to Turlock for the next concert where they'd be sharing the bill with someone else.

As we drove Randy said, "The guy who's playing tonight will really blow you away. His name's Barry McGuire."

Keith said, "You mean *the* Barry McGuire?"

"The guy who sang the hit song, 'Eve of Destruction'?" I added in surprise.

"Yeah, that's the one," Randy smiled.

"The Eve of Destruction" was an anti-war song from the '60s. It hit the top of the music charts all across America and we remembered it well enough to sing it in the car as we drove. It was hard to believe this guy was a Christian now and we were eager to see what he'd be like.

The Turlock concert was held in a high school gym. There were a few hundred people there when we arrived. After Randy's set, and Keith's, we settled back in our seats, anxious to hear Barry.

He'd made a Christian album, just like Randy. The whole idea of people recording whole albums of Christian songs sounded outrageous to us.

When Barry stepped out on stage to sing, we were immediately struck by his presence. At first glance, he looked a little rough around the edges—a big, burly guy with long hair and a bushy beard. He looked like he might ride to church on a Harley Davidson motorcycle or something. But as soon as he spoke, I was amazed at his meekness. He sang a few songs, playing the big guitar strapped around his shoulder. We were particularly impressed with one called "Bullfrogs and Butterflies". It was incredible to see this big hulk of a guy singing what sounded like a children's song. He explained it before he sang.

"What do bullfrogs and butterflies have in common? The frog

comes from a tadpole, and the butterfly emerges from a cocoon—but they both get born-again. And just like them, we need to experience a spiritual rebirth before we can really know God."

He sang and talked about God in a way that we never heard before. He made knowing God sound simple. Barry's mannerisms were so warm and easygoing that we were glued to every word he sang or spoke. When he was finished, we followed him back into the dressing room with hopes of talking to him before he had to leave. He was in a big hurry to catch an airplane, but he took a few minutes with us. Up close, he was kind and gentle—but it was more than that.

There was something about his eyes. They were like clear peaceful pools. His spirit was far different from his gruff-looking exterior—this was obviously a man who had been transformed. He was married, and he and his wife traveled all over the country telling people about Jesus—often living out of their small vehicle that had a camper shell on it. We were impressed by this "singing star" who was now following Jesus in such a humble, sacrificial way.

After that evening, Keith and I knew Barry McGuire had something we wanted. That special "something" in his spirit had caused the seed of an idea to burst open in Keith's heart—an idea that had once been planted there by another friend, named Randy Wimer.

Keith had felt an instant love for Barry, which he compared to the depth of relationship he'd had with Randy Wimer, who played in a band called MU. When Keith first met Randy, he was taken by his quiet spirit. Randy was a Seventh Day Adventist, and talked to Keith a lot about Jesus. Now some of the things he'd said about Jesus were starting to make more sense. Randy had told Keith that Jesus could take away sins once and for all—unlike the eastern and occult religions he'd studied.

As we drove home from Turlock, Randy's discussions with Keith all came back to him.

Many of the eastern religions teach the idea of multiple lives, and that your lot in the next life is determined by how "holy" you were in the lifetime before. If bad things started happening to you in one lifetime it was because you were paying for the sins of your past life. If you had "good karma" you'd have a happy life but "bad karma" meant you should expect hard times. We used to joke around when we saw someone do something wrong, saying, "That's gonna be a few years of bad karma!"

Now, Keith recalled something Randy Wimer had told him—that Jesus can wipe away your sins so you don't have to pay for them later. When we got back home Keith grabbed one of his older journals to find his notes from that conversation. When he found it he read the quote out loud to me:

Christ created us, the world, and the universe. His teaching is the way out of the cycle of death and rebirth (re-incarnation) and He is the way.

Keith concluded that he was more open than ever to the idea of Jesus being able to "cut your karma". And after hearing Barry McGuire, I had to admit that the idea of getting a "clean slate" and being born-again spiritually was starting to look like it might really be possible.

Unfortunately, our burst of inspiration was short-lived as the rockiness of newlywed life with no money hit. Keith closed at The Bla because, once again, he wasn't drawing a good crowd. But Keith felt he'd been there too long and needed a break, anyway. My mom cheered us up with a beautiful belated wedding reception at her house, where lots of friends and family came and loaded us down with lovely gifts. But even with all those blessings—even with our love—we felt like life was running out between our fingers, leaving us with nothing to show for our days.

Then in March, Keith played at another Christian coffee house with Randy Stonehill, near the beach in Pacific Palisades. The night proved to be another number on our growing list of disappointments. First Randy played, then Keith. Keith always loved to play new songs to "try them out" on an audience and this night was no exception. Two days earlier we'd written a humorous song about the energy crisis America was plunged into, called "Self-Service Mama". It was about a guy who meets a girl while they're "waiting in line at a self-service gas station". Part of the chorus contained some mildly-suggestive images. We just thought they were funny.

After Keith's set, Randy came up to him in a highly-agitated state. "What in the world are you doing, singing songs like *that* here? You've offended these people. This isn't The Bla Bla."

Keith was irritated, too. "What are you talking about? These people don't know a good song when they hear one. Don't Christians have a sense of humor?"

"You blew it man."

"Well, *excuse* me. Are you trying to tell me that 'Queen of the Rodeo' song you sang tonight had some kind of spiritual message?"

"Hey there's nothing wrong with a simple love song," Randy said defensively. "I'm just trying to help you."

"You can *help* me by trying to understand where I'm at and by getting off my case."

After that, Keith did become more cautious about the songs he sang for these "super-Christian" and un-funny people Randy was introducing us to. One that they especially seemed to like was a song Keith had been working on for a few years called, "The Prodigal Son". It was from a story in the Bible, about a young man who demanded his inheritance early from his father so he could go out and live on his own:

> *I was done hoeing,*
> *Out in the fields for the day.*
> *I was thinking of going.*
> *I had to leave right away.*
>
> *My father was reading*
> *The Holy books in his room.*
> *My heart was just bleeding,*
> *I knew I had to go soon. . . .*
>
> *I said, "Father there's so much to know,*
> *There's a world of things to see,*
> *And I'm ready to go and make a life for myself.*
> *If you give me what is mine,*
> *I will go if I can have your blessing.*
> *But if you won't bless my journey,*
> *I'm gonna leave anyway!"*

As the story goes, the father gives his son his share of money, and the son goes out and squanders it on wild living, gets used by his friends, and finally hits rock bottom. Then he realizes what he gave away by leaving a home where he was loved. It was a powerful song, with several movements to it.

At that time, I was working on a song with a similar theme, but a whole different feel. It was a song I started for Todd, because he was thinking of splitting from home in hopes of finding the truth about life somewhere "out there". It was called "Run To The End Of The Highway".

Since I'd gone all the way to Asia on my search and Keith had rifled through every spiritual option you could think of, it was appropriate that we finished the song together:

> *Well, you can run to the end of the highway*
> *And not find what you're looking for—*
> *No, it won't make your troubles disappear.*
>
> *And you can search to the end of the highway*
> *And come back no better than before.*
> *To find yourself you've got to start right here. . . .*

It was crazy in a way. Here we were writing songs about

people who needed to get their lives together, but our lives were slipping out of control again. Despite our heady, spiritual dialogues, we were once again falling back into the same old sloppy habits to deaden the pain of Keith's lack of success—not to mention our inner emptiness.

As Keith wrote, disgustedly, in his journal:

Took a downer, snorted coke—not good enough—smoked dope till the cows crowed.

Keith was really down on himself, and so was I. But a few days later at a party in a friend's gazebo we did it again. It was a beautiful day and after a small argument about whether we should or shouldn't, Keith and I ended up smoking large amounts of hash. The drugs made us miserable and only underscored the fact that we were lost and failing in our search for God. We were beginning to realize that all our good intentions were getting us nowhere fast.

Nothing really seemed to be working for us. We just knew we wanted to be pure and righteous and that we wanted to follow Jesus—but we seemed incapable of doing so. And so it seemed to go through much of 1974.

Keith wrote these two entries on the same day that summer:

JULY 29, 1974
Still Stoned
Always a rational reason why I can cloud up my clear sky and pretend that I'm getting "high". What a screw-up! Never believing in my will—a snort, a joint, a pill, will screw up my head until I let my angel(s) lead me away.
God
There is no one to talk to about how I feel. I love the Christ always—and Jesus and all the words and works. There's metaphysical Christians—and there's Jesus Freaks that scream, yell and chant his name, but there's no confused Christians like me—that I can see or meet. I love the goal so thoroughly that I'd give up anything to attain it if I were sure about the path. . . .Ah! My heart—It wants to break for the truth. . . .

It was clear that *something* had to break for us—and soon.

"There Is A Redeemer"

New believers. 1975

A S WE STUMBLED INTO OUR SECOND FULL YEAR OF MARRIAGE, in 1975, Keith had that old restlessness about him. Our life seemed to be rushing by at a crazy pace. We ran all over town, delivering the lead-sheets we'd been writing—and making demos. A blind singer, named Tom Sullivan, fell in love with one of Keith's songs, and the guy from Helen Reddy's management team picked six of his songs to send to her, including "Love With Me."

Still nothing materialized.

Personally, our relationship suffered many more tense moments. I was earning money with Keith on the lead-sheets, and we worked pretty well as a team in everything—well, almost everything.

When it came to the house we hit our big differences. I didn't want to be responsible for all the cooking, cleaning and laundry. It didn't seem fair to me. But Keith had other ideas.

JANUARY 9, 1975

We had a fight about Mel cooking for me and she wants it shared. I was still very mad at Mel cause she wouldn't take care of me.

My head was fighting between selfish chauvinism and sincere belief that Mel should take responsibility for the homey things. I don't know. I know I'm lazy and never liked housework, but neither does Melody. Please let me know, God.

I split . . . and called her and talked things out. She decided that she'd do the housewife trip for a while. It is resolved—temporarily.

Even more troubling, our "spiritual houses" needed a good cleaning up—but who did we call for that? It would be a lot easier if we could open the phone book and get the number for "Charlie's Cosmic Clean-Up". We wanted to live a life that would somehow put us in contact with God in a real way—but it seemed like we were just going backwards. The day after our "domestic" argument—while I cleaned the house—Keith poured out his spiritual frustrations in music. The song was called, "I Gotta Do Better Than This".

> *Lord I'm not living up to your expectations,*
> *I've gotta do better than this.*
> *I've got no excuses,*
> *No explanations,*
> *I've just gotta do better than this. . . .*

Keith and I kept fighting the urge to forget everything by smoking dope or dropping a few pills. But it was a battle we kept losing.

One night in early February, after a wild weekend of partying, something strange happened to Keith while he was playing a one-nighter back at The Bla. Albie had been in a pinch for "talent", and Keith had agreed to help him out.

We'd smoked some dope to help get us through the evening, and Keith was really getting off on his performance. There was one song in particular that I always loved. It was taken from a Bible story about "The Good Samaritan". Before, the term "good Samaritan" had symbolized some weak guy who'd always go out of his way for everyone, letting everyone use him. A totally uncool person. But Keith's song, "On the Road to Jericho", gave the story a whole new meaning for me. People sat down with their drinks. I could tell they were really listening as Keith sang with deep emotion:

> *I left Jerusalem last week for Jericho.*
> *In the afternoon, the sun was getting low.*
> *Then the bushes shook and out they came at me—*
> *They were robbing me half-naked*
> *As they beat me head to toe.*
> *Left me wounded on the road to Jericho.*
>
> *Lying almost dead and wounded by the road,*
> *Crying out in pain for a sympathetic soul.*
> *First a priest and then another of my kind,*
> *They were men I would have trusted,*
> *But they acted deaf and blind.*
> *They were strangers on the road to Jericho.*

As Keith sang it was as if *he* was the one crying out in pain. I could feel it—could see it on his face as he grimaced while he cried out the words. I could only think of the times I'd felt abandoned by those I'd trusted at one time or another. And then Keith's lament grew hopeful, as someone came to the aid of this wounded traveler. Only it wasn't who he expected:

> *Through the blood and tears I saw a worried face.*
> *He was from Samaria, my people hate his race.*
> *He bandaged up my wounds and laid me on his horse.*
> *Though my memory is cloudy,*
> *I can still feel his friendly glow—*
> *Such a kind man on the road to Jericho!*

It was a moving performance—but that's all I thought it was. I hadn't noticed anything out of the ordinary about Keith while he was singing. But later that night as we drove home he said, "Mel, this incredible thing happened tonight when I was playing 'Jericho'. I don't know if I can explain it—but I felt a touch from God."

Keith didn't elaborate so I wasn't exactly sure what happened, but I wondered if he wasn't seeing himself as that wounded traveler. Later that night, Keith confided to his journal:

Got stoned again. . . . Had religious experience while playing "Jericho." Decided to immediately stop smoking. God entered my life again. . . .

Out of the gloomy despair of a dope-clouded mind came to the call to New Life—the Christian calling again. After

forsaking the Lord to escape from my conscience and my path (my own self-discipline) for the cloudy shroud of constant smoking . . . I felt the despair surround me . . . and the Christian angel called me, saying—"Come to my fold" . . .

Praise God who never forgets—But always forgives. My perfect Father. I want to be with you and perfect, too.

I could only tell that Keith was once again caught up in his titanic, inner struggle. Privately, he wrote:

The Calling
Oh I feel the calling so strong tonight. To join the Holy army and fight the numbness in the world toward God. Even the very belief in the existence of God is a battle. But when I truly believe in God and I have to fight the insidious evils around me—and more horrifying, right inside me—I find myself feeling beaten, and hearing those Satanic words, "Give up— you're too human—only the saints, priest, monks and nuns are clean enough from the world and its forms to reach the Lord God and be chosen for Holy service."

Please God in Christ's name and teachings I want to be chosen to be with you . . . On your side only! No possibilities of any other master or side or path, or pseudo-light, belief or god.

I want to die for you God and be reborn a whole disciple. Living, emulating, and shining your will, teachings, and bearing fruits every day to everyone. . . . The devil hates me more every day. He despises me more, the more I get closer to you. He's losing his grip. Praise you, God. Your light is the only thing I want to see—And the only thing I want to reflect. . . .

In March, about a month after Keith's experience at The Bla, we decided we wanted to go to church. Since that was where most people who believed in Jesus hung out, we thought we'd give it a try. So we met Randy Stonehill and another Christian rock musician, Larry Norman, at the Little Brown Church for their Sunday morning service. I took my first Communion with soda crackers and grape juice. I left with a very warm feeling in my heart, and Keith had a fairly good experience too. He later wrote: "Stiff service but great, great sermon on giving."

However, going to a Christian church also made us face one of the major problems we saw with Christianity—the supposed deity of Jesus. Spiritual master, yes. *But God?*

We were reading in our chocolate-brown King James Bible

things like John 1:1, which said, " . . . the Word was with God and the Word *was* God." But we couldn't quite buy that. The idea even made Keith mad.

Once before, we'd tried going to a little Protestant church in Van Nuys. When we'd walked in, the usher in the back looked overjoyed—I guess not many hippies went to church there. We found some seats way in back and they started singing hymns. As we opened the hymnal, Keith flipped through it reading various lyrics. Suddenly, he stood and said loudly, "Let's get out of here!" By reading some of the words Keith realized these people believed Jesus was not only the *son* of God, but that he *was* God. We walked out rather abruptly, and I was embarrassed. Now we were facing the "God question" again.

While growing up, Keith had read that Jesus wasn't God—but a man who possessed the "true idea of God" more than all other men. As for me, I simply didn't see any way that a man who'd walked on the earth could be God. There was no way I was going to worship a man.

To make things interesting, our old friend Todd started talking about joining a group of Christians who believed Jesus *was* God. Keith tried to talk him out of it. "It's better to be right with God and be alone, than to be wrong about him and be wrong with hundreds of people."

But Todd was a seeker in his own right and was determined to follow his heart. He joined the group, and we started seeing a little less of him.

Then, just after Easter in '75, Keith started to get some measure of success musically. Teddy Neely, our *Jesus Christ, Superstar* friend asked Keith to play in his band for one of the hottest TV rock programs—"Midnight Special" on NBC. Then Keith landed another nightspot job at a place called "Goodbye Charlie's". Our CBS salary, which had been held up for several months because of some glitch, was about to be released, and it looked like we were going to have more money than we'd know what to do with.

Things were starting to cook—in more ways than one.

One evening near the end of April, Keith's friend Randy Wimer came over. Todd came over, too, and we ended up having what Keith called "a great Bible debate". The talk centered, of course, on God and Jesus. We were confused. If Jesus was God, did that make him his own father? That wasn't even logical. And why did people worship Jesus when the Bible says to only worship God?

Then Randy brought up a scripture we'd never heard. It was

out of the New Testament book of Hebrews, a book written to Jewish believers, so my ears perked up.

"God commanded all the angels to worship Jesus when he was born. Then it says, 'But of the Son he says, Thy throne O God, is forever and ever'."

Keith grabbed the Bible from Randy. "Let me see that. God calls *Jesus* God?"

"He sure does. God even calls Jesus *Lord* a few verses down." He took the Bible back, and read, "God says, 'Thou, Lord, in the beginning didst lay the foundation of the earth, and the heavens are the works of Thy hands'."

"You mean it says Jesus created the earth? That's something to think about. But I'm still not buying this Jesus is God stuff," Keith insisted.

The next night, Keith drove Randy Wimer to his parents' house, which was about an hour away. All the way there they argued about the scriptures and whether they were totally accurate and inspired word-for-word. To Keith it seemed impossible that the *whole* Bible could be absolutely true. How could men write a book that was perfect? Keith later wrote, "Randy kept claiming the Holy Spirit is the source of his translation and interpretation, and then something clicked inside and on the way home, tears filled my eyes and I was filled with the Holy Spirit."

A short time later he also wrote:

The Holy Ghost
Last Monday I discovered the knowledge of the existence of the Holy Ghost. As the personal vehicle through which the Son comes into our personal lives. . . . I feel so strong, my love for the Father and my trust in the Father. I am learning to love the son and only now seeing the need to acknowledge a third entity. Separate in identity, but one with the others in purpose. . . .

The day after Keith wrote that prayer we decided, with some uncertainty, to accept Todd's invitation to go to a service at the church he'd joined. Todd had taken a leap of faith and not only joined this church, he moved into their small community of believers—the ones who believed Jesus was God.

That evening when we arrived, the hall was fairly crowded and we took a seat on some folding chairs toward the back. Todd sat with us, and I could tell he was really pleased that we made the effort to come. The people looked normal enough, which took the edge off the moment. The last thing we wanted to do was spend the evening with a bunch of religious wackos.

A man went to the front and talked for several minutes. Then a young guy in blue jeans and a football T-shirt, who was sitting a few feet to our right, jumped up. He had a Bible in his hand and looked like he was about to read something. Instead, he started to *shout* out passages from the Bible at the top of his lungs!

Keith and I exchanged knowing glances, rolling our eyes a bit, and sunk down in our chairs. Our worst fears were confirmed. We just dug in for the duration, as people started popping up all over the place, yelling out scriptures. As soon as the first guy was done, an elderly woman with white hair pinned up in a bun stood and gave him a run for his money in the shouting department. It seemed more like a football game than a church service.

I leaned over and whispered in Keith's ear, "What are these people *shouting* for?" It was more of a statement of irritation than a question.

"Who knows," said Keith. "But one thing's for sure, these people are *straaange*."

Todd started shifting in his seat. Our disapproving whispers were not exactly subtle. Besides, Todd could read Keith like a book.

Suddenly, right in the middle of it all, Keith rose to his feet, his chair scraping against the cement floor as he stood. I held my breath wondering what he was going to do. He simply turned, walked up the aisle and right out the front door.

I was so surprised I wasn't sure what to do. Todd looked deflated. Neither of us said a word, but Todd was starting to cry a little. Finally I got up and walked outside. I found Keith pacing back and forth in the parking lot.

"Something's not right, Mel. It's not just the yelling. I can't put my finger on it."

"I think Todd's kinda upset that you left," I ventured.

"I had to get out of there. I felt like I was going to explode."

"Well, what do you want to do?"

"I'm not ready to go back yet. You go back in and I'll see you there in a few minutes."

I went back inside for what was left of the service, hoping the yelling was over. It was. I hung around the back of the hall until Keith returned and when the meeting ended, Todd slowly made his way over to us. I felt kind of bad for him and could tell he was embarrassed. But Keith didn't cut Todd any slack.

"Hey, Bro, why didn't you jump up and shout with the rest of them?"

"You know me," Todd said meekly, "I'm not one to put on a show."

Afterward we went out to eat with Todd, and he and Keith continued their ongoing arguments.

"What about Philippians chapter two?" Todd challenged.

He quoted a passage, that said Jesus was "in the form of God" though he came to earth as a humble servant. Because he had suffered death on the cross, the Bible said, "God . . . highly exalted him to the highest place and gave him a name that is above every name. . . ."

"Okay," Keith countered, "so I agree that God has exalted Jesus—but it still doesn't say he *was* God. Not directly anyway. You see, I can argue every one of your scriptures away," Keith said self-assuredly.

"But you don't really have any answers. You're just unwilling to believe," Todd replied angrily.

"I'm not willing to believe everything I *hear*. Todd, how can you live with those people? They're so strange. You need to get out of there."

"Hey, at least I'm doing something spiritual. What do you have that's better?"

As we drove home from the restaurant, Keith and I tried to sort through the whole evening. We decided that we were really turned-off by the church service, but we really liked being in a spiritual atmosphere, talking to spiritual people. Keith wanted to go back and check them out again the next week. But I suggested that we shop around a bit because the last thing I wanted was to get stuck in that group, like Todd seemed to be.

"Keith, if we're going to start going to church let's check out some more options. Maybe we should try that group Randy Stonehill invited us to go to."

Two days after our experience at Todd's church we called Randy Stonehill and found out where his Bible study was. They met in a private home on Coldwater Canyon on the other side of the mountain in Beverly Hills. Randy gave us directions and we drove over.

The Vineyard Christian Fellowship met in a fashionable part of town. There were no halls or churches in sight—just palm trees, manicured lawns, four-car garages, iron gates, security systems and an occasional uniformed nanny pushing a baby stroller. Coldwater Canyon was definitely on the "Map To The Movie Stars' Homes" that they sold down on Sunset Boulevard. I figured plenty of wealthy doctors and lawyers lived here, too.

We parked in front of a large yellow house that sat in a huge yard filled with flowers and trees. A white picket fence surrounded all of it. We got out of the car and opened the gate.

The house was not as fancy as some of the Spanish or Tudor homes nearby. But to me it spoke of family and commitment— and money. Lots of money.

Inside, we stepped into a large entryway just off the living room, where about thirty-five people were sitting on couches, chairs or on the thickly carpeted floor. We quietly found a spot on the floor, smiled a bit guardedly and waited for the meeting to start.

A young man went to the front of the room and sat by the fireplace. He introduced himself as Kenn Gulliksen. He had yellow-blond hair, a round friendly face, and his eyes were warm and smiling. He started speaking and his gentle manner immediately put me at ease. Keith looked relaxed too. As we sat cross-legged on the floor, Kenn led the group in some songs we'd never heard before. Not knowing any of the words, we just listened:

> *Father I adore you,*
> *Lay my life before you.*
> *How I love you. . . .*

The words just flowed over me. People broke into gentle harmonies that all seemed to weave in and out of each other. I felt a strange sense of peace start to wash over me—a peace that was like the intense emotions I'd felt the night, several years before, when I'd seen myself at the foot of the flaming cross. Only this time, it wasn't coming from a drug-induced hallucination. I closed my eyes and felt myself relaxing.

> *Jesus I adore you,*
> *Lay my life before you.*
> *How I love you. . . .*

As they sang about Jesus I could picture him in my mind's eye. It seemed so natural to think about him in this place. A moment ago, it had been a fancy Beverly Hills living room, but now it seemed like a place where the disciples of Jesus met. I almost felt like I could reach out and touch the fringe of Jesus' robe as he walked by. The spirit was catching, and the song was so easy to pick up that Keith and I started to sing along as they moved into it a second time. I felt so wonderful I thought I was going to fly off into heaven.

Kenn Gulliksen closed the time of singing with a simple prayer and started talking about God. "Just today I felt like I'd blown it with my wife by getting impatient. But you know, I realized that in 1 John 1:9 it says if we come to Jesus and confess our sins, he's faithful to forgive our sins. So I closed my eyes and simply said, 'Lord, please forgive me for offending Joni.' And then I went to Joni and asked her forgiveness, too. It was really beautiful."

I'd never heard anybody talk like that before. It just sounded so down to earth. He made Jesus sound like his best friend or something. It didn't seem abstract or mystical at all. I gave Keith a sideways glance to see if I could read his expression. He had that intent look on his face, the one where his eyes got deep and penetrating. He was totally absorbed.

Kenn also talked about how much God loved each one of us. "Just like I love my wife and children, and want to protect them and take care of them—that's how God loves you. He wants to be in a love relationship with you." He said being in a relationship with God would change our lives. That we could become new people by asking Jesus to forgive our sins and welcoming him into our hearts. There was nothing weird or spooky about anything he was saying. And the very best part was that he made it seem like getting to know God—*really* getting to know him—was totally possible. It sure seemed like *he* knew God.

Then he talked about how God sent his only son down to earth to live among us and show us the way to the Father. But we needed to be cleansed of our sins to be in a relationship with the Father—and that's where Jesus' death on the cross came in. People used to sacrifice animals to pay for their sins, but Jesus was the only one pure enough to be a sacrifice for the wrong things we've done that have hurt God and hurt others. So God allowed Jesus to be that sacrifice one time, for all of mankind. The only thing was, we needed to receive it. "It's like a beautiful present from a friend," Kenn said. "If you don't allow them to give it to you, you'll miss the blessing, and they'll be hurt. You need to open your heart to Jesus and let him come into your life."

Kenn spoke for about forty minutes, and when he was done he asked everyone to bow their heads and close their eyes. He asked, "Is there anyone here who wants to ask Jesus into your heart—to give your whole life to him? When you ask Jesus to forgive your sins, you'll become a brand new person. It's like being born again—only it's not a physical rebirth. It's a spiritual one."

You could almost hear hearts beating.

Then he said, "Just raise your hand if you want to receive Jesus." I sat with my eyes closed. It felt like lead balloons had been tied to my arms. My heart was pounding wildly, and I felt a pressure in my chest. The invitation was repeated but I could not raise my hand.

I felt Keith stir and I peeked out of the corner of one eye. To my surprise—and dismay—I saw his hand raised high into the air. Now I felt even more pressure to do the same thing, but I just couldn't get my arm to move. One part of me wanted to jump up and shout, "Jesus I want you! Please forgive me!" But another part of me was sitting back observing the whole scene and saying, "No way am I going to do this!"

After a minute or so, Kenn prayed right out loud for everyone who had their hand raised and asked them to repeat some things after him. I wanted that prayer to be for me, too, so I said it in my heart—but I knew I hadn't raised my hand. The moment was over now, and I'd missed my chance.

As the meeting closed, we had to leave right away because Keith had a gig that night at "Goodbye Charlie's". On the way out the door, someone said, "I'm glad you came tonight. I've been praying for you." It was a guy we'd briefly met at Randy Stonehill's birthday party a few months ago—and I couldn't believe he'd actually been *praying* for us. I'd never had anybody in my whole life tell me that. I thanked him and wondered why he'd want to pray for total strangers, and what kind of things he'd been praying for.

Keith and I jumped into "Victor" and headed off to work. Keith was elated and talking a mile-a-minute.

"Boy, it was really great tonight. I've never felt anything like it. This is really it, Mel. I feel like I finally found what I've been looking for."

I slouched down in what seemed to be my dark little corner of the van, feeling worse and worse as Keith went on. I felt so dejected, thinking, *Yeah you did it, but I blew it.* What if I'd blown my one big chance to get right with God? I should have raised my hand. *Oh God,* I prayed, *can I have a second chance? What if I go back next week?* I was happy for Keith but I felt miserable.

At "Goodbye Charlie's" I wasn't sure I was ready for the evening. This place felt a lot more like a bar than The Bla Bla, although it was decorated much nicer with red velvet cushions and mirrored walls. But the overall feeling was "sleaze". I noticed a sexy-looking blonde sitting on a barstool. Her skirt was hiked up and she was leaning toward some greasy guy who resembled a hungry shark getting ready for dinner. As we passed them, I heard him ask what her name was. It gave me an uneasy feeling to know people came here to get drunk and get picked up. What a switch from our time at the house in Coldwater Canyon.

Keith did his best, but tonight he seemed to be having a hard time. During one of his breaks, he looked at me and said, "I just can't do this anymore. Something's wrong. I don't know what it is, but I just don't fit in here." Keith had been really excited to get this job, but at the end of the evening Keith said goodbye to "Goodbye Charlie's" forever. He never went back.

That week was one of the longest I'd ever spent. As I stood in line at the market and ran around town with Keith, I kept thinking, *I want to go back to the Vineyard. I hope he asks us to raise our hands again. I hope it's not too late for me.* My mind seemed stuck and I could think of nothing else.

When Friday came around it seemed to drag on endlessly. Finally, that night, when we walked into that big yellow house the excitement in my heart was at an all-time high. We sat on the floor again, and when the singing started I could hardly wait for all the "preliminaries" to be over. Kenn spoke again, and then—at last!—he got to the hand-raising part.

"Is there anybody here that wants to give their heart to the Lord?" he asked.

To my surprise I hesitated. I thought, *This is crazy—I've been waiting all week.*

For the next few moments I went through an inner battle— something inside me did not want to be a Christian. Other hands were raised but I was thinking, *Maybe I'll just raise my hand next week.*

Just then, a gentle voice broke into my personal war-zone. "I believe there's another person here who needs to receive the Lord tonight," said Kenn patiently.

I *knew* he was talking about me. Then I thought, *That's impossible. How could he know?*

The room was totally quiet.

My heart was pounding in my chest and I thought, *It's now or never.* Something was tugging at me to open my heart totally to Jesus, but something else wanted me to keep my hands down. These forces were working against each other—right inside me! Then I knew that I had to make the choice. I thought, *If I don't raise my hand right now, nobody is going to do it for me. I need to choose sides.*

Quietly, I slipped my hand high into the air—just as I used to do in bed at night as a little girl. Only this time I knew what I was reaching for.

Kenn immediately prayed for all of us who were receiving the Lord that night, and a rush of peace filled my heart—a peace deeper than anything I'd ever experienced in my whole life.

—

"You Put This Love In My Heart"

River baptism by Keith.

WE *FINALLY* DID IT. IT WAS HARD TO BELIEVE WE WERE
really part of a Christian "fold", but it was true. Even though
we were excited about Jesus and the new way we'd opened
our hearts to him, we still had a lot of reservations about
Christianity in general. We'd spent so many years wading
through spiritual counterfeits and wandering down the wrong
paths that we were a bit wary of swallowing everything we heard. Just
because somebody says something is Christian doesn't mean it really is.
We wanted pure, undiluted Christianity—not the "slightly modified" version. For some time, though, it seemed like an unseen hand was at
work, bringing the right people into our lives—and keeping the wrong
people out.

Keith was painfully cautious about spending time with *anyone* who might influence him in a wrong way spiritually. In fact on the very day I raised my hand at the Vineyard Fellowship, an old friend of Keith's had come over to visit us. His name was Doug, and after catching up on old times Keith told him all about what we were going through spiritually and our recent visit to the Vineyard. Doug seemed to lean toward eastern thought forms, but as we talked about Christianity something seemed to click. Doug said, "I know somebody who's a Christian! He's really heavy-duty."

"Really?" said Keith. I was interested, too.

"Yeah! He's eighty-seven years old, and really wise."

"Where does he live?" asked Keith.

"He lives right here in Woodland Hills," Doug answered. Keith and I were still fairly new to this community, and the little house on Dolorosa Street. "I was going to go see him tomorrow. Do you want to meet him? His name's Richard Gene Lowe. He's Chinese."

Keith's face fell. "Chinese? Forget it!"

"Why?"

"I'm not into eastern religions anymore—all that stuff's occult. Forget it."

"But this guy's a *Christian*," Doug insisted.

"He's probably into some eastern mix of Christianity—with Jesus and Buddha and eastern mysticism all blended together. I don't want anything to do with that stuff."

I thought that was the end of the matter. However, the day after I'd given my heart to Jesus, there was a knock at our door. Keith jumped off the couch to answer it, and I was right behind him. There on our front porch was Doug with a sheepish grin on his face. Standing right next to him was a short, silver-haired Chinese man—obviously his friend, Richard Gene Lowe.

It was an awkward moment, but before Keith had a chance to react they both stepped inside. Once inside the door, Richard immediately gave each of us a big hug. Then both of his hands shot up into the air as he said joyfully, "Praise the Lord! Praise God!"

It was an odd thing. But for the first time, those words didn't sound weird at all. And something about Richard's face instantly drew me.

Richard Gene Lowe was radiant. His happy grin pushed his round cheeks up toward his eyes, making them all crinkled and laughing around the edges. It was almost as if there was some kind of a holy light streaming from this little man. He had something special. It was the kind of inner joy we wanted.

Somehow, I instinctively knew it was for real. Even Keith seemed to relax at once. I was thankful, because it wouldn't have been beyond Keith to throw them both out.

We were at once captivated by this little man, and we ended up spending the whole day together. Our conversation ranged from music to the deity of Jesus. We also learned from Doug that when he had told Richard about us, Richard insisted on being brought to our house so he could meet us. And now, we were very glad that he had.

Most especially, we were fascinated by the incredible story of Richard's life. Richard told us he'd become a Christian in China some seventy years before, when he was just fourteen. He almost married once but when he came to America his fiance changed her mind, and he never married. He also told us he never took any medicine. "Except an aspirin once," he said. "The Lord always heals me." Then he told us story after story of how he'd been healed.

Once, when he was younger and working with big diesel trucks, he'd jumped up on a running board and slipped. When he grabbed something, his hand wrapped around a hot exhaust pipe. The burn was so bad that his hand was bright red and the skin was peeling off. He prayed and asked God to heal him, and then wrapped it up. "The next day," he said, "it was totally healed. There was only a slight trace to show that it had ever been burned."

Richard was full of wonderful stories, and we eagerly listened to one after another—testimonies of his own healings and the healings of other Christians that he'd witnessed over the years. It was beyond mystical—it was miraculous! And he didn't seem to be making these stories up, either.

As he talked Keith kept looking at me with an astonished, "can-you-believe-this?" look on his face. Keith had been wondering if Christians believed in healing. Keith had seen healings while growing up, and read in his Christian Science studies that the sick are not healed simply by declaring there isn't any sickness, but by *knowing* there is none. Just a few months earlier Keith wrote in his journal,

I will not take any steps to cut myself off from Christian Science until I feel sure that its benefits of healing the sick are as plenty in a Christian's life. . . .

It seemed incredible that, immediately after making a commitment to Christ, Keith's questions about healing were being answered by this unlikely little man—someone who pursued us even when he knew we didn't want to meet him!

During the course of that first day with Richard, Keith brought up something that was weighing heavily on his heart— Todd.

Keith described the meeting we'd been to, where everyone was shouting out scriptures. He also mentioned the name of the group and their leader. "Ever heard of these people?"

Richard's eyebrows went up slightly and he nodded. "Oh yes, I've heard of them."

"Well what do you know about them?" Keith asked. "My best friend, Todd, is living with them. The last time we talked he told me he smashed and burned his amplifier and even burned the cross that was around his neck because this group is heavy-duty against materialism. What could be wrong with wearing a cross? It sounds weird to me."

Richard shook his head and said quietly, "It's not good. They are not true Christians. If he's your friend we need to pray. We must try to help him."

That was all Keith needed to hear. He was off the couch in a flash, dialing Todd's number. As soon as Todd was on the line, Keith made him promise to meet us at Shadow Ranch Park the following afternoon.

The next day Todd did meet us at Shadow Ranch Park and we cut Richard loose on him. We also told Todd all about our experiences with the Vineyard Fellowship and all the neat new people we'd been meeting. This impressed Todd because he'd prayed to receive Jesus too. But this group he was going to had told him they were the only true church. After what seemed like hours of talking and debate Todd saw that, out of his zeal to make a radical commitment, he'd gotten hooked up with the wrong people. Finally, he said, "All this really makes sense. I'm going to leave the group right away."

Keith was so relieved and I, too, was elated at this turn of events.

It was amazing to me how much satisfaction Keith got out of "rescuing" Todd out of that very dangerous spiritual situation. We now knew that the group was a cult. I might have taken a more passive route, figuring Todd would eventually see for himself that he was in the wrong place. But not Keith. He couldn't, *wouldn't* rest while he knew his friend needed help. That was the way he was. If there was anything he could do or say to help someone he loved, he always went for broke.

Things were really starting to happen fast. We were so

grateful for Richard. He became one of our best friends and the three of us, along with Todd, became inseparable for months. We spent hours and days together, running all over town. Richard had never learned how to drive, so we'd pick him up at his little bachelor apartment—which was so stacked with books and newspapers it was beyond clutter. We often went to garage sales, and once, for $5, he bought a suit that I altered to fit him. We also loved to pick up chili dogs at our favorite stand. Richard would laugh as he jumped into "Victor"—joking about how he kept up with us at his age. And the whole time Keith, Todd and I pumped Richard with questions about God and prayer. Richard was especially big on prayer. He loved telling us about the way it changes things.

"Prayer must be a two-way conversation," he insisted. "You talk, God listens. God talks, you listen."

"What do you mean God talks? Can you hear him?" Keith asked.

"Some people have heard his voice. I hear him in my heart. He speaks to me in a still small voice."

I asked, "How do you know it's just not your own thoughts you're hearing?"

"That's why you need to get to know God. So you can learn the difference."

In the midst of all our questions, we found out that Richard believed Jesus was God. Even though Keith and I were still skeptical on that point, it didn't turn us off to Richard like it might have in the past. In fact, it didn't change the way we felt about him at all. We loved him and there was no question that he loved us.

Since Keith was never one to keep a good thing to himself, he wanted all of our friends to meet Richard, too. We immediately started inviting people to our house so Richard could talk to them about God. Todd was usually there and so were some friends from The Bla Bla. Debbie Docis had been one of Keith's "fans", but she soon gave her heart to the Lord at one of these little studies. Since Richard loved to pray, he began teaching us how to talk to God. We'd all sit in a circle and hold hands. Then Richard would pray as we tentatively followed, offering some of the first prayers we'd ever said out loud. Richard said, "The reason we pray out loud sometimes is so we can all agree with each other's prayers."

Richard was always teaching us but he did it in a way that just seemed natural. He never made us feel bad about all the things we didn't know. Never made us feel like we needed a lot of help.

He just quietly and kindly helped us without pushing us further than we were able to go.

Not only was Richard an almost daily influence on us, but as we continued going to the Vineyard, Kenn Gulliksen was beginning to help us sort through our questions. In fact, it was Kenn who finally helped Keith settle the "God question".

One night after a meeting, Keith and I walked up to him and Keith said, "I know you believe Jesus is God—but what does that make the Father? There's only one God. Can you help me understand why you believe the way you do?"

Kenn smiled. "Keith, what you're struggling with is called the Trinity—the Father, the Son and the Holy Spirit. It really is a mystery. But I think I can shed *some* light on it for you."

Kenn picked up his Bible and turned toward the back, running his finger down the page until he found what he was looking for.

"Here, Keith, listen to this," Kenn said. "This scripture—Colossians chapter two, verse nine—is talking about Jesus: 'For in him all the fulness of deity dwells in bodily form . . .'"

Keith looked blank. "I still don't get it."

"Well, look at it this way. Just think of water, steam, and ice. They're all made out of exactly the same substance, but all three are distinctly different. God is a lot like that. But the analogy breaks down. An ice cube can't be a puddle of water and a puff of steam all at the same time—but God *is* all three at the same time!"

Nobody had ever said it to us quite so simply. I could tell something was clicking in Keith's mind as he listened. I wasn't sure how I felt, but as usual I was taking most of my cues from Keith. And he was keeping his thoughts to himself just now.

A short time later, we were visiting my mom one evening and Keith took a walk by himself after dark. When he came back in he looked very serious.

"I need to talk to you. Alone."

I was in the middle of trying to talk my mom into giving her heart to Jesus and felt a bit reluctant about just getting up and leaving. "Right now?"

Keith nodded his head. "Let's take a walk."

Once we got outside I could see how serious Keith really was. When we got down the steps and out onto the sidewalk he turned to me and simply said, "I bought it."

"You bought what? What do you mean?"

"I believe Jesus is God. I might not understand it totally right now, but something in my heart tells me it's true."

Now I was the one who got serious. I looked up at the moon

and wondered what Keith's decision would mean for me. I found out in two seconds.

"Mel, you need to accept it, too."

"I want to—if it's true. But I don't know if it is."

"Just do it Mel, just take a leap of faith if you need to. I think it's the thing that's been holding us back. I want you to believe with me. I don't want to leave you behind."

Kenn's analogy came back to me—water, steam, ice. It did make sense, in a mysterious sort of way. Since asking Jesus into my heart, it really did seem like I had a lot more faith. Actually I felt a little cornered, but I mustered up all the new-found faith I had at the moment and simply said, "Okay. I'll do my best to buy it, too."

We were over the edge. We were not only Christians, we found a group of people to learn about Jesus with, and two men we really trusted to help us along the way—Richard and Kenn.

We launched into Christianity with a bright burst of enthusiasm and optimism. It was like being shot out of a cannon—and we hit the ground running. Now all of a sudden we started noticing Christian symbols everywhere. While driving down the freeway we'd watch for cars with Praise The Lord bumper stickers on them so we could drive by and give them the "one way" sign we'd just learned—pointing our index finger to the sky, signifying there's only one way to heaven. Then we'd wave at them like they were long-lost relatives. Seeing a Christian bumper sticker meant someone who loved Jesus was driving that car!

We felt like we joined a big club with millions of people already in it, and we were excited about meeting all of them. We also noticed lots of people wearing "fish" and "dove" necklaces, pins, and T-shirts. We learned the "fish" was a secret sign for the early Church during their times of persecution, and the "dove" represented the Holy Spirit. I'd seen these "secret codes" before, but never knew what they meant. Now if we saw someone wearing a fish or a dove we'd walk up and eagerly say, "Hi. You're a Christian, aren't you? We are, too!"

So many things in our life started changing so fast that it was a real shock to everyone—including us. For one thing, instead of going to parties all the time, we started going to Bible studies almost every night. Besides the Vineyard, our favorite home study was up in the Hollywood Hills at a tiny, two-story house owned by the Cramers—a couple in show business. They had a goat tied up on their front porch, and in their loft they had a monkey in a large circus cage that chattered through our Bible studies. One "regular" there had starred in a movie with Liza Minnelli, and he was now a Christian recording artist. And Leo, their next door neighbor who had a drinking problem, was there whenever he was "dry." It was *almost* a typical Hollywood crowd—only it was different. These were the kinds of people we were used to getting together with, but this time it wasn't to have a party. It was to learn about following Jesus. And we learned about Jesus everywhere we could.

One night we went to Hillcrest Christian Church in Thousand Oaks with Richard and Todd. We heard a man named Hans Christian talk about the suffering church—that is, Christians who lived in Communist countries, who could not openly worship God. Many of them were murdered or put in hard-labor camps or insane asylums. We were shocked. I felt stirred in my heart, but something far more moving happened to Keith. He wrote:

My heart was speared by the Spirit to compassion. I cried for the suffering church and pledged to help take on some of that burden.

The next night Keith told some friends all about the suffering church to help get the word out and raise prayer support for persecuted believers. Keith also asked Kenn if Hans Christian could speak at the Vineyard. Kenn said yes. Two nights later Hans Christian spoke and Kenn gave everyone an opportunity to give toward this man's work with the suffering church. Five hundred dollars was collected! Keith was thrilled about playing a part in helping to ease the burden for others who were hurting. He also added the suffering church to his new prayer list.

After hearing about the suffering church we had some questions about why our pastor lived in such a huge house in such a wealthy neighborhood. We were relieved to hear that Kenn and his family were "house-sitting" for a friend. It was a big blessing to them because they barely had any money.

We were also totally gung ho all of a sudden about getting everyone we knew to "accept Jesus".

At first, though, we had better luck leading strangers to the Lord than we did our friends. Except for our friend Debbie Docis from The Bla Bla—who was so radiantly excited about Jesus we called her a "lightbulb on legs"—few of our friends were interested. One night in June we had a late dinner with some of our new Christian friends, then we all played penny-ante poker for fun. We were on a winning streak and Keith started joking about driving to Las Vegas.

"Hey, we're on a roll," Keith said, with a gleam in his eye. "Let's go to Vegas!"

One of the guys said, "You're crazy. It's already after ten."

"Come on. It'll be fun. I can make it there in four hours."

Keith was starting to sound more serious and I was a little worried because I didn't know if real gambling was okay now that we were Christians. But I was always up for an adventure.

Keith ended up persuading everyone and even phoned Debbie and talked her into calling in sick the next day so she could go with us. We headed out, and by midnight we hit the desert. We were all praying and singing as we drove. One guy picked up his Bible and it happened to fall open at Isaiah 42, which talks about praising God in the desert. He read it out loud and we really got excited then. Just as he closed his Bible we saw two hitchhikers, barely visible in the dark desert night.

Keith prayed, "Lord, please send someone to pick them up."

Immediately, he hit the brakes and pulled off to the side, saying, "God just told me the someone was us!"

A young couple climbed into the back of "Victor". Keith laughed and said, "You just fell into a den of Christians!"

"We don't mind," they said as they got comfortable. Their names were Scott and Lori, and as we drove on we learned that they weren't married but were living together. I also noticed that Lori was holding her head in pain. She told us she had a blood clot on her brain that was too big to remove. The doctors only gave her about six months to live. We all glanced at each other and started praying silently.

After a while Scott said, "Hey, this is kinda strange, but for the last couple of days I've had a terrible backache. When we got in, it was killing me. But suddenly—just like that—the pain disappeared." We told them we'd been praying for Lori and he must have got a healing instead! We talked to them nonstop about God's love on the whole ride up north.

When we got to Las Vegas, we headed straight for a casino— and left them a few dollars richer. Near dawn, we all checked into one room and just lounged around. Scott and Lori were still with us and it was natural to start praying for each other. One guy had a cold and after our prayers he said he felt better. My heart started pounding as I thought about praying for Lori. What if God wanted to heal her blood clot? I finally said, "Lori, do you want us to pray for you?"

"Oh, yes. Please . . ."

We gathered around her and laid our hands on her back and

shoulders and prayed for about five minutes. When we stopped, Lori started to cry.

"Why are you crying?" Keith asked.

"It's gone! The clot is gone! It was really big and I can't feel it anymore!" she said. Then she began to sob.

All the time she was talking she was hitting the back of her head really hard—on the spot where the blood clot apparently had been. When we realized that God had healed her we *all* started crying for joy.

Lori got up and took a prescription bottle out of her purse and walked into the bathroom with it. I saw her pour some little pills that thinned her blood into the toilet. "I won't be needing these anymore," she announced.

We were all in awe of what had just happened. We'd been talking to them about becoming Christians on the whole drive down. Lori's dad was a minister. She'd slipped away from God, but now saw that she needed to make a new commitment. Scott wanted to receive the Lord, too. Then Keith tackled another subject.

"You know, it's wrong for you to be living together without being married. If you really love each other, you need to get married."

To our surprise, they decided to get married on the spot. Keith opened the phone book and found a preacher who did "house calls" and he came and married them under a palm tree by the pool of the Thunderbird Hotel, where we were staying. What a time! Getting two people saved, healed, and married in less than twenty-four hours! We didn't see how it could get much better than that!

Later that day, we gave the newlyweds some extra cash, dropped them off at the freeway entrance so they could continue their journey north, and headed back home so we wouldn't miss our Friday night fellowship at the Vineyard.

Two weeks later, Scott and Lori came to visit us and we took them to the Friday night meeting at the Vineyard. Kenn gave Lori a few minutes to share and she told their incredible story—along with the clincher.

"I went to see my doctor and didn't tell him about the healing. He took an X-ray as usual and I waited for the results. Then he came in and clipped the film on the light board in front of me."

"Tell me what you see," he said.

"Nothing."

"That's right, nothing! But these things don't just go away."

"I know, but it's gone!"

The doctor had called in three other experts, and Lori told them all the whole story about how God healed her. "They all walked out shaking their heads," she reported, smiling.

Then her doctor told her to make another appointment, but when she got into the reception area the nurse gave her another doctor's number. "The nurse told me my doctor was so upset that he didn't want to see me anymore! I just give God the glory for my healing. My doctors gave me no hope, but Jesus gave me new life!"

The whole room burst into cheers and applause for the goodness and faithfulness of God. Keith and I were so thrilled to know that the healing had been verified by her doctors. Scott and Lori came to our house after the Vineyard to spend the night. And we began to sense that things weren't going too well in their relationship. Scott went to bed first and Lori confided to us that Scott did not want to follow Jesus anymore. He was getting drunk and saying he didn't want anything to do with God. Lori was heartbroken.

We spent quite a bit of time encouraging Lori and praying with her before we went to bed. But once we were alone we tried to make some sense out of the situation.

Keith said it first. "How could this happen? How can Scott turn from God?"

"I don't know. When he prayed with us in Las Vegas it seemed like he meant it."

"He saw God heal Lori, too."

"I can't figure it out," I replied.

The next day Keith wrote, "Lori is still on fire, but Scott has fallen away."

Before they left the next day, Keith talked with Scott, but didn't feel he got through to him. We told Lori we'd be praying for them and to keep in touch with us. We expected everyone who loved Jesus to be as excited as we were. We never dreamed that there might be some Christians who weren't really excited about God. Even though we couldn't figure out what went wrong with Scott, it didn't stop us from telling others about Jesus.

The next evening, we invited Debbie and her parents over for dinner so they could meet Richard. Another guy we'd already led to the Lord was there, too. He called his mom who lived on the east coast and led her to the Lord over the phone. Later on, Matt and Bonnie, two fans from The Bla Bla, came over. Frank, a Christian we'd picked up hitchhiking who was staying with us, helped us tell them about Jesus. Keith wrote, "Frank got Matt to pray with him and I got Bonnie to pray with me. But something was trying to stop her from saying the name of Jesus. She split after being totally freaked out." This kind of evening was quickly becoming "typical" at our house.

Soon, we were having all-night prayer meetings in our living room a few nights a week—inviting those who believed and those who didn't. We also kept several crosses and Bibles on hand to give to those who received the Lord. We never minded it when we had to buy "new supplies" because it meant we'd gained a new brother or sister in the Lord.

Yet Keith and I were aware that, just a few short weeks before, we'd been lost and seeking, too. Keith was so sensitive on this point that he penned this prayer:

JULY 27, 1975

Not A Fanatic

Please Lord, keep me sensitive to the spiritual needs of those who need your salvation. . . . People can get wary of my company if I go off the deep end and only witness from my "plane" instead of going to where they are and showing them I care for them individually. Lord, change me, get rid of any radical tendencies. Help me control my "overwhelming enthusiasm." Make me unselfish, unproud, quiet and full of humility and gentleness.

Father I love You. You showed your gift to me—Jesus.

If we ever thought our lives might cool down a bit, we were mistaken. What we were going through was nothing compared to the fire we were headed into.

"When There's Love"

Sparrow promo shot.

SHORTLY AFTER WE BECAME CHRISTIANS, KEITH AND I TOOK TWO of our favorite people to one of our favorite places—Sequoia National Park. Keith had known Peter and Cag for years. He even lived with them for a while in their large, rustic home overlooking downtown Hollywood. Peter was a record producer, but we had more than music on our minds as we wound up the mountain roads toward Sequoia.

A big moon had already risen high over the redwoods when we arrived, but as soon as we got into our cabins we made chili dogs and started telling them why they needed to become Christians. Peter and Cag were Jewish, and two of the most loving people we knew. I had become very proud of my Jewish heritage once I became a Christian and realized the spiritual significance of it. In our eagerness to explain all that we'd been learning about being Jewish and believing in Jesus, we unloaded both barrels on this beautiful couple. Keith took the first shot.

"God sent Jesus to the Jews first, because they were the only people who believed in the one true God. Everyone else back then worshipped idols!"

Then I chimed in. "Yeah, Jesus was Jewish, and almost everyone in the early Church was Jewish, too. Later on God allowed the message of his son to go out to the Gentiles. The Messiah the Jews are waiting for has already come—and he's coming again, too."

Peter and Cag listened patiently as we went on, telling them how Jesus might return at any minute and that's why it was so important that they accept his sacrifice and his love. We wanted them to be in heaven with us when that happened.

Keith said, "We'd really like you to pray with us and accept Jesus as your Messiah. That's all you need to do. It's as simple as that to get born-again!"

I don't think they'd ever heard a gospel message quite like that. Peter and Cag kindly but firmly declined our invitation. And if they hadn't loved us as much as they did, we could have totally destroyed our friendship in that one evening. We applied quite a bit of pressure. As it was things were a little tense between us for the next few days of our trip.

After we got back home we remained very good friends, but we were disappointed that we couldn't get them to pray "the sinner's prayer" and find what we had found.

We had just learned about this thing called "the sinner's prayer", and our goal was to get everybody we knew to pray it with us. It could be said in several different ways. It just needed to contain a few important things. The person had to recognize they were lost without Jesus, and to repent of their sins and of living their life without God. Third, they needed to ask for God's forgiveness. And last but not least, they needed to ask Jesus into their heart as their personal Savior. We thought if someone believed those things enough to pray the prayer they'd be saved. We had begun to lead people to the Lord that way—assuring them that's all it took.

It was so exciting to see these "baby Christians" come to fellowship meetings and start to learn about Jesus and the Bible. If they started to miss some meetings Keith would always call them to remind them to come, to offer them a ride—anything that would encourage them to keep their commitment to God.

Some people seemed to blossom once they became Christians. Their lives started opening up like beautiful, scented buds. That was wonderful. To us, there was nothing better than being able to help someone come to that place with God.

Everything had such a sense of urgency to it—especially when we discovered what a crucial moment in history we were facing. We'd learned that Jesus might return at any moment to catch all the Christians into the air with him and take them to heaven—and time runs out for mankind after that. No one can get right with God past that point. We'd even seen a movie about it, called *A Thief In The Night*. There wasn't any time to waste when so many of our friends would be left behind if Jesus returned.

In fact, there was one day when Keith and I got separated in the supermarket and I began to panic. My heart started to pound as I hunted up and down the aisles, but couldn't find him. I thought maybe Jesus returned and took Keith—but that I'd been left behind because I wasn't really saved after all. To my great relief, I finally found Keith in frozen foods with a Sara Lee box cake in his hand—but that frantic, lost feeling stuck with me as a reminder to keep telling others about Jesus.

Keith and I got more and more involved with the Vineyard. However, Keith purposely held off doing any kind of concert for them, as he normally would for a new group of people. He wanted to just be accepted for who he was—minus the music. But after about a month he played at a Sunday morning service—the same service where Kenn talked about baptism. When we heard about getting baptized we knew it was our next step. That afternoon Kenn had a baptism service at the beach near Sunset Boulevard—at Lifeguard Station 15. We figured the Pacific Ocean was a good place to lay our old lives to rest.

We all went down to the beach and we got baptized. It was so fantastic, Mel and I were baptized together. We were all so close, I'll never forget it.

At the beach that day, we found out the Vineyard was about to lose its temporary building. Since the weather was really nice, Kenn announced that we'd start having our Sunday services at that very lifeguard station—with the ocean and sky as our backdrop! We met there for several months, which was great with us. People would ask, "Where do you go to church?" And we'd reply, "We go to church on the beach!" It was non-traditional, and that had a strong appeal. However, we found that there were some rules we *didn't* want to see broken.

One day we overheard some of our Christian friends talking about a party. We were immediately curious. One of them said, "Keith, we don't think you'd be interested in going. It's pretty wild."

"What do you mean *wild*?"

"It's at Leo's house. Sometimes he has lots of booze and dope around. Some people from the study will probably be there."

We knew Leo had a drinking problem, but we thought he was fighting it. We didn't believe he'd throw a wild party and invite other *Christians*. The next night, Keith and I decided to go and see for ourselves.

As we walked up the stairs we heard blasting music. Inside, it was wall-to-wall people, most of them lying on the floor or on big pillows. Carefully stepping over the guests, we took one sweep through the house—there were a few kegs of beer, some people smoking dope and, sure enough, there were a few people there from the Bible study—and they weren't just passing through. We left right away feeling very upset.

"I can't believe it," said Keith as we drove.

"What can we do?"

We had such strong feelings about seeing Christians getting loaded, but we felt helpless. We wondered what we were supposed to do when we saw other Christians making wrong choices.

A short time later we felt like we found some answers at the Cramers' Bible study. The monkey was chattering in the background, but we were tuned in to the message. It was from the Old Testament book of Ezekiel, in a passage about a watchman who had the job of sitting on the wall of an ancient city. His job was to alert the people in the city if he saw danger coming. If the people heard the watchman's warning but ignored it, then it was their own fault if they ended up getting hurt. The Bible said their blood would be "on their own head". But if the watchman fell asleep and neglected to warn the people about approaching danger, it was the watchman's fault if they got hurt—and the blood of the people would be on the watchman's hands. He would be held accountable.

The Bible teacher went on to say that as Christians we are the watchmen. God wants us to warn others if we see disaster coming their way—and what could be more of a disaster than living in a way that would separate you from God eternally? We left the study feeling like the weight of the world was on our shoulders. One of the reasons we were so troubled was because we had a Christian friend, Tom, whom we really loved, and we knew he was having a hard time breaking off with an old girlfriend—and they would sometimes sleep together.

That night another friend came home with us and we all sat on the floor in Keith's music room wondering what to do. The thing that made it so heavy for us was that Tom sometimes helped to lead Bible studies in another church where he was really outspoken about the need to accept Christ. He sometimes came to the Vineyard, too, and Kenn knew him. It was only because of our close friendship with Tom that we knew what was going on. What if Jesus returned *tonight,* before Tom had a chance to repent? He might be separated from God—forever! And his blood would be on *our* hands. We knew we were responsible to say something right away.

So, sitting on the floor in front of the old upright piano, Keith came up with an idea. "One of us should phone Tom and warn him right away."

I thought Keith should be the one, since he had the most nerve. Besides it was his idea. But Keith's eyes lit up. "Let's draw lots," he said. "They did that in the Bible."

Keith rifled through the scattering of half-finished lead-sheets on the piano and found three different sized pencils. He tucked them into his hand, making them all even at the top. Wouldn't you know who came up with the short one—*me*! I protested that one of the guys should phone, but I knew that we all had equal responsibility before the Lord in this situation. Anyway, I was never one to back down from a challenge and if God had chosen me to sound the alarm I was determined to do it. I dialed the phone.

My heart was pounding as it started to ring. After the first ring I thought, *Maybe I should hang up.* . . . It rang again. I said, "Keith, it's late. He's probably already in bed."

Then someone picked up the phone. A groggy voice said, "Hello . . ."

"Uh, hi. It's Melody. Did I wake you?"

"It's okay. What's up?"

I could feel my face getting warm. "I'm sorry I woke you, but we went to this Bible study tonight. It was about being watchmen and . . . Well . . . uh . . . of course we know what's going on . . . and well, we just wanted to tell you that the Bible says you really shouldn't be doing that."

"Yeah, I know," Tom said softly. "I'm getting some counsel from my pastor. And I'll be taking care of it really soon."

"Okay. I just wanted to tell you. Good night."

"Thanks. Good night."

I hung up the phone and couldn't believe I'd really done it.

Keith said, "Wow, I'm really proud of you, Mel. You did great!"

I was just relieved that it was over. I knew I'd done the right thing, but it was really hard. And I was a bit puzzled. I couldn't figure out why Tom was getting counsel. What was there to get counsel *about*? The Bible was clear on the subject of having sex outside of marriage. What was there to talk about?

The next time we saw Kenn, on the following Friday night, we were excited to tell him we'd taken the watchman teaching we'd just heard to heart.

"Did you hear we called Tom?" Keith said, expectantly.

Kenn paused for a minute and looked thoughtful.

"Well, actually, I did hear about it . . ."

Keith happily went on to explain about the Bible study and the watchman and my phone call.

Then Kenn said, gently, "You know, you probably shouldn't have called."

Probably shouldn't have called? We were shocked.

"What do you mean?" Keith asked, incredulously.

"Well, maybe it would have been better if you'd just prayed."

As we drove home that night we were really confused. Just prayed? What kind of advice was that? If Jesus came back before Tom got things right, he'd be separated from God forever—and we were supposed to "just pray" and not even talk to Tom? We were hearing all these things about living holy lives, practicing what we preach, being watchmen . . . and now this? It seemed to us that watchmen were supposed to sound an alarm, not "just pray" about sounding one!

We loved Kenn so much—and really respected him. We knew he was a man of God, and that he understood God's unconditional love. But we were confused. Did unconditional love mean that you ignored sin? Maybe there were things he and Tom's pastor knew about the situation that we didn't. Still, it didn't make sense.

"First the wild party at Leo's. Now Tom. I can't believe this," said Keith. "The Church is just *filled* with sinners!"

I couldn't believe it either. But something told me Keith's reaction might be a little strong.

"We've met some really great Christians in the past few months," I countered. "It can't be *all* bad."

"I know, I know. But I'm beginning to feel like this is just the tip of the iceberg," Keith said thoughtfully. "I know we're not perfect, but we're trying. It's not just Tom. It's a lot of people. They know the right words to say, but their lives don't match up."

As I said, in the beginning it seemed to us that some people just seemed to blossom and grow. But after several months, it appeared that quite a few of those "blossoms" had already withered. Sometimes, after leading someone to the Lord, we'd run into them weeks later at Topanga Plaza and they didn't even want to look us in the eye. Then we'd learn that they were back on drugs and sleeping around, as if they'd never even seen the light. Keith was never afraid of confrontation and he'd try to reason with them. A few, we convinced to return to God. Others we couldn't. And the few who returned to church still lived the same old lives.

Why was this happening? They'd prayed the sinner's prayer, but they weren't acting very saved. Why did some Christians "stick" and some just fall away? We started to think that just giving your heart to the Lord in a prayer might not be enough.

One day, a Christian friend named Robin asked me to pray for her brother. We really looked up to her because she'd already known the Lord for eight years—which to me seemed forever. I asked her why we needed to pray for her brother.

"Oh, he's saved. He's just out of fellowship." She went on to give me more details. "He used to come to church all the time. But he's living with his girlfriend now and back on drugs. I know he'll go to heaven—but he won't have any rewards in heaven if he keeps this up. I really want to see him back in fellowship. I know he'll be happier then."

I wondered about this. Is losing "heavenly rewards" the only thing we need to worry about after we pray the sinner's prayer? What about living for God now?

I told Robin I'd pray, but I felt really odd inside. I figured she knew what she was talking about since she'd been a Christian a lot longer than me, but something didn't add up.

Later on, Keith and I talked about it, voicing the questions that were collecting in our minds. If you prayed and asked Jesus into your heart, was there ever a point where he might leave you? What if *you* decided to leave him? And if you asked Jesus to save you, could you keep living in sin—and just be automatically forgiven of everything? All we knew was that we were getting really frustrated with what we were seeing around us.

One day, after trying to figure out how to pray for Robin's brother, Keith spent the whole morning telling Feather, a young hippie girl, about the Lord. In fact, that day it brought all our questions to a head.

Feather was very skeptical about Christians, and she gave Keith a run for his money.

"I don't think they're any better than I am. The Christians I've known have all been a bunch of hypocrites. They say one thing and do another."

"Real Christians aren't like that," insisted Keith. "They really love the Lord and they live holy lives."

"Well, I don't need a list of do's and don'ts in my life. I believe there's a supreme being, but I don't want anybody telling me what to do."

"If you had a child you'd want to protect him, not control him. God loves you so much that he doesn't want you to do things that will cause you pain. I know. I really blew it before I was a Christian. I hurt a lot of people, but mostly I hurt myself."

As Keith started to share from his own life I could tell Feather had really started listening. We both knew exactly where she was at, because we'd been there ourselves once. The more open Keith got about himself, the more I could see she started to believe him.

Keith said, "God wants to be in a relationship with you. I think he's been speaking to you for a long time. You need to start listening."

As her attitude grew softer Keith really encouraged her to open her heart to the Lord.

"Just pray with me. You don't have anything to lose—and you have everything to gain."

Finally, after a few hours, she came to a point where she was willing to pray and ask Jesus into her life. Keith led her in a really precious prayer, and then wanted to take her to meet some of our friends. He said, "I want to introduce you to some of your new brothers and sisters who really love God. We want you to meet some *real* Christians."

We jumped into "Victor", drove up to Hollywood and ended up at the home of our friends the Cramers, but they weren't around. The Cramers happened to live next door to Leo, and now we heard some noise coming from Leo's backyard, so we walked over. There were a few people from the Bible study swimming in Leo's pool, and we pulled up a few chairs at poolside, all the while telling our new sister, Feather, how great being a Christian was. She was starting to look more relaxed and I knew we were getting through to her at last.

We were only there a few minutes when the sliding glass door from Leo's house flung open wide. A new Christian we'd met at the Cramers' home came charging out at full speed. He ran across the concrete with his arms raised over his head, yelling—"Praise the Lord!"—and dove into the pool. There was only one problem. He was totally naked.

Now there he was, swimming around in front of us, with nothing on but a big smile. I quickly glanced at Feather to see her reaction. She looked upset.

Keith immediately jumped to his feet. Standing on the edge of the pool he said firmly, "Get out of there, right now!" Then he had immediate second thoughts. "No! Don't get out. Where are your pants?"

The guy didn't want to tell Keith where his pants were, but Keith insisted. He gave in and Keith went into the house to get them. Then he brought them out to the pool and handed them to this happy streaker.

"Put them on!"

He did.

Leo was really angry when he heard what Keith had done. He thought Keith had a lot of nerve to tell a guest at his house that he needed to put his clothes on. But we were really upset, too.

The incident had unraveled our whole testimony to Feather, who was just hours old in the Lord. Even though nudity was widely accepted among hippies, we'd told her Christians were different. We never saw her again after that day and we knew it was because of what happened at the pool. Everything we'd told her about Christianity had been ruined. We didn't know if she'd ever believe another Christian again, and our hearts really hurt for her.

This, coupled with the time we "raided" Leo's beer blast, served to fuel Keith's quickly growing reputation as some kind of radical. It also earned us the name "The God Squad". The name didn't stick, but these things stuck in our minds and caused us to be really troubled.

It was apparent now that the attitude of many Christians was pretty lax. It seemed like you could be a Christian and do almost anything you wanted—sleep around, smoke dope and swim nude in mixed company. And it seemed as if nobody was objecting.

Keith fell into a real depression over what we were seeing.

"Something's really wrong here," he said. "I've struggled too long and too hard to find Jesus. I'm not gonna quit now," Keith said. "But I'll tell you one thing, I'm not going to compromise what I know is right, no matter what people around us are doing."

"It seems so crazy to play games with God," I added.

"Yeah," Keith concluded, "we have to give God more than lip-service—we need to give him life-service."

We were wrestling with some big questions—like what it meant to really be a Christian. The Bible says, " . . . if you confess [Jesus] with your mouth you will be saved." But is just *saying* you're a Christian enough? Anybody could do that. Does something more need to happen to "prove" you're a Christian? Even though we had a lot of unanswered questions, something in us really began to hurt for other people who'd been just like us. People who were trying to find something real in life—a reason to live. We had an aching desire to reach out to those who were looking in all the same places we did—drugs, occult, free love. We knew how they felt and understood how hurt some of them were. We wanted to help them find the peace and hope they were longing to find.

Since Keith loved to tell people about Jesus, we usually made a point of going out to find people to talk to—anywhere. One Sunday, a few friends were over and we argued about where we should go to find some hurting people to lead to the Lord. It was between Muscle Beach in Santa Monica and Tapia Park in the foothills. The beach came out the winner and off we went!

True to its name, Muscle Beach was filled with flexing masses of manhood—posturing, lifting weights and balancing girls in very small bikinis far above their heads—in swan-dive positions! We plopped ourselves down on the grass right in the middle of all this and Keith started playing some worship songs on his acoustic guitar. We all sang out loudly and with a lot of enthusiasm. A small crowd started to gather around us as Keith's energetic playing drew people like a magnet.

After singing for a while I noticed one blond girl who was sitting several feet away. Her head was down and it looked like she might be crying. I got up, went over and sat down by her. She *was* crying.

I sat there for a minute unsure of what to do. Finally, I said softly, "Excuse me. You seem kind of upset. Is there anything I can do to help?"

She lifted her head. Her eyes were red and questioning.

"I know you don't know me," I ventured, "but that's my husband playing the guitar over there. I just felt like I was supposed to come over and talk to you."

Her lip quivered a little as she started to speak. "I . . . I just don't know what to do. I'm pregnant and I don't *want* this baby."

"Why don't you want it?"

A sob caught in her throat. Then she said, "My husband and I are separated, and I can't take care of a baby by myself."

Her light hair and delicate features made her look too young to even *be* married, let alone pregnant. She continued with her story and I played with the grass, silently praying that God would help me to help her. Bit by bit her story unfolded.

Her name was Cassie, and she and her husband had gotten involved in some kind of strange group that was very repressive— especially toward women. She could only wear a certain type of clothing and had extremely limited privileges. Then to make things even worse, her husband started beating her.

She dropped her face into her hands and started sobbing. "I went to the leaders and told them he was beating me and that I was afraid. But they told me I couldn't separate myself from him. I was so afraid. And . . . and then I found out I was pregnant."

She really broke then, and just wept. I looked away. Muscle men were still tossing tanned bathing beauties around. Little kids were running by with corn-dogs and lemonade. And Keith was still playing his guitar and singing about Jesus.

Cassie lifted her head in a moment. "In spite of all the threats, I left and moved into a Salvation Army unwed mothers' home in Los Angeles. The reason I'm so upset is because today's Sunday."

"What's so upsetting about that?"

"On Tuesday I'm scheduled to have an abortion."

My heart broke for her. Before becoming a Christian I would have thought getting an abortion was a good solution to an unwanted pregnancy. Now I knew better. Destroying her baby was not Cassie's answer. I talked hard and fast, knowing I might be her last hope. I told her not to get an abortion, but that bit of advice seemed kind of empty considering her whole situation.

Hoping that Keith might know what to do, I went and told him everything. Keith immediately got up and went to her side. His eyes were filled with compassion as he said a few comforting words of encouragement. She really responded to his kindness. And then I heard him say, "Why don't you come home with us? Come and live with us. We'll help you."

I was probably as surprised as Cassie by Keith's invitation. I thought, *Come and live with us? Is he serious? We don't even know her.*

But as I thought about it for a minute, I realized that Keith saw exactly what she needed—someone to love her enough to take her in and walk through this terrible time with her. And there was also a second little life at stake. It really seemed like God brought us together so we could help her, and I was glad Keith asked her to move in with us.

We drove to the unwed mothers' home to get her things and it was a very depressing place—filled with some really young girls, who were *very* pregnant. We helped Cassie pack and took her to our house in Woodland Hills, assuring her she'd have a nice room all to herself.

Cassie looked relieved as we turned onto Dolorosa Street and she could see it was a nice family-type neighborhood. She seemed to love our little house with its warm sunny-yellow kitchen and big picture windows in the living room. We had three bedrooms off a narrow hallway—with the only bathroom at the end. We showed Cassie to her room and helped her get settled.

By Tuesday, we had actually talked Cassie into cancelling her abortion. On Wednesday her baby was still alive. We also led her to the Lord, and talked for hours on end about Jesus, and her husband, and baby.

Then one morning, Cassie was nowhere to be found. She returned late that night and told us she hitchhiked down to Muscle Beach. And after she'd been with us about two weeks, we woke up and she was gone again. Only this time she didn't come back.

We often wondered what happened to her and worried that she might have scheduled the abortion after all. We had no way of knowing.

One night at a Bible study we met a young mom, named Cindy, whose husband had moved in with another woman. Now Cindy was raising her three-year-old daughter, Kelly, alone. Kelly was real cute and looked like a miniature version of her very pretty mom. We became friends and did a lot of things together. Cindy was sweet and vulnerable—as a new Christian she was always trying to help others.

One night when she came out of the bar she was working in, there was a drunk guy by her car. She talked to him about Jesus and the next night she picked him up and brought him to a Bible study. When he got angry at the teacher and stormed out in the middle of the study, Cindy started to chase after him. But Keith blocked her way at the door.

"Let him go," Keith said firmly.

"But I brought him. I feel responsible to drive him back home . . ." she insisted.

"He's a big boy. He can find his way home. It's just not safe."

Later that night we all sat down and had a talk. Cindy had

recently looked up an old boyfriend who wasn't a Christian—and yet she was struggling to keep strong in the Lord.

"You know, it would really be good for you and Kelly if you lived in more of a Christian environment," Keith offered.

"The only people I could think of living with is you and Melody."

"Well, we'll just pray about that!" Keith told her.

Keith and I did pray that night, and the next day we told her she and Kelly could move in with us if they wanted. They did. As soon as they moved in, Keith sat down with her and they had a long discussion far into the night. There were a few guys wanting to take Cindy out but Keith told her he didn't think she should be dating anyone because she was still a married woman. He also pointed out that she should look for another job because by working in a bar she was helping people get drunk. Cindy really wanted to do what was right, and she took his counsel on both points. Now she and Kelly shared one of our three bedrooms, leaving the one remaining bedroom for us, and a music room.

But there was still more room at the inn.

A short time later, I struck up a conversation with a young woman at the health club Keith and I belonged to. We were always trying to keep in shape, but I admit I spent most of my time in the jacuzzi. In fact, that's where I was when I met Maureen. She looked sad, and we got to talking. She was going through a personal crisis and was very open when I started to talk about Jesus. We invited her to church with us—and, well, one thing led to another. Pretty soon, I was asking Keith if she could come and live with us, too.

Some people thought we were crazy for having so many people move in with us. We'd often hear comments from people at church. They'd say things like, "You guys are nuts. You haven't even been married that long. You need time alone." It was true we were young in our marriage, and even younger in the Lord—but it just didn't seem like the urgent needs of these people were going to wait. Where else were they going to go while we made sure we got our time alone? So we did what we felt the Lord wanted us to do—we kept our home and our hearts open to anyone who needed help. It gave us a deep sense of joy to know we could be used to make a difference in someone else's life.

In the process of seeing other people's lives change, our lives were radically changing, too. We used to go to all-night parties and run around doing whatever we wanted. Now that people were moving into our house, Keith and I were spending a lot more time trying to help them grow in the Lord and overcome the effects of the past. Cindy, for instance, seemed to be having problems with her jobs.

After she'd quit her job at the bar, Cindy started waitressing in a deli. But now her boss told her if she wanted to keep her job she'd have to stop reporting the full amount of her weekly tips to the IRS. The other waitresses were complaining because Cindy was consistently reporting a much higher figure than they were and they were afraid they'd get caught cheating.

Once again Keith sat up late at night and talked with her.

"What am I going to do?" Cindy asked, desperately. "They want me to lie."

"You can't lie. And it wouldn't be right to cheat the government."

"I don't want to lie. But I need my job."

"It's more important to do what's right."

After much discussion, Cindy came to a firm resolve and made a decision we were all really proud about. Keith wrote in his journal that Cindy "had to quit because they wouldn't let her be honest."

Not only were we staying up half the night counseling people, there were other meetings taking place at our house, as Christianity soaked into every nook and cranny of our lives. One night, after a Friday meeting at the Vineyard, Kenn announced, "Everyone's invited to an all-night prayer meeting at Keith Green's house!" Keith's natural leadership was starting to surface again.

So here we were, having all-night prayer meetings when we barely knew how to pray ourselves! But Keith had read books about giants in the faith who prayed all night. One man used to go out in knee-deep snow and pray all night for the Indian tribes he was trying to reach. Another man would crawl into a hollow log in the woods to pray all night. We figured if all-night prayer helped make them strong, it would help make us strong too— even in our comfortable living room!

One night, something unusual happened. It was sometime in the gray, pre-dawn hours. We had lost ourselves singing songs of praise. Gently, slowly, it seemed like the whole atmosphere in the room changed as we worshiped the Lord with our friends. An overwhelming sense of peace settled on us—the air was thick with it. In fact at one point we all looked at each other and saw what looked like a misty fog gently hovering in the room. We all saw it at the same time. The Holy Spirit seemed to be with us in a very sweet way, and we could feel the closeness of God.

When we weren't meeting at home or at the beach, we could often be found at one of Keith's favorite restaurants—talking about Jesus with friends while trying to get our waitress saved. In fact, Keith would go anywhere, anytime, if it meant being with Christians or reaching someone for the Lord.

One time, Keith even went so far as to drive a guy we'd just met all the way to Arizona. We met Ray through some Christian friends, but he wasn't a Christian. He was a genuinely nice guy—a clean-cut, all-American type—but that didn't matter to Keith. Ray still needed the Lord. When Keith heard he was taking a Greyhound Bus to Tucson the next day, he announced, "God just told me to drive you!" Everyone, including Ray, kept telling Keith he was crazy. But Keith figured how could he measure a few days drive against the value of someone's eternal soul? Their mutual friend Jerry Houser, who was an accomplished actor, went along so Keith wouldn't have to drive back alone—or maybe he went so Ray wouldn't have to be alone with Keith!

At any rate, Keith returned a few days later, road-weary but excited. "We've got a new brother in the Lord!" he announced, bursting in the front door.

Even though we saw lives being turned around, like Ray's and Cindy's, we were still troubled by the friends who didn't stick. A few more had dropped out and weren't around anymore. We wondered where they went. And more importantly, *why* they went. What made them fall away? Was there some attitude in their hearts that they hadn't dealt with? It made us question our own hearts and attitudes.

Keith could be painfully self-examining. Quite often, he was much harder on himself than he was on anyone else. He would say, "If they could go cold toward God, what about me?" We realized that outward changes were the easiest—things like giving up drugs and drinking or cleaning up our language. The inner changes were the hardest. Some of our attitudes were a lot more subtle and harder to detect. Were there things we hadn't dealt with in our own lives?

In particular, Keith started to question his music. One day, he said to me, "If my life is going to be totally submitted to the Lord, what does that mean about my music?"

I was amazed that he was even open to this question. For years he'd believed part of his destiny was to use his music as a platform to deliver a spiritual message. It was a sense he'd had long before he was a Christian. But now that he really *knew* the Lord, Keith felt he needed a new "go-ahead" from him. Singing for people seemed like the natural thing for someone with Keith's talent to do—but he didn't want to assume anything.

This was an excruciating question for Keith. His music was

more than a hobby—he'd been singing all his life. Music was who he was. And it was most certainly our means of support. A lifetime of hopes and dreams were wrapped up in his music. Was it possible that after so many years of searching for acclaim and musical success that Keith might not ever sing before an audience again? We talked about it more than once.

"You know Mel, since I was a little kid, music has been a part of my life. My grandfather taught me my first rock-and-roll chords, my parents have stood with me. . . . But I'm not sure anymore if God wants me involved in music."

"Keith," I countered, "God gave you your music. Wouldn't he want you to use it?"

"I don't know. Why should I think Jesus wants me doing music just because I've always done it? Because it's the thing I do best? That's not enough of a reason. Maybe he wants me to go get a job making hamburgers at McDonalds."

I didn't know what to think. How could he *not* do music? On the other hand, I knew it was always important to obey God. But this seemed like a pretty high price to pay.

"You need to do whatever you think God's telling you to do," I said finally.

Keith spent many hours, even days, agonizing over his decision. Finally, he announced his decision.

"Mel, the only way to know for sure if God is giving me my music is to give it up. I need to let it go. I think it's okay to keep writing for CBS and to play at home—but I'm laying down all of my public performing at the foot of the cross. I won't pick it up again unless God tells me to."

I swallowed hard. "Are you sure?"

"I'm sure," he replied. "I don't want to presume upon the Lord." Then he got an intensely serious look in his eyes.

"Mel . . . I don't really know if God will ever let me pick it up again. Once I lay it down that may be it forever."

If anything left me with an uneasy, open-ended feeling, it was that decision. We were getting down to the roots of big issues. That was really scary.

But Keith had made his mind up. As far as he was concerned, Keith Green would never play in public again. The old Keith—the one with the dream of being acclaimed as a singer—was dead.

"Your Love Broke Through"

Santa Monica Beach with Dawn.

THROUGHOUT THE SUMMER OF 1975, KEITH TURNED DOWN ANY concert offers that came his way. He confined himself to his upright piano at home. This put a bit of a strain on our finances, but Keith was determined not to budge from his decision.

For me, it was really a strange feeling to have something that was such a part of your life be dead. I was surprised to find how much I missed the music—but it was obviously a much greater sacrifice for Keith. However, it did seem like some neat things were going on in Keith's heart.

One starry night, we took a walk to the neighborhood donut shop. Holding hands on the way, we looked up at the moon and stars and began to wonder about what might happen in the future. Of course,

Keith's music was one of the first things to come up.

"Music is such a part of who you are," I began. "It's hard to imagine you without it forever."

"I've been thinking about that," he agreed. "But you know, maybe my music has been a crutch."

"What do you mean, a crutch?"

"When I was growing up, my talent always opened doors for me. I never really had to work at having 'social graces', like other people did. I knew I could win people over if I could just get to a piano. Music has always been my calling card."

"You sure blew me away when you played for me on our first date," I said, squeezing his hand.

"That was the whole idea," Keith said, with a grin. "But now I want to be accepted because I reflect the Lord, not because I blow everyone away with my music."

We reached the donut shop—and we were in luck. They had some hot ones cooling on racks. We got several in a bag and went outside to sit on the curb. It was such a nice night and, with other people always in the house, we had so little chance to talk alone.

"All the talent in the world won't buy me a godly character," Keith was saying, "and that's what I want more than anything."

I agreed. That's what I wanted, too.

After we got back home, Keith went into his music room and closed the door. I could hear him playing a beautiful new melody on the piano. I could tell Keith was playing it just for the Lord— and I silently wondered if the Lord and I would be the only ones ever to hear it.

Keith's twenty-second birthday came and went in October, and we were busier than ever with the new people in our lives.

Just before we'd become Christians—which was now about six months ago—our good friend Karen Bender had come over with her daughter, Dawn. Karen had met a guy she really liked and he wanted her and Dawn to move to Colorado with him. They'd come to say goodbye, and we'd sat on our front lawn to smoke a "goodbye joint" together.

Now Karen and Dawn were back from Colorado. Karen came back first and moved back to Hollywood, but Dawn stayed in Colorado with her grandparents. When Karen returned without Dawn she rented an apartment in an adults-only building. Since then, however, Dawn had returned so she could be with her mom—which presented two problems. First, no one under eighteen could live in the building and the manager told Karen she was going to have to find another place to live now that Dawn was back. Second, Karen was working a split-shift at the phone company, which meant little Dawn was home alone many evenings.

Keith and I had become Christians while they were gone. Since we wanted to spend some extra time with Dawn now, we decided to take her with us to some evening Bible studies. She really wanted to go.

"When I was living with my grandma and grandpa," she told us happily, "I went to church with them on Sundays. I told them I wanted to be a Christian, so they phoned the pastor to come over and pray with me. I got baptized, too!"

We took Dawn with us to as many meetings as we could over the next few weeks.

One night I was standing at the sink doing the dishes, and Dawn phoned. Keith spoke with her a few minutes and then came into the kitchen and announced, "Dawn's moving in with us."

I stood there silently for a moment, the tap water still running.

"Moving in with us? What do you mean?"

"Dawn called to say goodbye," Keith explained. "Since Karen can't keep her in the apartment, she was going to send Dawn to live with some of her relatives." When he told me *which* relatives, I winced. Karen had told us about these particular folks. They had a lot of problems—drinking and smoking dope at all hours of the day and night.

"They're leaving tomorrow morning to move up north into the woods somewhere, and Karen wanted to send Dawn to live with them. Mel, you should have heard Dawnie's voice. She didn't want to go. She asked if she could come and live with us instead."

"And you said . . . ?" I just wanted to confirm what I'd heard.

"I told her she could."

I was silent again for a moment. I could feel something rising up inside of my chest. On one hand, I really loved Dawn and had a lot of compassion for her situation. On the other hand, Keith didn't even ask me how I might feel about it. True, it wouldn't be a good thing for Dawn to go off to the woods and live with people who were struggling with major problems. And Dawn was so young—young in the Lord, too. Still, I wished Keith would have talked to me before telling her she could move in. After all, she was a minor, and the responsibility was pretty big.

But in the same moment, I resolved not to even mention it to Keith. I knew I would have said yes anyway. I really loved Dawn and felt very protective of her. It was obviously the best thing to do. And in those few moments of silence I felt a sense of peace

—

123

rush into my heart. Maybe that was the Lord's way of telling me we were making the right decision.

And so Dawn moved in with us just a few weeks after her eleventh birthday. She said happily, "I've always wanted to live in a real house, with a backyard, and a dog." And even though we told her to just keep calling us Keith and Melody, she started calling us Mom and Dad right away.

Mom and Dad . . . Keith and I had talked about having children, but it was a short conversation. Neither of us had any burning desire to be parents just yet. And now, here we were—the parents of a beautiful, bouncing, pre-teen daughter. We knew *zero* about being parents—especially to an eleven-year-old. But we loved Dawn. She had taken root in our hearts. Dawn moved into Cindy and Kelly's room, and now there were five of us in the little house on Dolorosa Street.

About the same time Dawn moved in, Keith was asked to perform at a benefit for the Hollywood Free Theater—made up of a group of Christian actors who met to encourage each other in the Lord and to work on their acting skills. In fact, Keith and I had gone to a few classes there. Neither one of us showed any "star" quality, but it was fun and they were a great group.

It had been nearly three months since Keith laid aside his performing. He'd quickly turned down other opportunities, but this time he felt torn. He wasn't trying to slip out of his commitment, but he did have a desire to help raise money for this group of Christians. Finally, he felt it was okay to at least *ask* the Lord about it. He prayed a lot, because he didn't want his own desires to get in the way of hearing God. At last, Keith thought he had some direction.

"I believe God is giving me the 'go-ahead' to accept this *one* invitation," Keith told me. "He didn't tell me to pick up my music again—I think maybe he's letting me do this because it's for a good cause. It's a one time thing. After that I'm totally going back to my commitment."

The benefit was going to be held in the heart of Beverly Hills at a very "in" nightspot, called The Daisy. On the night of the benefit, late in September, we jumped into "Victor" and headed up Wilshire Boulevard, past the famous Brown Derby restaurant, then turned onto North Rodeo Drive and into the parking lot of The Daisy.

The place was packed when we arrived, but not with the usual crowd. We immediately saw many familiar faces from the Vineyard—Randy Stonehill, Larry Norman, Jerry Houser, and a Christian recording artist named Jamie Owens. And then there were famous faces we were seeing up-close for the first time—Pat Boone, Dale Evans, and Julie Harris, who'd just starred in the movie *The Hiding Place*.

The place was alive with energy and excitement. Light glittered off the chandeliers and mirrors, and Christian music was playing in the background. The long, mirrored bar against the far wall held only trays of fruit juice and soft drinks tonight.

Keith and I found a small table for two. He was slotted near the end, just before Pat Boone and Julie Harris. Keith usually had nerves of steel, but I knew he felt a lot of pressure tonight. He wanted his performance to bring glory to the Lord—and only to the Lord.

When Keith's turn came at last, he walked up into the bright spotlight and sat down at the piano. The room fell into a polite hush. He looked out at the audience as he started playing softly on the piano and talking.

"This song I'm about to sing is *my* song. This is *your* song. It's for everyone who's ever left the loving arms of their heavenly Father to go out on their own.

"I was a prodigal son," he explained. "But I'm not running anymore. I came home covered with mud and dirt from the world, and my Father in heaven picked me up, washed me off and sat me on his lap."

As Keith launched into "The Prodigal Son Suite", the meandering conversations ceased. I remembered the hours Keith put into polishing the lyrics to "The Prodigal Son" during that stony time almost a year-and-a-half ago. Now, people set down their soft drinks, and turned their attention to the stage. I sensed at once that *something* was happening up there with Keith. This wasn't just a performance. It was as if, through Keith, God was portraying his heart to us—a father's heart that longed for his children to come home.

When Keith came to the part where the now-broken prodigal son returns home, there was such a trembling cry in his voice, my throat tightened. At the table next to me, a woman had tears running down her face. . . .

> *I was near home,*
> *In sight of the house.*
> *My father just stared—*
> *Dropped open his mouth.*
> *He ran up the road*
> *And fell at my feet,*
> *And cried . . . and cried . . .*
>
> *Father I've sinned.*
> *Heaven's ashamed.*
> *I'm no longer worthy*

To bear your name.
I've learned that my home
Is right where you are
Oh, Father, take me in. . . .

People all over this beautiful ballroom were dabbing at their tears. And then, Keith broke into the last movement—the part where the father, with joy, forgives his son and calls for a celebration. . . .

Bring the best robe,
Put it on my son!
Shoes for his feet—
Hurry! Put them on!

This is my son
Who I thought had died!
Prepare a feast
For my son's alive!
My son's returned,
In the hands of God!

When the song ended Keith threw his head and body forward over the keys to emphasize it was finished. There was a moment of stunned silence—then the whole room exploded in applause and cheers. Many people jumped to their feet in a standing ovation. But Keith got up from the piano at once and quietly made his way back to our table, barely looking up.

Once the program ended, many people came up to Keith to encourage him and tell him how the Lord touched them while he was singing. Keith looked pleased, but he was a bit reserved. Later, on the way home, I found out why.

"I wasn't sure how to respond when everyone was so excited," he said, shaking his head.

I was elated. "Keith, you were incredible. I really saw the Lord *in* you, in a more powerful way tonight."

"I *felt* the Lord in a new way, too." Then he hesitated for a moment. "Mel, I think the Lord gave me back my music while I was playing tonight. I was in the middle of the song and I just felt a peace and an assurance that I was right in the center of God's will—doing exactly what he created me to do."

"That's wonderful!"

"Yeah. It's hard to believe, but I think God really wants me to play for him and for his glory—and *only* for his glory."

When Keith received his music back it was the go-ahead from the Lord that he'd been waiting for—but it was another three months before he really picked it up and started running with it.

But when he did, word about his music ministry quickly spread, through our friends in the Christian music world. And by the end of 1975, Keith was getting asked to do concerts in some of the churches in southern California. It was a whole new world to us. Except for the few concerts he'd done with Randy Stonehill, Keith had only played his music in nightclubs, colleges, hippie vegetarian restaurants and recording studios—along with a few television appearances when he was younger. Playing in churches posed some new challenges—and interesting transitions—for us.

Our first big question was, how much money do you ask from a church that invites you to do a concert? In the secular world, everyone always struggles to make more money. Besides the money itself, the amount you receive is a yardstick to measure your worth and popularity. The better you are, the more you get. Even though Keith was never in it "just for the money", it was his trade and it paid our bills. And we still had bills to pay! Our CBS salary helped, but our growing household had become a hub of activity, and we were often busy with what seemed to be a continual "feeding of the five thousand".

We were just learning about finances from a Christian point-of-view. Keith had always had the highest integrity when it came to money—but the idea of tithing was new to us. In fact, we got a fiery baptism on tithing when a seven-month delay in our CBS salary eventually came in—with a check for $7,000! After we got over the initial shock of giving away $700 in tithe all at once, we were glad to follow biblical principles about giving. At least they were clear. But what were the biblical principles about charging for concerts? Where were they found in the Bible?

Our inquiries didn't help much. Other Christian musicians were all over the map when it came to this matter. Some sold tickets, some asked for a certain amount up-front, and others went for love offerings. We heard stories galore. They weren't all good. We had a few tough experiences of our own.

There was the time Keith was called at the last minute to play at a very large church about an hour-and-a-half away from us. He was told on the phone they would give him $20 to come. Keith balked, because he figured that would just cover his gas for the three-hour round trip. They were such a large church, he felt they could afford to give a little more. But they stood firm, probably thinking the opportunity to play for a few thousand people would help give Keith's ministry greater exposure. That was true, but Keith still didn't feel it was the "brotherly" way to do things. Still, he felt the Lord wanted him to go anyway, even though he didn't think they were being fair. Besides, it *was* a good opportunity to minister to a lot of people.

By the standards we were used to, we wouldn't have run an *errand* that far away for that price—let alone do a full concert. But this was not the show-biz world. This was ministry. Yet, we were confused.

So we set out, feeling our way along in the dark. Now that we were Christians we instinctively knew the money rules had changed in some way—but we really didn't know how. Keith's music was no longer a "career". He considered himself a minister and we wanted to see people come to the Lord. But music was Keith's trade and we had big household expenses every week. Keith was an accomplished performer, so it seemed like he should ask for more than somebody who'd just taken a few guitar lessons. But as a minister, should Keith even care about how much he made?

It was a question we'd have to wrestle with for some time.

Even with these questions, our excitement about Jesus continued to grow and touch every area of our lives—especially our music. New songs just tumbled out one after another.

Keith was constantly writing—either alone, with me or Todd, or with some other new musical friend. Sometimes a combination of us wrote together, which made it even more fun. Many songs were inspiring calls to worship God in Spirit and truth, some were light-hearted expressions of joy—and then there were the funny ones.

Keith didn't believe that being a Christian meant you lost your sense of humor or your ability to have a good time.

One day our friend Wendell Burton came over and he and Keith ended up in the music room. Wendell went to the Vineyard and usually led worship at the house with the monkey. He was also a very talented singer and songwriter, and he and Keith decided to try and write something together. What resulted was a funny song about some heroes of the faith who trusted God even when the odds were against them—"He'll Take Care of the Rest":

> *You just think about Moses*
> *In front of the burnin' bush,*
> *Barefoot on the holy ground,*
> *You know, he must have been thinkin',*
> *Hey, what's an old dude like me*
> *Gonna tell 'em all when I go down?*
> *(Go down, Moses!)*
> *But the Lord said, "Hey, Mo!*
> *Don't you worry 'bout your going down south,*

I'll be saying every word that comes out of your mouth!" . . .

You just think about Noah,
Totin' his umbrella
When there wasn't a cloud in the sky.
All his neighbors would laugh
At his pet giraffe
And they would (ho, ho)
Snicker as he passed by.
But the Lord said,
"Hey, Noah, be cool.
Just keep buildin' 'dat boat.
It's just a matter of time
'Til they see who's gonna float!"
"You just keep doin' your best
And pray that it's blessed.
Hey, Noah, I'll take care of the rest—
I'm the Weather Man!"

Then there were a few songs that Keith wrote right away to express his own pure joy at finally finding the truth that set him free. Now, Keith was shining a light that drew people to him. He wrote this song to the Lord to tell him that, whenever anyone asked why he looked so happy, he had the honor of pointing the way to the Source of that light and simply say it's "Because of You!"

It's because of You
People smile at me
And they say, "What a lucky guy!"
Because of You
I can raise my hands to the sky
And say, "I'm only happy
Because of You!"

Another song Keith wrote during this time talked about the supernatural touch from God he felt in his heart. Keith said, "It's like chocolate ice cream. How do you describe the taste to someone who's never tasted chocolate?" "You Put This Love In My Heart" expressed Keith's gratitude for that miraculous touch.

Is all this real or a dream?
I feel so good I could scream!
You put this love in my heart.

Well, I know the loneliness I had before
Is gone now, I'll never feel it anymore.
'Cause Your lovin' has released me
From all that's in my past,
And I know I can believe You
When you say I'll never be forsaken
Your love is gonna last!

One day, Keith walked into the music room while I was

working on a new song. He listened as I played what I had of it on the piano—and sang the few sketchy words. . . .

When I hear the music start, I wanna sing it for You
Music that will fill Your heart, I wanna bring it to You

"Pretty good, so far, Mel."

I showed him the rough chords I was playing and he started fiddling with it. A few days later, Keith sat down to write but nothing was coming. He was walking around the house pretty frustrated about it. After he went back into the music room, I had an impression—words seemed to form in my mind. Was the Lord trying to say something to Keith—through *me*? I wrote down the words and took the piece of paper to Keith. He opened the note and read, "Rest quietly before me, and I will give you a song."

Pretty soon I heard music. Keith was singing a song, with the same chorus melody I'd written—but it had a whole different theme. Keith walked out and said, "The Lord just gave me a love song—from him to me."

My son, My son,
Why are you striving?
You can't add one thing
To what's been done for you.
I did it all while I was dying.
Rest in your faith
My peace will come to you.

When I hear the praises start,
I wanna rain upon you
Blessings that will fill your heart.
I see no stain upon you
Because you are My child
And you know Me.
To Me you're only holy,
Nothing that you've done remains,
Only what you do for Me.

My child, My child
Why are you weeping?
You will not have to wait forever.
That day and that hour is in My keeping—
The day I'll bring you´ into heaven. . . .

Another song we wrote together was inspired by something we read in the newspaper. It was the story of a priest who was trying to cast demons out of a woman who was possessed. The priest said that one time the demons started laughing and talking to him through this lady. He claimed that they were boasting, saying, "We have all the power because nobody believes in us any more!"

As soon as Keith and I had become Christians, we knew there was a real God—and a real devil. It certainly explained the dark force that took control of Harmony outside The Bla Bla that hot night a few years ago. So many people in southern California—and across America—were dipping into the occult without realizing the demonic powers behind it. We now knew that Satan was a for-real, hardball-playing bad guy, who was determined to capture and destroy every unsuspecting soul he could.

I drove to the market after reading about the priest, and his words kept coming back to me. I found myself scratching lyrics on a scrap of paper with one hand, while driving with the other. After I got home I put a fresh copy of the words, all sung from Satan's point-of-view, on Keith's piano. He added a few more words and some music and the result was called "Satan's Boast:"

Oh, my job keeps gettin' easier
As time keeps slippin' away.
I can imitate the brightest light
And make your night look just like day.
I put some truth in every lie
To tickle itchin' ears.
I'm drawin' people just like flies
'Cause they like what they hear.

I'm gainin' power by the hour,
They're fallin' by the score.
You know, it's gettin' very simple now
Since no one believes in me any more.

Oh heaven's just a state of mind
My books read on your shelf.
Oh, have you heard that God is dead?
I made that one up myself!
They're dabblin' in magic spells,
They get their fortunes read,
They heard the truth but turned away
And followed me instead . . .

Everyone likes a winner.
With my help you're guaranteed to win.
Hey, man, you ain't no sinner, no!
You've got the truth within.
And as your life slips by you believe the lie
That you did it on your own.
But I'll be there to help you share

Our dark eternal home—
Our dark eternal home.

Another influence was the Christian literature we were discovering. Keith was constantly reading and one of his favorites was a classic allegory called, "Hind's Feet On High Places", by Hannah Hurnard. Keith was thinking about the trials and testings the Lord had brought him through when he wrote the song, "Trials Turned To Gold".

He's brought me low
So I could know
The way to reach the heights.
To forsake my dreams
My self-esteem
And give up all my rights.
With each one that I lay down,
A jewel's placed in my crown.
Because His love
The things above—
Is all we'll ever need.

He's brought me here
Where things are clear,
And trials turn to gold.

He also wrote this journal entry:

Where Things Are Clear
We are nothing but dust. Our lives are not ours. Our bodies are not ours. Our future is in Your hands. The Lord is making me ready to die—completely—I don't deserve to live—so come Spirit of the holy God—live instead of me. There is no joy left in life but to realize I am nothing and let God be what He is— all.
Tears cannot express nor laughter His grace/gifts. I am His. Please Keith! Don't ever go back—look up.

Probably the greatest boost to our growth as songwriters was meeting other Christian musicians. Keith's first Christian recording session was playing piano on the *Growing Pains* album by Jamie Owens. Then through Jamie, Keith met a guy named Terry Talbot. Keith and Terry hit it off immediately.

Terry and his brother, John, had been in a famous rock band called Mason Proffit. Terry was working on a musical called "Firewind", and he asked Keith to sing one of the lead vocals on a song called,"Walk and Talk". Interestingly, it was going to be a duet with Barry McGuire. Keith couldn't believe it, since Barry had made such an impression on us a few years ago in Turlock—and now Keith was going to sing his first recorded Christian song with him! It seemed like so many little threads were starting to weave together.

Keith was really excited about this recording session because he was going to get to meet so many other Christian artists. From the story I heard later, Keith must have made quite a first impression himself.

Before Annie Herring from The Second Chapter of Acts even came to the session, Jamie Owens had told her, "Wait until you meet Keith Green. He's so filled with energy and his heart is just full of the Lord. You're going to love him!"

When Annie walked into the studio, Keith was working on his solo with the recording engineer. She suppressed a laugh, because Keith was trying to sing his lines with energy and feeling—and at the same time trying to explain to the engineer where to punch between words. The engineer finally got it, and did it just as Keith said. Annie thought, *Boy, he sure knows how to take charge!*

A little while later Billy Ray Hearn of Sparrow Records showed up, because "Firewind" was going to be released on his label. Keith did what he *always* did when he met the president of a record company. He dragged Billy Ray over to the piano and said, "Listen to this!" Then he proceeded to play a few songs. That wasn't all. Keith told him, "You gotta come to one of my concerts! There's a whole different spirit during a concert!" Billy Ray told Keith he'd try to come to a concert—sometime.

Besides getting to know Terry and Barry much better that day, Keith met Annie and the rest of Second Chapter—Annie's brother and sister, Matt and Nelly Ward—and Nelly's boyfriend Steve Greisen. They all had a great time getting to know each other and joking around. In fact, Annie made a lasting impression on Keith.

They'd been joking around and Annie, who was used to holding her own in a large family full of brothers, gave him what she considered to be "just a loving punch". When Keith came home he said, "Annie slugged me in the arm—hard!"

A week later, Keith met Annie's husband, Buck Herring, who was the producer for Second Chapter. Buck and Annie had only been married for a few years when her dad died. At that point Annie's youngest brother and sister, who'd been living with their dad, came to live with her and Buck. A short time later, Nelly, Matt and Annie discovered they could sing together.

The first time I met Second Chapter, I was so new to Christian music that I'd never even *heard* of them—even though they were nationally famous. Keith took me to their house in Northridge, and when we walked in Buck was listening to one of their albums. I was blown away. I walked into the kitchen and Annie was standing at the sink with an apron on, doing dishes. I didn't know what to say, so I said the first thing that came to my mind.

"I just heard your album. I've never heard you before. It's incredible. You . . . you sound like *angels!*"

"Oh, thank you!" Annie said with great delight.

Immediately, I felt really stupid. How embarrassing to tell a famous singer that you've never even heard them! I wanted to fall through the floor. I was really in awe of this beautiful woman with the elegant, high cheekbones and dark, dancing eyes—this woman of God, who sang like an angel and did dishes like a normal person! And I was standing in her kitchen. I wasn't sure how to act.

But Annie was so kind and warm—and seemed genuinely encouraged by my remarks. I guessed she was used to people getting a bit flustered around her. She made me feel welcome at once.

Meanwhile, Keith and Buck were off in the corner talking about music, producing and making albums. Keith had so many questions, especially about *who* he was supposed to sing to. I could hear them talking in the background as I helped Annie wipe the counter.

"I really believe I'm supposed to make an album." Keith was picking Buck's brain. "But I'm not sure if it's supposed to be a *Christian* album or not. What do you think?"

"What else would you do?" Buck said.

"Well, I want to lift up the name of the Lord. But it seems like Christians have plenty of music already. Anyway, why sing about Jesus to Christians? They already know him."

"Evangelism is important, Keith. But it's not the only reason God gave us music," Buck responded.

"I know, but it's the thing that's most important to me. I really want to do an album with a Christian message—for people who don't know the Lord yet."

"We tried it, brother. Our first contract was with MGM, and the secular machinery didn't know what to do with an album full of Christian songs."

"Maybe so, but at least the album will have a better chance of making it. I can always tell when I hit the Christian radio station—even before I hear the words. It just really bothers me that Christian records have such low budgets you can't get good sounds."

"It won't matter how good your album sounds," Buck shrugged, "a secular label still won't know what to do with it."

"I'm not into singing *just* for Christians. I really want my music to bring people to the Lord."

"Then I'm sure the Lord will show you what he wants you to do," Buck said simply.

Later that evening, as we drove home, Keith was deep in thought. I could tell his conversation with Buck didn't convince him. Keith wanted to reach people outside the church. But I knew he wouldn't rest until the question was settled.

Our musical family kept growing, as we met people like Chuck Girard, Phil Keaggy, Mike and Kathy Deasy, Kelly Willard, Karen Lafferty, and Andrae Crouch. We also listened to tons of tapes by people like Bob Ayala, a group called Mustard Seed Faith, and a girl with the name of Honeytree. We were totally impressed that they'd given their talent to sing only for the Lord—and yet we were still torn over what path Keith's musical ministry might take.

It was during this time, too, that one friendship where there had been long-standing tension was finally resolved.

Keith bumped into Randy Stonehill unexpectedly one day at the Vineyard offices. They were both glad to see each other, and Keith invited him over to our house. Because of some heated conversations before we were Christians, the friendship had been strained. They were still friends, and Keith even played at Randy's wedding—but things hadn't been quite right.

When Randy arrived with his guitar case, they headed straight into the music room. I was in the kitchen with Cindy, Kelly, and Dawn, and I could hear them laughing, talking, and playing music. Then it got very quiet for a long time. Later that night, Keith told me what happened.

"Things between me and Randy finally got worked out. I told him how upset I've been, thinking that I would have become a Christian a lot sooner if he would have *really* shared more about Jesus with me."

"What did Randy say?"

"He said he *did* try to tell me, but because he wasn't living out his faith consistently, he knew his words probably didn't have a lot of power. He said he knew actions speak louder than words sometimes. Randy said he was sorry."

"That was pretty neat of him to be so open with you. What did you say?"

Keith smiled. "My heart just melted, and I saw some of *my* mistakes. I know sometimes it was hard for him to have a two-way conversation with me. I'm not always the best listener. I forgave him, and I asked him to forgive me, too."

"Well, it *was* Randy who invited us to the Vineyard."

"Yeah. We were both teary-eyed. Then we got really excited. I ended up pulling out the melody Todd and I wrote a few days ago, and we worked on the words together. It's called 'Your Love Broke Through.' It's really hot!"

Later, Keith wrote:

MARCH 21, 1976

Randy played me some new songs and then we started talking and one thing led to another and it finally ended up in a big confession. . . . IT WAS A MIRACLE and an answer to prayer.

It really seemed like the Lord was starting to tie some loose ends together. We were hoping the next thing God would tie together would be Keith's music. It always amazed me that some major record company didn't snatch Keith up after one listen. I'd often seen him play his heart out for some executive, giving a performance that would take their breath away, but nothing ever came of it.

Now I wondered: Was something blocking the way before? Had the Lord been waiting for Keith to become a Christian before letting his career take off? What if, now that we were Christians, God would blow open doors, unplug ears, and help Keith find a record company that believed in him?

The dream of "making it" musically was not dead—it just had a slightly different slant to it now. Keith continued to make demos of his songs, and run them all over town still trying to get a record deal with a secular label.

And then, it seemed like our dream was going to take off.

One afternoon, about two months after meeting Buck, Keith went into Hollywood to meet with the people at Arista Records. Arista was a well-respected secular label that was turning out hit records with top-name artists. He played them some of his songs and they got very excited.

When Keith got home he bounced through the door. "Melody! Guess what?"

When I hurried into the living room, Keith was smiling from ear to ear.

"Mel, Arista wants to send me to New York next week!"

"New York! You're kidding!"

"They want me to meet with *Clive Davis*—straight to the top! They're paying my way out and everything. This might be it. Maybe God is going to open some doors after all!"

The following week I drove Keith to LAX and gave him a kiss goodbye, wishing I could go with him. Keith was so charged up I knew he was going to blow Clive Davis out of the water when he sang for him. I wished I could be there to see his face. It seemed like that long-awaited record contract was finally at Keith's finger tips.

Once Keith arrived in New York he settled into his hotel room anticipating his big meeting with Arista the next day. Keith later wrote:

APRIL 9, 1976

Clive Davis . . . kept me waiting for almost two hours. It was a failure, but I took it so well I couldn't believe it . . . kept telling myself that the Lord wanted me to do a Christian album. It depressed me, but I kept my chin up.

The following afternoon, my phone rang. Keith was calling from New York.

"How'd it go?" I asked eagerly.

"Well—I think God wants me to do a Christian album."

"You're kidding?"

"No. My interview was a flop. I was really upset at first, but I'm kinda starting to feel relieved now. At least I finally have a clear answer from the Lord. Hey, do you want me to bring a New York pizza home for you?"

"That would be great!"

The dream was dead—the one that had been in Keith's heart since he was a child. Some dreams are so deep they seem to become a part of the very fabric of your being. When they die, a part of you dies too. This should have been the biggest disappointment in Keith's life. But it wasn't. I saw the grace of God in Keith in such a strong way. After the initial depression lifted, Keith was actually excited. His prayers had been answered at last.

Now Keith knew why things had never really come together with his secular music. He saw even more clearly how his life-plans needed to be anchored in the reality of God's will—otherwise they would never be anything but fantasy. And the song Keith had written just a few months earlier with Randy and Todd had an even deeper meaning:

Like a foolish dreamer
Trying to build a highway
To the sky,
All my hopes would come tumblin' down
And I never knew just why.
Until today,
When You pulled away the clouds
That hung like curtains on my eyes.
I've been blind all these wasted years,
When I thought I was so wise.
But then You took me by surprise . . .

All my life I've been searching
For that crazy missing part,
And with one touch
You just rolled away
The stone that held my heart.
And now I see that the answer
Was as easy as just asking You in,
And I am so sure
I could never doubt
Your gentle touch again.
It's like the power of the wind!

Like waking up from the longest dream
How real it seemed!
Until Your love broke through.
I've been lost in a fantasy
That blinded me,
Until Your love broke through!

Keith was sure at last that the Lord wanted him to sing his music to Christians—probably even make a Christian album.

Mostly, he was wondering what God might want him to *say* to all these Christians. We'd seen some glaring inconsistencies. A lot of people were going to church and to Christian concerts—but not many of them seemed really excited about Jesus. Keith wondered how God felt about that.

And his heart was heavy whenever he thought about it.

"For Him Who Has Ears To Hear"

Keith sang and the Spirit moved.

FTER THE DOORS SLAMMED SHUT ON THE RECORD DEAL WITH Arista, Keith launched out in a whole new direction. He still didn't know if he was really ready for the church. Or, for that matter, if they were ready for *him*—and the unorthodox way he looked. He didn't even *own* a suit or a tie. But Keith figured they'd have to take him like he was.

Since "Victor" wasn't really cut out for the road, we bought another vehicle we tagged the "The Pregnant Blue Guppy". It was an old blue van, and the previous owner had extended the back about four feet. The extension kind of bubbled out, which gave it the pregnant-fish look. It had a big bed in back and bucket seats in the front. Now we were ready to go on the road—only we weren't sure where!

Since neither of us had a church background, we had no idea where to go. Other musicians told us which churches did concerts and helped us get going. Chuck Girard, the lead singer of the group, Love Song, gave Keith a jump-start. Love Song often had to turn down invitations because they had so many requests. Whenever that happened, Chuck recommended Keith to that church—so we got all their overflow, which was a big help.

By the spring of 1976, Keith was ready to go out on the road, doing church concerts up and down the west coast. He had a lot of different kinds of songs—serious, funny, inspiring. We were about to find out what being in a public music ministry was all about.

One night, Keith did a concert in a church that probably held a few hundred people. At the end, the pastor stood and encouraged everyone to give generously, because it was all going to be given to Keith. "Let's bless him back for the great time of ministry!" About half-an-hour later, we wandered out to the "Blue Guppy" and opened up the envelope we'd been given. We were stunned by the amount inside. We obviously hadn't received *all* that was given. Keith didn't know what to do.

At first Keith said, "I'll just let it go. I'm not going to make a big deal out of this." But after a few minutes, he realized he couldn't drive off without talking to the pastor. It wasn't just the money—it was the *principle*. Keith felt he should be given the whole offering because that's what people were *told*. Everyone gave with that in mind.

When Keith told me he was going to go back in and talk to the pastor, I nearly died. I probably wouldn't have gone, because I'd be afraid to look like I was just being greedy. But Keith was determined.

"We always take all of our expenses out of the offering," the pastor said, in reply to Keith's inquiry.

"Then you should have *told* everyone that was going to happen when you took the offering. Then it would have been fine."

"Well, no one's complained before. . . ."

Keith stood firm. "I just don't think it's right. Everyone was told the offering was going to be given to me, and that's who they thought they were giving to."

I could tell he felt awkward, knowing he was probably being misunderstood. "I'm not trying to be greedy—but I feel the givers were misled, whether it was intentional or not," he concluded.

I don't remember if Keith was given the rest of the offering, but he did what he felt was right. That was the most important thing to him.

Our real concern about finances was centered in the fact that we had more and more people floating through our home. A woman in her forties, who was extremely depressed and suicidal, moved in for a few months. Another guy who was on and off heroin stayed with us, along with his wife and two little kids. He robbed us, then showed up at our next prayer meeting to pray for "the robber". Later, his wife told on him and we forgave him. Then there was the young, Spanish girl who was kicking an addiction to Seconal—or downers. And then a friend of ours met a girl in Beverly Hills who was selling roses for the Moonies, a cult run by Sun Myung Moon. Our friend phoned us immediately.

"Hey you guys. There's a girl with me who wants to get out of this cult and find Jesus. She's just traveling through from out-of-state. I don't know what to do with her. Can I bring her over?"

The answer was, "Of course!"

Everywhere we turned there were desperate or wounded people who needed help. While Keith was wrestling with the question of what it was the Lord wanted him to actually *say* to the church, we'd been having "message-shaping" experiences. Some were pretty vivid. The nude-bathing incident was definitely one of them. And so was our experience with a young woman who went by the name Mistiana.

Keith and I had flown up to Seattle. There were a lot of people up there who were already into his music because of all the clubs he'd played in every time he ran away from home. He capitalized on his popularity by doing a concert at Everett College, preaching a strong evangelistic message to the unsuspecting students. We also went up to Bellingham, where Keith did a concert at his old, Washington State hang-out—a place called Mama Sunday's. But this time instead of playing songs about searching—he sang and talked about what he had found.

It was during this trip that we met Mistiana. You couldn't miss her when she walked in a room. At first glance, she looked like a gypsy, with her long-flowing skirt and black velvet jacket. Her dark flashing eyes, framed on each side by her long-feathered earrings, caught our attention with interest. We talked to her for a long time, and found out she was going to be driving home to San Francisco. We wanted more time with her and asked if we could ride along as far as Portland. She agreed to take us.

The next day, during our drive, Mistiana told us she was into witchcraft. Actually, she was a bonafide, spell-casting witch. Keith began talking so hard and fast about God that she became angry, feeling like she was a captive in her own car. But before we pulled into Portland, Keith was leading her in a prayer to receive the Lord.

We wound up riding all the way back to California with Mistiana, and before long we'd talked her into coming home with us rather than returning to San Francisco right away. We knew she was weak and probably wouldn't make it as a Christian if she went home alone. For hours in the car, we kept talking to her about our past involvement in the occult and drugs and all the wonderful ways God had set us free. Even though she'd prayed to accept Christ, something about her still seemed kind of strange.

Immediately when we got back home, Keith grabbed a book off our shelf. It was called *Jesus Is Coming Soon,* and it talked about the end-times when Jesus would return—but he wasn't going to return for everyone. The book said anyone involved in idolatry, fornication or witchcraft, to name a few, would be swept away in the Day of Judgment.

As Keith read from this book and quoted from the Bible, Mistiana's dark eyes got bigger and bigger. Suddenly, she put up her hands and said, "That's enough. I have some things I want to get rid of—*right now.*"

Keith closed the book. "Sure! Let's do it. What do you want to get rid of?"

"Well I've got my astrology chart, some tarot cards, and some books. They're in my trunk. I'll get them—but what should we do with them?"

Keith thought for a moment, and then his eyes lit up like they always did when he had a good idea. "Let's burn them!"

Mistiana grabbed all her occult trappings, and we piled them in our driveway. As Keith set them on fire, we rejoiced at the goodness of God and at Mistiana's obedience. I don't know if our suburban neighbors driving by on Dolorosa Street were rejoicing or not—but they were at least getting used to seeing strange happenings at our house.

In a couple of months, however, Mistiana moved to another small Christian community led by a very special pastor named Reverend Glenn. He pastored the Topanga Canyon Community Church up in the mountains. It was real "hippieville" up there, and Reverend Glenn had a heart that was open to people many other Christians ignored. It was a sacrificial, bare-bones kind of ministry. Reverend Glenn lived with his wife and kids in this old beat-up church. He hardly owned anything, but they kept their doors open day and night. Often, there were kids sleeping in the pews because they had no place else to go, and no one else who cared.

So Mistiana moved up to Topanga and, not too long after, got engaged to a guy she led in the sinner's prayer in a bar. He was an alcoholic and untested in his Christian commitment. It didn't seem like either one of them was ready to get married. Keith tried to talk Mistiana out of marrying him. When that didn't work, he went to Reverend Glenn, who was going to do the ceremony.

"Please, don't marry them," Keith begged. "They're both new Christians. They barely know each other. I'm telling you this guy is *not* committed. Counsel them against it. Please tell them to wait."

But for whatever reasons, Reverend Glenn decided to marry them. We went to the wedding because we loved them. Keith hoped his hunch was wrong, and that they'd live "happily ever after". And we still loved Reverend Glenn, too—even though we were afraid he might have missed it on this one. Only time would really tell.

And we wondered if there was anything we could have said to Mistiana that would have prepared her to make wiser decisions. We didn't know. But more than ever, the experience underscored our question: Why didn't leading someone in "the sinner's prayer" revolutionize their life right away?

Our house was continually swelling with people. Cindy no longer had an outside job. Keith and I told her we'd take care of her and Kelly if she wanted to stay home to help us cook and run the household, which was a full-time job now. With so many people in and out I didn't know what our neighbors thought— especially if we were going to have bonfires in our driveway! But it looked like they were going to have to get used to us, because we decided to buy our house.

Now the question of what to charge for a concert was becoming more of a pressing issue. We tried several different ways. Sometimes a church wanted to take a "love offering" for Keith. And sometimes they wanted Keith to tell them how much he'd charge to come. In these instances Keith set a small fee for going. One night, he asked for about $50, but later on he really struggled. He knew other less-accomplished music ministers got a lot more. He was trying to figure out if he should start asking for $75 or even $100 a night. At least then he'd know what he'd be getting and didn't have to worry about scanty offerings. However, an offering gave the Lord a chance to bless you where a set fee did not. More than that, Keith was trying to figure out where all the boundaries were. Did you not go minister somewhere because they couldn't pay you enough? And how much was enough?

In some ways, the Christian music ministry was beginning to appear similar to the secular music business we'd just stepped out of—record companies, contracts, concert tours—we were even beginning to see that there was a pecking-order of artist popularity. But in other ways it was a whole new animal. And when you were invited somewhere, what should you expect to receive in return? Some churches were obviously wealthy, others were poor. How do you deal with the differences? Maybe asking for a minimum amount would settle the issue.

"And yet," Keith said, "I can't imagine Paul telling the Corinthian church, 'Sorry guys, I can't come unless you promise me 5,000 sheckels and two first-class chariot fares!'"

But the money issue was not going to immobilize Keith from delivering the things in his heart. The work seemed so urgent. In June of 1976, Keith did a concert in Ashland, Oregon. What he told the audience impressed me because I saw how much Keith was changing.

"It's getting darker outside" he said, during one of his piano rambles.

"Twenty years ago you couldn't tell the difference between a Christian and a moral heathen. There were a lot of . . . upstanding people and they had high moral codes. . . . But today if you don't live with someone before you get married, you're considered stupid by the world. . . .

"In L.A. right now on the streets there are rows, and rows, and rows of pornographic newspapers. For fifty cents—right at the eye level of little kids. There's women lying with women right on the front covers. Men lying with men. It's Sodom and Gomorrah time!

"Jesus said, 'It shall be in the last days as it was with Sodom and Gomorrah.' The only sin listed [for Sodom and Gomorrah] was homosexual gang rape. . . .Two months ago, there were two crimes never before recorded in the history of Los Angeles crime—Two homosexual gang rapes. . . .We're at the doors. The Lord is returning soon."

While Keith felt so strongly about the sin of homosexuality, he really felt compassion for the person caught in that lifestyle. In fact, one day after a concert at a church, we wound up talking to a young guy from the church. It became obvious that he was struggling with some things and, within a few minutes, he was confessing to us. Even though he was active in the church, he was a practicing homosexual. Far from being turned off, Keith reached out to him with an offer of help.

When it seemed like this young man was open to getting help, Keith went to the nearest phone and called our friends at Jesus People USA in Chicago to see if they would take him in. We knew they'd had success in helping others in the same situation. As Keith continued talking to this guy, all I could see in his eyes was an overwhelming desire to see this young man set free.

Early in 1977, Keith was offered a record deal by Billy Ray Hearn of Sparrow Records. Sometime after the "Firewind" session, where they first met, Billy Ray took Keith up on his offer to come see him in one of the many church concerts he was doing. Keith was playing at the Vineyard, and Billy Ray slipped in unannounced. He had been shocked to find the place packed out, and even had to crawl over people just to find a place on the floor in an aisle. It was not protocol for record company presidents, but he stayed to see what it was about Keith that had drawn so many people.

It was a powerful night of music and ministry. Billy Ray was more than mildly interested, and that kicked off a long process of conversations and negotiations with Keith and his father over the proposed contract. Keith asked Todd to play bass on the album, but who would produce it? Earlier Keith had asked Buck Herring to produce him, but Buck figured that he and Keith were both too intense to try working together. Instead, a young man named Bill Maxwell was suggested.

Bill Maxwell was a hot drummer and an excellent producer. He'd co-produced with Andrae Crouch on his albums for a while, and he was a committed Christian. When Bill came over to our house to meet us, we were taken with his warm, open manner. He looked like he was in his late twenties, with light brown shoulder-length hair and southern tones in his voice. He was decidedly unassuming for someone who came so highly recommended.

Keith played Bill all of his demos—and then played some songs on the piano for him. Bill's response was very direct. "You sound so much better in person than you do on your demos. You've got so much more energy and style when you play and sing at the same time. That's what needs to come across in the recording," Bill said.

Keith and I had also noticed that before—but how did you capture Keith's energy and style on tape? More importantly, how did you capture the unusual sense of what God was doing *inside* Keith himself as he sang? Could it be done?

Keith and I were learning the value of prayer, and so at Keith's concerts he began asking people to pray for the album project. "I really need your prayers more than anything," he'd say, "because I've pretty much got the songs picked out, and the producer, and some of the musicians. But in the studio, a spiritual song can sometimes lose its anointing. I want the Holy Spirit to come through. I want to make sure the Spirit is producing it, and recording it. If you all would just put me on your prayer list . . . I need that!"

By the time we went into the studio, some weeks later, Bill had seen Keith in concert several times. He knew exactly what Keith could do and was committed to capturing it on tape—if it could be done. Usually the instrumental tracks are laid down before a singer overdubs his vocals. Keith made his demos that way, too. But Bill wanted to try something different. He sat Keith at the piano, with a headset and a mike, and said, "We're going to do this 'live'." Then Bill came into the control booth where I was watching through the glass.

The tapes were rolling now, and Bill gave Keith the nod.

Keith was only halfway through the first verse when Bill and I exchanged wide-eyed looks. Something sparked! The song definitely had life!

Bill had pinpointed that indefinable something that made the difference between the slick homogenized demos Keith had had produced for years, and a vibrant, exciting recording. Of course! Keith always sang and played at the same time. His voice played off of the energy and rhythm he was feeling from the piano—and vice versa. Now we were cooking!

As Keith expected with making a Christian album, there wasn't a big budget compared to the tens, and sometimes hundreds of thousands that go into a secular album. We only had $15,000 to work with. But there are some things money can't buy. Together, Bill and Keith were capturing Keith's raw energy, emotions, and spiritual heart cry. The songs were fresh and the delivery was powerful. And when you listened, you had an uncanny sense that you were hearing from someone more than just Keith Green.

Besides the prayer support Keith had been asking for at his concerts, the people who lived with us formed prayer teams. They faithfully prayed during every studio session throughout the whole recording.

While Keith and Bill were mixing the tracks one afternoon, Keith said confidently, "God told me this is going to be one of the biggest selling Christian albums ever!"

Bill raised an eyebrow skeptically. "How do you know that?"

"Because I told the Lord I'd give the money I made back to him to use for his work—and not just put it all into my own pocket. So I know he's going to bless it."

Bill could sense Keith wasn't speaking out of arrogance, but from a sincere desire to help others. This really touched Bill—but a history-making Christian album? Only time would tell.

Keith fittingly named the album, *For Him Who Has Ears To Hear*, taken from the beginning of The Book of Revelation: "For him who has ears to hear, let him hear what the Spirit is saying to the churches. . . ." Who has ears to hear what God is saying? Obviously, it is supposed to be the Church. But was it possible to have the right "equipment" and still be deaf to the voice of God? Keith wanted to sing to the people who were in-tune with God— or be used as a tool to help unplug the ears of the ones who weren't.

By the summer of 1977, Keith's debut album was in the bookstores. And we had a big mailing party at our house to send out the albums to the 6,000 people who had pre-ordered it at concerts over the past several months. Keith told everyone he'd send it to them "hot off the press"—and he did.

Rather than just throw away the names of 6,000 people who seemed to be interested in receiving further encouragement and ministry, Keith said, "Let's just keep in touch with all these people and put together a little newsletter to encourage them in their walk with the Lord." And so, *The Last Days Newsletter* was born.

Just before Keith's album was released he started working with Steve Greisen, who was engaged to Nelly Ward of Second Chapter of Acts. Buck Herring and Steve wanted to help lesser-known artists with valid ministries get out on the road. Steve would do the bookings, and they took Keith on. Buck wrote a letter of recommendation, which was a big help because Keith was only well known on the west coast. As usual, Keith had big ideas.

"I want to tour the *whole* country this summer!" Keith directed Steve. "Can you set it up?"

Steve set up a fifty-two-city tour, and off we went! We'd even retired the "Blue Guppy" and bought a thirty-two-foot motor home we dubbed "The Ark". That way we had enough room to take several new Christians along with us. During our nine weeks on the road we had plenty of time to counsel them and encourage them in the Lord. And they became our "road team" which was a big help to us, too.

What a tour.

Keith's album had just been released, so he was still unknown.

He ended up singing to a lot of "built-in" audiences at coffee houses, youth group meetings, and regular church services. Often Keith would joke about his hair, beard, and less-than-brand-new blue jeans to relax all the gray-haired saints who came not knowing what kind of music Keith was going to play.

"Somebody drug their grandmother here tonight," he'd say, "and she's looking over at me saying, 'Do you bear witness to *this*?' I just wanna say that God works in mysterious ways, and *I* am one of his mysterious ways. I know you haven't seen this much hair up on the pulpit before—but God doesn't look on the outside to see what kind of a Christian you are. He looks on the inside.

"Now I don't wanna upset anybody who's used to listening to Lawrence Welk a lot because I *do* get into the piano. Aren't you glad I'm not playing electric guitar?"

Usually, by this time, he'd put everyone at ease.

But there were some very difficult aspects to this tour. Some nights, the promised housing didn't happen and we had to rent our own rooms unexpectedly. And it seemed that adequate sound systems and tuned pianos were rare commodities. Over all, the audiences were sparse and some nights we'd make little or nothing. One pastor who brought Keith in told Steve in advance, "He can come, but Chuck Girard is in town the same night and I know who *I'd* rather go see." But God was teaching us to be grateful in all things—the big and the small. Shortly after we returned, Keith reflected on the tour to a concert crowd in southern California.

"I just got back from the road," he told them. "I've heard people say, 'It's worth it when only one person comes forward to receive the Lord.' I say, yeah, it is worth it. There were some real humbling concerts. Like twenty people. *One* person would come forward. I'd sit down at the end of the stage and when they'd come forward I'd say, 'You're the whole reason why I came to this town.'

"And then there were other really beautiful times. I played an Army base in Fort Leonardwood, Missouri, for about 500 young recruits. They felt a little bit out of place. They didn't have any hair, and they were all about eighteen. Under their breath they were saying, 'I want my mommy!' And they were all sitting there freaking out about being in the Army. And the Lord got to them in that state, because 350 got up and received Jesus!"

We had learned at the Vineyard that every trial was an opportunity to grow—and we certainly grew on that nine-week tour.

We were growing at home, too. Because now there were over *a dozen* new Christians with us. So as money came in from Keith's concerts, studio sessions, and album sales it was poured back into helping the people who had come to live with us.

We'd moved Keith's piano into our bedroom and turned his music room into a dormitory. Counseling, helping, encouraging, witnessing—it pervaded every part of our life. And the best part about it was how much fun it was! It was an adventure every day—wondering what would happen next. If someone wanted to give their life to the Lord, or serve God in a deeper way, we'd do whatever we needed to do to help make it happen. And I knew I needed to stay as flexible as possible, since Keith was so naturally "spontaneous".

As every available sleeping space in the house slowly filled, Keith had a growing desire to move out into the country. We thought it would be wonderful to get the people who needed help out of the big city and into a place that would be peaceful and restful—somewhere that wasn't filled with so many glaring, easy-access temptations. Besides, we didn't know how long our neighbors would put up with our endless streams of what, by their standards, probably looked like a group of aliens.

Keith and I both loved the Pacific Northwest, and thought for sure we could find a farm or ranch for sale up there. Keith really wanted to live in the woods, while I wanted to live by the ocean. I hoped we could find a little place nestled in the trees—with an ocean view!

On our next concert tour to the Pacific Northwest late in the summer, we continued to spy out the land for possible places to move. One of our stops was in a little town called Sweethome, Oregon. A family from the small church where Keith was playing housed us, and they lived out on a beautiful farm. It was haying season and they were out on their tractors—wearing straw hats, and bonnets, and praying it wouldn't rain between the time they cut the hay and got it baled. In spite of our hippie, "whole-earth" orientation, we were really new to being in the country, so it was an incredible scene to behold. We felt like we were staying at the Little House on the Prairie!

The family loaned us their motorcycle and told us we could take it for a ride in the woods. There was only one problem—the roads weren't paved and we kept getting stuck in the mud. We also got lost. And the motorcycle kept dying on us. So there we were, lost out in the backwoods, with a dead, muddy bike.

Just when I started to think, *Oh Keith, what have you gotten us into now,* a guy came wandering out of the woods. He was thin, with shoulder-length blond hair. The only thing he was wearing was a leather headband and a very skimpy loincloth, but he was carrying a clipboard and a pencil. He was actually talking to the trees, obviously high on something. His name was Rick. We talked with him for a few minutes and he told us he lived alone in a tepee in the woods.

Right there, in the middle of nowhere, Keith and I began talking to this blond "primitive" about Jesus. Fortunately, by the time we had to leave, Rick was clearheaded enough to tell us how to find our way out!

As it turned out, Rick came—at our invitation—to the concert that evening. He had on some jeans and a red flannel shirt—and we were grateful for that! Still, he was one of a kind in that country congregation, and I prayed he wouldn't panic and leave before Keith asked for commitments to Jesus.

Rick did give his life to the Lord that night and—you guessed it—he accompanied us back to southern California. The only place for him to sleep, however, was in our garage now because our house was packed full of women—all except for a young neighbor boy, who was only twelve. Jeff was having some problems at home and his mom wanted him to stay with us temporarily. The only place for him was sleeping in a sleeping bag on the floor of our bedroom.

So now we had something like *fourteen* people living with us in our little three-bedroom house with only one bathroom! You couldn't go anywhere in the house without running into someone—and I do mean running into them—who needed counseling.

And we still kept meeting people who needed a place to stay so they could escape a bad situation and get grounded in their new faith in Jesus. Only there wasn't any place left at our house. Not only did Keith no longer have a private place to write music, he could barely get a turn in the bathroom with all the women in the house! What could we do? Our answer came in an unexpected way.

When Dawn came to live with us, a few years before, we had needed to obtain some type of legal authority to enroll her in school. Karen approved of us becoming Dawn's foster parents, but the State of California needed to approve us as well. We didn't accept the regular foster parent money the state provided, which meant they wouldn't visit us as much. But we still had to pass a housing inspection because government standards required a certain amount of "airspace" in Dawn's bedroom. We had passed everything with flying colors—*then*.

Now it was time for another visit from Dawn's social worker, and we knew our crowded living conditions would make her eyes bug out. We were in quite a dilemma. There was no way we were going to lose Dawn. But we also knew we couldn't put everyone else out into the streets. What were we going to do? One afternoon, Keith and I had a rare moment alone to talk about it.

"What are we going to do?" I began. "We need more space—that's all there is to it."

"I've got an idea," Keith said, his face brightening. "Let's rent another house."

"It might work," I replied, thoughtfully. "But—wait a minute. We've been here almost three years and I've never even *seen* a house for rent in this neighborhood. Everybody owns their own home."

Keith's brow was furrowed in thought. "There are those apartments about a mile away," Keith said. "—but they'll *never* rent one to a bunch of wild-looking, single hippies. . . . Hey, I've got an idea. Why don't *we* rent one!"

"You mean move out of our own house?"

"Yeah, they'll for sure rent one of those places to a nice family with a teenage daughter!"

We did have some extra money because of Keith's new album. Later that day, we drove over and looked at a two-bedroom apartment. It wasn't far away so we'd still be close to people back at the house, and Dawn could have her own room which would make the State of California happy. We put a deposit on the apartment and went home.

The whole thing seemed kind of crazy, but it was also really exciting. We were scheduled to move in a few weeks and my mind was getting into gear for packing. But before we had a chance to make the move, the strangest thing happened.

We were driving though our neighborhood one day, and suddenly Keith said, "Mel, look! A 'For Rent' sign!"

Sure enough. It was right in front of a nice-looking house with a big tree in the front yard. Unbelievable.

We rented it immediately. It was a nice three-bedroom place with a den. We moved all the singles over there, and cleared out a bedroom for Dawn in our house. Dawn's social worker came and went—and so, by the end of 1977, we had become a "two house" family.

We needed a name for the new house so that when we talked about it we'd be able to separate it from our house on Dolorosa Street. The new house was on Sale Street, so we just called it The Sale House.

In no time, it seemed, we had filled up both houses again.

These were powerful times. These were innocent times. We just did what was in our hearts to do. We were always on the run—and unaware of how our lives were about to change, one more time.

Keith closed the year by playing at The Daisy—but this night in particular was strangely different. It was a New Year's celebration and I was sipping some kind of fruit juice, watching Keith minister. He was only about twelve feet away so I could see him clearly. By now I'd watched Keith play hundreds of times, but this night burned in my memory.

The spotlight was bright white—flooding Keith's face with light. His eyes were aching as he sang. Overflowing with unspoken feelings as he poured out his very soul. But as he sang, he was not looking at the audience. He was looking up into the light, as if he were looking directly at God. He seemed transfixed in time . . . like there was something holy or significant about the moment. His eyes were the bluest of blue, sparkling, yet crying out. His skin like milk. He looked like a little boy. But his eyes. His eyes were haunting as he looked up into the light. I had the strangest sensation while watching him.

When the thought first came I shook it away. But it came back. As I sat and watched I was captured by the moment and thought, *Keith Green—you're not long for this earth. . . .*

Immediately I wondered where that thought came from. It was crazy to even think such a thing.

I didn't know what Keith was thinking, or hearing from the Lord, in those moments. Later I didn't ask him—and I didn't tell him what I had thought either. But it would not be the last time I had feelings like that about him . . .

"Asleep In The Light"

Keith and newborn Josiah. 1978

FOR HIM WHO HAS EARS TO HEAR** DID TAKE OFF! VERY QUICKLY, it moved up the chart of bestselling Christian records to become the biggest debut album in the history of Christian recording— with over 300,000 copies distributed.

The net effect was that, by the end of 1977, requests for concert bookings started flooding in from all across the country. It was exciting. In the space of a few short months, Keith rocketed from being an "unknown" to becoming one of the most popular and sought-after singers on the Christian scene.

But very little of the "flap" about his popularity reached Keith at all—not in his heart anyway. He disliked being referred to as a recording "artist", since that term seemed to carry with it the connotation of being on a higher level than other people. And more than that, I could tell that Keith was starting to get caught up with inner questions that, for him, held more importance than his popularity rating.

"Mel," he said to me one morning, as I packed him for another concert tour, "I feel like the Lord is calling me to make an even deeper commitment to him. I don't want to get caught up in everything that's happening to us and become a "celebrity" in the church. I can already feel the pull to go out there on stage and manipulate the crowd by saying things I know will move people emotionally. I don't want to get soulish."

In particular, Keith felt he needed to count the cost if he was really going to be a true follower of Christ. He was beginning to struggle with the thought that something might happen to me. There had been this rumor kicking around about a devastating earthquake God was going to send to southern California. It was supposed to destroy Los Angeles. Whether or not there really was going to be an earthquake, Keith considered what he would do if something happened to me.

While Keith was on the road alone for a few days, he wrote a prayer to the Lord:

JANUARY 22, 1978

. . . I only pray You let me keep my wife Melody for I need her love and help although Your grace is sufficient unto me. Please spare her to stay with me, I will give You far more love than I give her, and all my love for her is for You Jesus.

Take anything, but leave my Melody. Please God, but I am willing to suffer all loss if it is Your precious will. I am Yours.

Bye bye Lord—Your baby.

Keith returned home thoughtful. Would a tragedy cause him to lose his faith? If he wasn't willing to lay even the deepest loves of his life before God, what did that say about the roots of his faith?

When Keith told me what was bothering him, he said firmly, "I've decided that whatever it takes to get deeper with the Lord I'm going to do—even if it means praying and saying, 'Lord, Melody's really yours.'"

Keith's wrestling with giving everything to the Lord had another dimension to it, too—because we'd just had some great news. I was pregnant! Shortly before, I'd had a miscarriage—but this time it looked like there were none of the early distress signs I'd had with my first pregnancy. We were really thrilled! Now all we had to do was wait out the nine months.

Those nine months weren't spent passively, however. We were on the road, running through airports to catch planes and staying up half the night to counsel our ever-growing community in Woodland Hills. And I wasn't alone in my pregnancy. There were three other pregnant women with us!

With so many people who were badly in need of help, it was a relief to have some more stable people joining us, people who needed a place to stay while they learned how to make a full commitment to the Lord. Kathleen Griffin was one of those. She had just moved in with us from down south, and we thought she was one of the most caring people we knew. Her thick, blond hair and California-girl complexion made her one of the prettiest, too. She seemed to represent the kind of Christian commitment we wanted to encourage others to make. After you become a Christian—what do you *do* about it? Did you keep the blessing to yourself or, like Kathleen, pour yourself out for others?

There was already talk about a second album, and Keith believed it was supposed to be more than a "nice" collection of upbeat, inspiring songs. A stray comment he made one day really stuck with me

A few of us were in our living room one day, talking about how necessary it was to pray. Keith offhandedly said, "Our whole life should be a prayer!"

The words just rang in my ears. I kept hearing the phrase over and over in my mind, "Our whole life should be a prayer!"

Later, alone in our room, I sat down at the piano and just started playing. A melody just came to me, and also some words, flowing together with unusual ease. I played the few simple chords and I started to sing what Keith had said—only now it was in the form of a prayer—with hardly any forethought:

> *Make my life a prayer to You.*
> *I wanna do what You want me to. . . .*

I reached for a pencil and pad of paper and started jotting down the lyrics as fast as I could. Then I started playing the piano again. There were a few false starts, but basically the whole song flowed out in about twenty minutes.

When it was finished, I was overjoyed. I'd never experienced the Lord's help and creativity in my writing quite like that before. I almost felt like I had just taken dictation. "Make My Life A Prayer To You" seemed to be born of the Spirit in a special way.

Keith loved the song and started singing it in concert right away. Then it really came alive because it was, of course, Keith's prayer, too. One night, Steve and Nelly—now Mr. and Mrs. Greisen—came to a concert. Nelly was so moved by the song, she asked me if she could sing it on the next Second Chapter of Acts album. What an encouragement! I couldn't help but remember the days of tears and wadded up lyrics in the trash.

Through the months of April, May, and June 1978—while "Ears To Hear" was number one on the charts—we were in and out of the studio recording Keith's second album. The only problem was he still didn't have an album title that felt right. Sparrow was eager to release the album and we needed a concept so the artists could get busy with a cover. Nothing was clicking. Then one day, when Keith was looking through all the song lyrics for what seemed to be the tenth time he suddenly glanced at me with excitement.

"Hey, Mel, what about these words in your song?" He quoted:

> *Make my life a prayer to You.*
> *I wanna do what You want me to.*
> *No empty words*
> *And no white lies,*
> *No token prayers,*
> *No compromise. . . .*

"No token prayers, no compromise," he repeated. "Let's just call the album *No Compromise!*"

It seemed to capture the heart of what Keith wanted to say to other Christians—that they needed to quit compromising, stop listening to the voice of the world, and start living committed lives.

Even the artwork was going to reflect the "No Compromise" theme—one man, standing up in the midst of a crowd that was bowing to an earthly king who obviously wanted to be worshipped. One of the guards was angrily pointing at the lone man with a look that said, "You've had it!" The picture reminded you of Daniel in Babylon.

Keith's idea was to shake Christians awake from the comfortable "slumber" we'd seen. Sure we weren't faced with anything as obvious as the choice between bowing to a false god, or death. But Christians are continually tempted to bow to other "false gods"—to go with the crowd, to *not* speak out for what is right, to be ashamed of our convictions. So we compromise. We bow to invisible idols of acceptability, fear, pride, lust, greed and secret sin. Keith wanted other Christians to face the need to have these things cleaned out of their lives—just as he was facing the need in his own life.

Keith was so convinced of the urgency of this message that, as with the first album, people were rallied to pray. During each session, day or night—sometimes *all* night—there were people from the community in the studio with their heads constantly bowed in prayer. If the recording engineer was having trouble getting the right sounds, they prayed. If Keith was trying to hit some difficult notes, they prayed. If we were working on guitar parts, or background parts, they prayed. There was constant prayer—asking for God's help and grace. We sensed this was a special project and a difficult message. It was going to need the smoothing oil of the Holy Spirit to slip the strong things Keith was saying into peoples' hearts.

As always, I was right at Keith's side. Keith trusted my judgment and he'd often ask, "Mel, how was that?" Or he might say, "Do you have any ideas for background vocals?" And Bill Maxwell was so pitch-sensitive he could always tell if any notes were even slightly off-key. Bill seemed to know how to bring the best out of Keith. And our good friend, Peter Granet—the one we'd dropped our "gospel bombs" on in Sequoia a few years ago—even came to lend his support by being the recording engineer. It was one big happy family!

And speaking of family, I was very pregnant by this time. Whenever Bill played the drums my baby kicked me without mercy—often, right in time with the music!

But there were a few points on which Keith and I were *not* side-by-side. One of Keith's new songs was called "To Obey Is Better Than Sacrifice". Actually, I loved the song—but there was one line that really bothered me. The whole song was sung as if it was the Lord speaking. At the end of the third verse, there was an especially troubling line:

> *To obey is better than sacrifice—*
> *I want more than Sundays*
> *And Wednesday nights.*
> *'Cause if you can't come*
> *To Me everyday,*
> *Then don't bother coming at all.*

In the studio, Keith and Bill had a long discussion about it before the final vocal was laid down.

"Keith, I really feel like that statement is going to make people feel condemned," he objected, "especially people who might not know the Lord."

"It's mainly for Christians who should *know* better," Keith replied. "I really believe I need to say it that strongly to make the point."

157

"But it's a hard line to draw," Bill came back, shaking his head.

"Well, it's the line *I'm* walking," Keith replied.

I had already voiced my concerns about it to Keith by this time. I knew Keith wanted to make a strong statement—but I wondered if there was another way he could do it. Some people were going to be offended, but even that wasn't my main concern. The bottom line for me was, did the statement really represent God's heart toward us? Of course, he wants us to come to him every day. But even when we blow it, I couldn't imagine God saying, "Don't bother coming at all!" I felt really torn. I knew that, for Keith, it was like he was trying to shake people who were sleeping through a fire.

When I'd told him my concerns, he said, "If you saw a child about to get hit by a truck and the best you could do was kick him out of the way just before impact, you'd do it. He might end up with a few broken ribs but at least he'd be alive. And any parent would thank you for saving his life—they wouldn't be angry about the broken ribs! You did the most loving thing you could do."

In the end, the decision was made to record the song as it stood. Even though the lyric never really sat right with me, I also wanted to see religious apathy shaken at its core—even in my own life. And in that, I totally supported Keith's heart in the message he wanted to convey.

Another song that carried a "strong-punch" message for Christians was called "Asleep In The Light". None of us had any trouble with the lyrics in this one.

Keith got the idea for the song from a phrase in the book *Why Revival Tarries* written by a man named Leonard Ravenhill, who had come to America in 1950 after being involved in many revivals in Great Britain. Keith just happened to find the book on someone's coffee table, during a time when he was asking God to help him be less intense. After finishing it he said, "What is God doing? Letting me read this book was like pouring gasoline on a fire!" Keith was so stirred he took the concepts from the book and put them into a song—hoping the fire would spread.

Do you see, do you see,
All the people sinking down?
Don't you care, don't you care,
Are you gonna let them drown?

How can you be so numb
Not to care if they come?
You close your eyes
And pretend the job's done . . .

158

The world is sleeping in the dark
That the church just can't fight
'Cause it's asleep in the light.
How can you be so dead
When you've been so well fed?

It was true that Bill and I—and many others we knew—were behind the warning Keith was trying to sound. But what about the Christian public? What would they think about this message that was growing stronger in Keith's heart every day? We'd soon find out.

That summer, while the album was being pressed, Keith was invited to sing at a festival in Oregon, called "Jesus Northwest". It normally drew about 20,000 people—but this year, an estimated 35,000 people were there!

A traffic jam clogged the roads for two or three miles, and the police were frantic. The campsites were overflowing. It was all one, big, glorious confusion!

Because the festival went on over several days, in open fields under a blazing sun, many people stripped down to the bare minimum to beat the heat. Keith and I thought it looked like a mini-Woodstock.

It was great that so many people were there enjoying the Lord and enjoying each other—but something seemed a bit amiss. It was a huge success and the promoters were blown away. But the real question was, what would the outcome be from an eternal perspective? Would everyone go home thinking, "Wow, that was a lot of fun!" Or was there something God wanted to say to everyone? In fact, inside the hospitality trailer, the man who put the festival together expressed his concern to Keith.

"We have a success in numbers, but I'm not sure what's happening in the Spirit."

On the last evening of the event, several of us gathered in the trailer to pray before Keith's turn to go on-stage. Our friend Winkie Pratney, who lived in east Texas, was there with his wife, Fae, because Winkie had been a main speaker. By now, Keith and Winkie had developed a certain closeness. Winkie was like an older brother to him. He was probably the only person who would have put up with Keith's late night phone calls—sometimes at 1:00 or 2:00 in the morning—just to say "hi". A New Zealander, Winkie had a quick, brilliant wit and a keen mind. His dark eyes flashed brightly when he laughed, and he laughed often. But beneath the humor was a drive to see men, women and young people commit themselves to Jesus Christ. For years, he'd written books and articles, spoken and travelled around the world as a true ambassador for the Lord. So Keith's spirit meshed with his readily.

And just now, they were both troubled—not about what had happened at the festival, but what *hadn't* happened. We'd heard that the emphasis of the festival had been on music—lots of it, and loud. There were some speakers, too, but hardly anyone had given a challenge for change or commitment. The place was packed, but some were saying there had been no real move of God, and that it was just one big party. Keith and Winkie felt strongly that if nothing happened then, it was a waste of a festival.

There was a piano in the trailer, and Keith crawled under it to "get alone" with God and pray. He'd be closing out the festival in just a few minutes. From where I was praying, I could hear Keith softly crying.

There was a tentative knock at the trailer door. Someone summoned Winkie outside to see a young, blond girl who had asked to speak with him. She had tears in her eyes. Winkie recognized her from the Youth With A Mission booth there at the festival. She was timid, but at the same time had a gentle boldness about her as she spoke.

"Excuse me, but I've felt a little grieved during this festival, because it doesn't seem like God has been given a chance to speak what's on his heart. There's been no breakthrough. We've had counseling tents and prayer meetings, but nobody from the stage has said anything about getting right with God."

While Winkie was outside, I looked over at Keith. I could hear loud weeping and choking sobs coming out from under the piano. In between the sobbing, Keith prayed out loud, "Oh God, what do you want me to say? What do you want me to do?"

When Winkie walked back inside the trailer, he was holding a small piece of paper in one hand.

At the same moment, Keith's head popped out from under the piano and he said, "Winkie, isn't there a scripture somewhere about festivals?"

Winkie looked up from the paper in shock. "Yes," he said, "I just happen to have one. A young girl gave it to me."

When Keith read the slip of paper, his mouth dropped open. A few minutes later, he carried it on stage with him.

When Keith walked into the spotlight, the crowd burst into a prolonged roar of applause, whistles, and cheers. Keith sat at the piano and adjusted the microphone, waiting for things to settle down a bit. Then he turned to he crowd and, still wiping a few tears away, started talking:

"Have you ever felt the Lord was sad? Most people think, 'No,

—
160

no, the Lord's always happy'. Well, tonight I was praying and I kind of felt the Lord inside me, weeping. So I started to cry.

"And I got to thinking about all the people that give God one day a week. How would you like it if your wife gave you one day a week? 'Well dear, I'm here for the weekly visit.' People like to visit God from ten to eleven on Sunday mornings. . . ."

I'd gone over to the side of the crowd to watch Keith on-stage. As with any outdoors event, the crowd was a little restless. I knew they were waiting for Keith to sing, and so he did. But the song he chose to open with was anything but lighthearted—"To Obey Is Better Than Sacrifice". As soon as he finished, he started talking again. . . .

"In the Old Testament it says, 'These people draw near with their words and honor me with their lips, but they remove their hearts far from me.' I was listening to everybody singing worship songs before. And nobody deserves praise and worship but Jesus. It's a beautiful thing.

"But what if your wife said 'I love you' but you knew she didn't honor you and love you in her heart? That you weren't the most important person on earth to her. And in fact, she had a couple of other men she liked to look at and think about more than you. How sick would it be for you to hear, 'Oh darling, I love you!' What do the words 'I love you' mean? If you praise and worship Jesus with your mouth and your life does not praise and worship him, there's something wrong.

"I don't want you to go away from here under condemnation. But I want you to get broken before God, because unless you're a broken vessel he can't put you back together the way he wants you. . . ."

The crowd had gotten quiet now. I noticed one young guy toward the front, wearing cut-offs and a "Jesus Is Lord" T-shirt. He leaned forward, with a serious look on his face. It was then Keith reached into his pocket and pulled out the slip of paper Winkie had given him. I suspected things were going to get even more serious, as he started to read. . . .

"This scripture is out of Amos. 'Thus saith the Lord, I hate, I reject your festivals, nor do I delight in your solemn assemblies, even though you offer up to Me burnt offerings. . . . I will not accept them. . . . Take away from Me the noise of your songs, I will not even listen to the sound of your harps. But let justice roll down like waters, and righteousness like an ever-flowing stream.'

"Does anybody understand what that means? Some of you do. Among 35,000 so-called Christians there's always a remnant of real ones peppered in. My job as a minister is to make sure that

---

161

every person here leaves a real one. But I can't do it, I'm nothing but dust."

Keith looked to the sky and said, "I depend on you, Lord Jesus . . ."

Keith's words had the effect of a shotgun blast. The crowd sat in stunned silence—the first silence I'd heard all night. I glanced quickly at the guy in the Jesus T-shirt again. He was just sitting there with his mouth open. I wondered what he was thinking, as Keith continued. . . .

"How many of us care about the people living next door to us? How many of your neighbors have never seen anything more than a little fish on your car? They think you work at the fish market. . . . What's going on?

"As for me, I repent of ever having made a record or ever having sung a song unless it's provoked people to follow Jesus, to lay down their whole life before him, to give him everything. It doesn't cost you much to follow Jesus—just everything!"

Keith did sing a few more songs—"The Sheep and the Goats" and "Asleep in the Light"—but they only served to underscore his hard-hitting message. Then he sang "My Eyes Are Dry", and taught it to everyone. As he sang he started to weep, his voice cracking with emotion:

My eyes are dry, my faith is old,
My heart is hard, my prayers are cold.
And I know how I ought to be—
Alive to You and dead to me.
Oh, what can be done with an old heart like mine?
Soften it up with oil and wine!
The oil is You, Your Spirit of love,
Please wash me anew in the wine of Your blood. . . .

Then with tears streaming down his face, Keith prayed, "Lord, we're sorry! Lord, we're sorry for having such deceitful hearts and such weak flesh. For being children of our own desires instead of being children of your desires. Children of religion rather than children of truth. Lord Jesus, please save us from ourselves and from institutions. . . . Lord, corner our flesh—crucify our flesh, kill our own desires. . . ."

He turned back to the crowd:

"Do you know the rich young ruler would be accepted in any church today? But Jesus wouldn't accept him. . . .Why? Because he had an idol in his life.

"Do you know who the Christian idols are? I happen to be one of them. So is Andrae Crouch, Evie and B.J. Thomas. You can even idolize your pastor. They don't want to be idolized, they never asked for it. Remember that applause you gave me when I walked out? I didn't hear you applaud the Lord like that anytime today. . . .We're more excited about a Second Chapter of Acts concert than we are about the Second Coming! SIN! . . ."

This was tough stuff. I wondered what everyone was thinking about Keith's message. How did a bunch of people who thought they were Christians feel about having their salvation challenged? It seemed to me it needed a good challenge. And if the young fellow I'd been watching was any indication, the Lord was doing good things. He had his arms wrapped around his legs, his head bowed on his knees. . . .

"The rich young ruler came to Jesus, and Jesus said, 'You still lack something. Go away, I can't take you right now.' Who today would say, 'I'm sorry brother, I can't lead you in the sinner's prayer. You've gotta give up your dope, your selfishness, your love of possessions, your clingy-ness to family and friends—and your life'? Aren't you a little disappointed at how Jesus handled such a sinner? Didn't the Lord know how to lead a soul to himself?

"The requirement for salvation is not just a prayer. The requirement is an open, totally empty heart that's ready to be full of Jesus Christ. After saying 'the sinner's prayer'—if in a few months your friends can't tell that you're born again, if your relatives can't see a change in you, if your teacher can't see that you're a Christian, you're probably not!

"Because let me tell you something, when someone's born again, they get excited! It changes the way they live, what they do, how they speak, how they act, what they do with their money, their cars, their girlfriends—it's all different! Then how come it looks the same? How come Christians are trying to ride the line?

"I challenge everybody who calls himself a Christian, which means 'little Christ', to live as Jesus did. Or else sometime Somebody might say, 'I never knew you'. . . . I'm gonna get on my knees every day and say 'God, search my heart and see if there be any wicked way in me. I don't want to go astray. I want to be with you.'

"You can't get to heaven by being a nice guy. You might end up to be the nicest guy in hell!"

Finally, Keith gave a challenge to everyone in the audience— first, to people who had never given their lives to Christ, and then to people who considered themselves Christians, but who'd never given Jesus every hope, dream, possession, every friend and loved one.

I looked at the young guy I'd been watching to see if his

hand was up. Instead he was flat on his face along with many others! Other hands were up everywhere. Not only that, weeping and loud crying was breaking out all across the open, grassy field. It was awesome. I could hear people sobbing and choking prayers out to God.

Then Keith asked everyone who was making Jesus Lord of their life for the first time to stand. To my shock, almost everyone in the crowd stood. Keith was so surprised, he thought they must not have understood him. So he clarified it:

"This is *not* a rededication. This is the first time, the *first* time you've ever understood what making Jesus Lord really meant. Do you really mean it? Wow! How many people here realize that when they get home they have a lot of things to get rid of and a lot of things to change in their lives? . . . A brother down front here says he has to remodel his whole bedroom. You've gotta remodel your whole heart, then the outside's gonna change!"

Then Keith called Winkie, Fae and me up on the stage, and we all led worship with Keith for about half an hour. And that's the way the festival ended. Keith came down from the stage, exhausted. I knew he'd delivered his soul. I was the first one to encourage him about how powerfully the Lord used him. But there were many others waiting to tell him the same thing. It was a bit overwhelming for Keith.

As we were driving back to our hotel we saw some people still out in the fields—praying.

Even with great results, Keith came away from the festival quite disturbed. What was the purpose of a festival anyway? Was it just a place for Christians to get together and have a party? Or maybe it was just another way to market the gospel. The promoters did seem to have good hearts, but were the people who came receiving it in the right way? Or did the responsibility of the spiritual tone of the event rest with each invited minister?

And for Keith, personally, his night of ministry left him with many questions. It took raw obedience to tell 35,000 people who were all "having a good time" that God hated their festival. The pressure to please a crowd that large is overwhelming—to be popular and loved. Even to sell a lot of records or make a "good" name for yourself. In obeying God, Keith figured his "hard message" would turn people off. That would have been easier for him to live with. But to become like a "celebrity" in spite of his strong words was, in some ways, frightening.

"Mel, I left all that stuff behind three years ago when I became a Christian. The groupies, the fans, the praise of men—I don't want to get sucked back into that again."

Keith's quick rise to popularity had been unsettling enough. He was worried about getting entrenched in a system that might eventually cause him to forget about God—or cause others to focus on him instead of the Lord. Keith was also worried about the power of his own charisma. Even though he didn't want to, what if he was "making things happen" in his own strength? How did he know if people at any given concert were responding to a move of the Lord, or if they were just responding to the performance skills he'd acquired over a lifetime of training?

For Keith these were more than passing questions. They were deep concerns. He had major questions about the Christian music industry—but even more troubling were the questions he had about himself. Keith really felt he needed to take some time off to sort through everything. We'd been on a non-stop schedule of traveling and recording for months. Besides that Keith figured it would be a great time to do some studying.

Winkie Pratney had bought Keith a whole library, because he saw his hunger for the Lord and his confusion over the intensity of his feelings. Winkie felt that Keith needed to study church history. Winkie told him, "Lots of Christians have felt like you do—and they've written some really great stuff. You need to read what they had to say." Then he took us to a bookstore and bought Keith a shopping cart full of books.

So, shortly after we returned home from "Jesus Northwest", Keith announced, "I'm taking a sabbatical—starting right now!"

"For how long?" I asked.

"I don't know, maybe a year. I might do a few concerts, but no major touring. I need some time. I want to get into the Word of God more—and all those books Winkie gave me. I just need to figure some things out."

It was nice to have Keith at home more as my September due date approached. We were so excited about this baby. We'd already read several name books, along with flipping through the Bible, to help us find some names we liked. We were taking natural childbirth classes to learn how to survive the "unknowns" of my first labor. Keith's mom even gave us Keith's original baby dresser! He'd painted it with a bunch of hippie stuff several years ago, so I spent a few days stripping off the paint, oiling it, and putting on a smooth satin varnish. Things were coming together!

Preparing to be parents brought us to a whole new level of counting the cost of living the type of life we were living. We both felt excited, however, about raising our child in a busy ministry. It seemed to us like the best way for a child to have an understanding of how to serve God was to grow up doing it. Still, we hoped we'd be good parents and be sensitive to our child's needs. Up to this point, we both thought producing an album was a much harder task than producing a baby. But that idea, at least from my point of view, was about to change drastically.

When my first labor pains hit—two weeks ahead of schedule—we phoned our doctor. Nothing happened that first day, though, and the next day Keith set up prayer teams from our community.

At one point in my early labor, about twenty people from the community came to see me, bringing a bunch of wrapped gifts with them. Since I'd started labor early I was going to "miss" the baby shower they'd planned. I opened the gifts between contractions, but it sure was hard to smile at that point!

Finally, the next day I was taken to the hospital. Once there, things started to speed up—some. Keith was by my side, watching the contractions on the monitor and telling me to "breathe" and to "relax". I was beginning to wonder if this baby was *ever* going to be born, and I was already totally exhausted. Keith would try to encourage me periodically.

"Pretty soon we're gonna have a baby to hold!"

"Really?" I was beginning to have my doubts.

"Hang in there, honey. We'll have our baby in no time. Just think! *Our baby!*"

Finally—after forty-nine hours of labor—I made it through the final few pushes and heard our doctor say, "It's a boy!"

He had lots of curly hair, and Keith kept exclaiming, "Wow, a boy! Honey, a little boy! Oh, thank you Jesus! Thank you!" He nearly danced around the room beaming and thanking the Lord, every inch the proud father.

The doctor wrapped our little blond-haired baby boy in a blanket. I was in awe as I inspected his little fingers and toes and looked into his blue eyes. Keith and I just looked at each other. How did God do this miracle?

We named our son—our son!—Josiah David, after two great kings. Josiah was the child-king, and the Bible said he always did what was right in the eyes of the Lord, never turning to the right or to the left. And David was known as a man after God's own heart. It already seemed like Josiah David looked a lot like Keith—who looked a lot like *his* dad. Keith was thrilled about that because of his deep love for his father. The feeling of being wheeled out of the hospital with such a precious gift in my arms was incredible.

Meanwhile our other "family" was growing, too. By now we had incorporated and we were calling ourselves "Last Days

Ministries". About this time it seemed like the Lord was bringing more people who would help us build our growing ministry.

The day Wayne Dillard drove up was a big event because he was the only one who'd ever shown up driving a new car! He'd written us from South Carolina after being deeply moved at one of Keith's concerts, saying, "My friends call me 'Mr. Fix-It' and I'm willing to do anything you need." We told him to come right away! And Jerry Bryant, who had a radio program in Illinois, came with his young son after sponsoring one of Keith's concerts in Carbondale.

Not everyone came from such a great distance. Martin Bennett decided to move into the ministry after coming to a few of our home Bible studies. Carol Hoehn was also from the area, along with Francine Weisberg, and Pam Wible. Keith and I had also taken in a teenage girl who had a background of physical abuse and who needed some parenting. She shared a room with Dawn. By now Michelle Brandes, our old friend from The Bla, had become Keith's secretary.

So, more and more, people were starting to pour in.

Along with the "people explosion", of course, we needed a "housing explosion" as well. We bought the house next door to us, formerly owned by a guy named Harvey. We made a gate through the backyard fence and it became a girls "dorm"—even though we continued to call it by the unlikely name of Harvey's House. We also rented another house on Dolorosa Street and called it The Rental. Then another house on Sale Street became known as The School House because it was across the street from a school. The Pool House was named for obvious reasons, and The Glass House got its name because it was full of sliding glass doors and windows. Within short space of time we went from twenty-five people in three houses, to seventy people in seven houses!

Although we were experimenting with community living and everyone living out of "one pot", Keith and I were underwriting almost one-hundred percent of the expenses with our own money. But God was really blessing us financially and we wanted to bless him by pouring it back into ministry. To give everybody at least a little feeling of independence everyone got $5 a month for "mad money", and we did a lot of activities together like going out to Little Tony's for pizza, or Solley's Delicatessen for hot fudge sundaes.

To bring in some extra money we put together a housecleaning service and teams of girls went out. The guys had a gardening service. We kept leading more people to the Lord and we'd baptize them wherever we could—in swimming pools, at the

—

beach, in jacuzzis—and Carol even got baptized in the bathtub at The School House. Everyone crowded into the small bathroom for the event, and I stood on the toilet lid to watch as Keith did the honors.

Mealtimes were always interesting because much of our food was donated. We ate things like squid, tongue, and graham crackers spread with cake frosting for dessert. Sometimes we'd just open a bunch of unlabeled cans to see what was for dinner. As we shuffled from house to house for meals and almost nightly Bible studies, I wondered more than ever what our neighbors thought about us. We were such a motley crew of ex-bikers, unwed mothers, and ex-drug-users. We'd walk along the street in clumps of ten or fifteen, past kids on skateboards and dads mowing the lawn in bermuda shorts—a bunch of post-hippies trying to follow God.

We decided the neighbors must think it was all pretty strange. So we sent teams out door to door through the whole neighborhood to let them know who we were and what we were doing. We also invited them to come to any of our Bible studies or Friday night potluck dinners. We'd say, "We'll always be available to pray with you. If you ever need help with anything, just let us know."

At our Friday night potlucks, we'd usually have some type of concert after dinner. Sometimes Keith would play, or one of our friends like Randy Stonehill, or Phil Keaggy. Then Keith, Richard Gene Lowe, or Reverend Glenn would preach. We saw many people come to the Lord—even whole families with their children. Todd's mother and father received the Lord as well.

But there was another side to community living.

Because many of the people who were staying with us had come from some pretty rough backgrounds their lives were generally out-of-control. We had to make a lot of rules to build in some strong structure. For instance, everyone had a "buddy" to go places with, because some people couldn't go to the corner store alone without sneaking cigarettes, or beer, or scoring some drugs. Some of the rules even seemed kind of crazy, but we needed them. For instance, it was against the rules to pull wheelies on the bicycles, because the tires got bent and people got hurt. It was against the rules to eat special donated foods without permission. And in order to keep some semblance of order we actually had to hand out demerits when people didn't make their beds or clean their rooms.

Even though we knew other rehabilitation type ministries had similar rules, Keith was really struggling with having so many people under his authority. He confided to his journal:

I'm so afraid of power. Not God's power . . . my fleshly desire to rule others. In my heart of hearts I only want to serve! To present the babes as mature men and women of God. I want more than anything else to pour myself out for them, for Jesus. But then there's my old nature that wants to control everything.

Lord, I repent of my old nature and I give my fear of power to you. For you are the only true power, Jesus!! Control my life with your Spirit. Control the sheep's lives with your Spirit—and if you use me, let me give thanks to you!! Let me continue to grow less important to me. . . .

In the midst of all this, Keith continued to explore the questions that had arisen after "Jesus Northwest". He plunged into a time of soul-searching and reflection—praying for revival in his own heart. He was fasting regularly as he buried himself in the Word and the writings of Christian leaders of the past and present. The pages were worn and underlined by the time Keith got done with them. He'd often grab the nearest person and read the "good parts" to them out loud.

Keith was exceptionally fidgety and restless now, too. When he wasn't fasting, I'd catch him poking his head in the freezer looking for his favorite chocolate ice cream. Then he'd pace the floor—the carton in one hand and a spoon in the other. He hated it when his weight was out of control, but his nervous energy got the best of him sometimes.

Early in October of 1978, I dressed Josiah for one of his first big outings—only the event wasn't exactly as we'd have chosen. Richard Gene Lowe, our first teacher and our good friend, had been on his way home from a big conference somewhere. It was late at night, and he was sleeping in the passenger seat of his friend's car. A truck coming in the opposite direction hit them head on. The doctors said Richard never knew what hit him. But we were shaken, even though we knew Richard was with the One he betrothed himself to years ago—his beloved Jesus. Keith really thought the Lord took Richard home in such a merciful way.

"Boy, that's the way to go!" he said, "No laying around in a hospital with some long drawn out disease. You just fall asleep and wake up in the presence of the Lord!"

"Yeah, Richard didn't feel a thing," I said.

"When my time comes that's the way I wanna go," Keith said as he snapped his fingers. "Earth to heaven in an instant!"

Keith's words went right by me at the time. There would come a day, though, when they would come back. For the moment, I busily tucked the blanket around Josiah as we headed out the front door for Richard's memorial service.

One day, a short time later, Keith walked into our bedroom looking more serious than usual—and that was saying a lot. He was holding the book, *Rees Howells: Intercessor,* in his hand as he flopped on the bed.

"Did you know Rees Howells and his wife *gave* their infant son away so they could go to Africa as missionaries?"

"They gave him away . . . ," I repeated, flatly. Already I didn't like the sound of this.

"They gave him to relatives," Keith continued, "and God told them they 'could never claim him again'. Years later, after he graduated from college, he joined his father in the ministry in Africa. But he was already all grown up."

"That's really heavy." Wasn't there something else we could be talking about?

"Yeah. God told him to do it."

"I sure *hope* it was God," I said, and now I bit my lip, wondering what Keith was leading up to.

"Mel, what if God told us to give Josiah away?"

"I can't see how that could ever be the Lord's will," I shot back at once. "I mean, do you really think he would ask us to do that?"

"I don't know. He might. God can do anything he wants."

"Well, I always want to obey the Lord, no matter what it costs. But that would be a hard one. Are you saying you would be willing?" I pressed him.

"It would be the hardest thing I've ever done," he said, seriously. "But if I was one hundred percent positive it was God, I'd do it."

By now, my heart was so heavy it could have burst. I was afraid Keith was going to do something crazy. *What if he tells me he thinks God wants us to give Josiah to somebody else?* I was thinking, *What would I do? You don't just give kids away, do you?* My emotions were rocking.

Things had been so much easier when it was "just us and our stereo". We'd always said we would give the Lord everything. But it seemed a lot easier to give God things like money, comfort, and time. How do you give your child? Rees Howells found out. So did

Abraham, with his son Isaac. The enormity of their commitment was staggering to me.

Fortunately, it wasn't a question we needed an immediate answer to. We weren't going to put Josiah up for adoption or anything. Still, our parent-hearts were being painfully tested. And for the next few months Keith, in particular, was going through a deeper testing than I knew about until much later.

JANUARY 15, 1979

Lord, Help Again!

My Jesus, please pour your strong life out on me. . . . I'm almost dead. . . . I need and desire to be close to you. . . . Please, God, you know I'm serious about this. Send your angel to answer.

One evening, in February 1979, Keith was poking through his bookshelf—pulling books out, scanning a few pages, then putting them back. I noticed that he kept at it, until one book seemed to capture his interest. Keith carried it over to his favorite chair—a $5 Naugahyde recliner we "scored" at the resale store—and kicked back to read for a while. I smiled and shook my head. Keith was always tackling books that frightened me off just by their size.

It seemed like he was only half a chapter into it when he called me over.

"Mel, do you remember this book?"

It didn't look familiar. "No. What's it about?"

"It's all about revivals! *Real* ones!"

I did remember what he was talking about now. The book was called *Revival Lectures* and it was written by a nineteenth-century revivalist named Charles Finney. One night about a year ago, Keith had phoned me from the road, sobbing into the phone. He had read me a whole chapter of that book over the phone! Keith had been reading more Finney lately and, tonight, he had rediscovered this particular book.

He went back to his reading now—no long passages to read out loud, I guessed—and I got ready for bed.

When I walked out into the living room to say goodnight, Keith was still engrossed in reading. But by this time, his expression had changed from excitement to total sobriety. Keith was so absorbed that he barely looked up as he mumbled a goodnight to me. I went in our room and turned out the light.

The next thing I knew Keith was shaking me awake. I was so groggy I could hardly understand what he was saying.

"Mel, wake up. You need to get up."

"Uh . . . why?"

"It's happened! Get up. We're gonna have a special meeting right away."

Our voices woke Josiah up and he started to cry for my attention. It was barely daylight and through the haze of grogginess I wondered what on earth Keith was going on about.

"I've got to go to the other houses," he was saying. "I'll be back."

As I turned my attention to Josiah, the front door slammed and Keith took off in the gray morning light. One of the first places he went was one of the men's dorms. Wayne Dillard and a few other guys were awakened the same way I'd been. Later on Wayne told me what happened when Keith shook him awake.

"As soon as I got my eyes half-way opened, I could see his face—it was like he was smiling from the inside out. He was radiant."

"Wayne, wake up!" Keith said. "We've got to have a meeting."

"Okay," Wayne mumbled, "but what time is it?"

"It's about six. Listen, I was out in 'The Ark' praying all night. And I just got saved."

"You *what*?"

"*I just got saved!*"

"Rushing Wind"

Direct challenge.

BY THE TIME ALL SEVEN HOUSES HEARD ABOUT THE SPECIAL meeting, our community was buzzing with curiosity. Having an early morning meeting was in itself a shock. Usually, no one even saw Keith before 10 a.m. because of his late-night schedule. I watched everyone quietly drift into The School House—throwing questioning glances at each other. It looked like all seventy of us were there—crammed into the living room, and spilling over into the hall and kitchen, anxiously waiting to find out what was going on.

As soon as I saw Keith's face I knew something big was going on. His eyes were clear and bright and his whole face was lit with a broad grin. *Something* had happened to him!

"You know I've been struggling with a lot of questions about my ministry and the Lord's will for my life," he began, "I've been really wanting God to be more real. Well, I was up all night in 'The Ark' and God showed me so much sin in my life that I spent the whole night weeping and crying out to Him. I told the Lord I wasn't going to leave 'The Ark' until I had a breakthrough—no matter how long it took. Finally, it happened. I had a touch from the Lord like I've never had in my whole life. And I know I just got saved—I just got saved last night."

Keith's words stunned everyone as much as they stunned me. I could see it in their faces. Just got saved? I thought, *What have you been if you haven't been saved?* But Keith just kept talking, either ignoring or not noticing the wide-eyed surprise on everyone's face.

"Last night I was reading Finney, and I just couldn't get past a chapter called 'Breaking Up The Fallow Ground'. God convicted me of so much fallow ground in my life—ground that's hard and crusty and needs to be broken up for Him. . . ."

Now the happiness in Keith's eyes clouded over as they started to fill with tears. Blinking them back, Keith pulled some sheets of paper out of his Bible and unfolded them as he kept talking.

"I've already gotten these things right with God, now I want to confess them to you and ask for your forgiveness because my sins have affected you. First of all, I know I haven't been a very good leader. I've wounded some of you with my words and my crummy attitudes. . . ."

Now Keith broke and really started to cry, but he controlled himself enough to go on.

"The Lord has also shown me areas of pride and unbelief in my life. I don't read my Bible enough and I don't pray enough, either. And I'm so undisciplined. I've been a bad example to all of you. I have no excuse except for being lazy and loving myself more than I really love God. . . ."

He went on for several minutes, pouring his heart out and crying.

"Another area God has convicted me in is not trusting him for finances. When we offered the cassette of my 'Jesus Northwest' concert in the newsletter, we said we'd send it for free, or for a donation. The Lord showed me we shouldn't have even mentioned donations after promising not to solicit funds—so we're going to send everybody's money *back* to them right away.

"I know my sin has broken God's heart. I know it's hurt you, too—and I'm really, really sorry. I'm not worthy to bear the holy name of Christian. Please forgive me."

Then Keith picked up his Bible and read a scripture to us from Hosea: "Break up your fallow ground, for it is time to seek the Lord until He comes to rain righteousness on you. . . ." Keith continued, "Fallow ground is ground that was once tilled, but has since gotten hard and unusable. Before it can receive seed it needs to be broken up and made soft again. Finney says to break up the fallow ground of our heart we need to examine our motives, actions, and state of mind very carefully."

Then picking up the Finney book, Keith read to us. "Many people never seem to think about doing this. They pay no attention to their own hearts, and never know whether they are doing well in their walk with the Lord or not—whether they are bearing fruit or are totally barren."

Keith explained the two kinds of sin Finney talks about. Sins of *commission* are the things we do that we shouldn't. Included on Finney's list were—lying, cheating, gossip, wasting time, slandering others, love of possessions, vanity, envy, bitterness, hypocrisy, having a bad temper, and hindering the usefulness of others. Keith added in a few areas that Finney didn't list because they weren't as prevalent in his day—things like sexual sin, drugs, and involvement with false religions.

And if that wasn't enough, there were the sins of *omission*— the things we *don't* do that we should. Included in these were lack of love for God, for the Bible, for prayer, for the poor and needy, and for the lost all around us and in foreign lands. Also listed were the sins of ingratitude, neglecting to be careful about our words and actions, and a neglect of self-denial.

Then—Finney again. "There are many professing Christians who are willing to do almost anything in religion that does not require self-denial. They are so far from realizing that self-denial is a condition of discipleship, that they do not even know what it is!"

As Keith was talking an awesome sense had been coming over me. Instead of thinking that the things he'd done were so terrible, I found myself starting to examine my own heart, thinking, *if God put the searchlight on Keith, what does all this mean for me?* By now I was starting to make a mental list. A long one.

Keith went on to read the whole chapter out loud to us. It was a real "outline" for a point-by-point examination of our own hearts. Finney said that "general" confessions of sin are not good enough. Since our sins were committed one by one, as much as possible they need to be repented of one by one—confessing to God those sins committed against him, and confessing to other men the sins committed against them. No shortcuts allowed! Then Keith paused and seemed to take a deep breath before he continued.

"I believe God wants to do something powerful in all of our lives. What God did for me, he wants to do for you. He wants all of us to have pure hearts that are soft and open to him. We all need to humble ourselves and break up the 'fallow ground' of our hearts so God can be glorified. I believe we all need to have a breakthrough with God. I really think we all need to pray now."

Everybody bowed their heads and closed their eyes. Then Keith started praying a very powerful prayer and a hush fell over the room. In just a moment something began to happen.

Suddenly one of the women burst into tears. She'd been sitting on the floor and now she was on her face, her whole body heaving with deep uncontrollable sobs. A few others started to weep, and the next thing we knew we were all on our faces, crying, and calling out to God. Actually, some of us could do little more than moan. The feelings were so deep it was hard to even put them into words. It was a gut-wrenching time of conviction and soul-searching. The sound of wailing started to rise and fill the room—and it went on and on.

After a long time, Keith asked everyone to go and take some time alone with God. "Go home and make out a list. List every area of sin that the Lord is showing you and will continue to show you. List it in detail. Let the Lord shine his spotlight into your hearts."

We met again later that evening and over the next few days— day and night. We had hours of prayer, weeping, and humble open confession. Everyone was being broken. They'd read their list of sins and ask forgiveness of God and those who'd been affected. There was such an awesome sense of God's presence in the room, sometimes overwhelming. And more often than not after someone shared, tears of sorrow ignited into tears of joy— and even laughter as many broke through to God at deeper levels than ever before. They said they felt cleansed and refreshed in a brand new way—like their souls had just come alive and the weight of the world was lifted off their shoulders. It seemed like, one by one, this was happening to everybody.

Everybody, that is, except me.

After a few days, so many people had experienced their "breakthrough" I started to worry about when I'd get mine. Keith was beginning to worry about me, too. He'd walk over to me while I was lying on the floor praying and say, "Do you think you might be getting close?" He was so excited and had waited so long for this to happen, he wanted to be sure it happened for me, too.

One of the first people Keith phoned was Winkie. "It's happened!" he told him. "We're having a powerful move of God!"

Meanwhile, word was getting out locally, and some people from the Vineyard showed up at our ongoing meetings. Even some neighbors came. All with the same results—deep conviction of sin and a fresh touch from the Lord.

One night a brother from another ministry came and taught us about God's sacrificial love. At the end of his teaching he shared a story with us.

It seemed there was a man with the job of raising and lowering a drawbridge so passenger trains could cross a deep canyon. This man had one child, a son, that he loved very much. One day the little boy wandered toward the bridge without his father noticing.

Soon the father heard a train whistle. As he started to pull the lever to lower the bridge, he looked out the window and saw that his son had crawled down into the big heavy gears. If he pulled the lever his son would be crushed!

There were only seconds to decide. Hundreds of people would die if he didn't lower the bridge—all sons and daughters loved by someone. He took a deep breath and his heart screaming with pain, he pulled the lever.

The bereaved father stood helplessly at the window, beating on it with both fists and screaming out in anguish, as the train zipped quickly over the bridge. The passengers saw him and thought he was waving—so they waved happily back without realizing the price that father had just paid for them.

When the story was over, every face looked stricken. As the meeting was dismissed I started crying. Running out into the dark night, I fell on my knees in the backyard with my face pressed into the grass. I still hadn't had a "breakthrough" like all the others, but with this story, I'd felt the heart-crushing pain of the father. In my mind's eye, I could only see my curly-haired Josiah in those gears.

"Oh Lord," I cried, "please give me a clear picture of what it cost you to send your only Son to earth. I'm so sorry for taking your sacrifice for granted—and for not loving you the way you deserve to be loved. Please forgive me!"

The next day, I left the meeting and went to sit in a car parked near The School House. I decided I wouldn't leave until I got my breakthrough. That worked for Keith, so maybe it would work for me. I didn't know what else to do.

I'd already made a long list of my sins and shared them with the ministry, repenting to God and man. I confessed to everyone that sometimes I got really tired of living in community. Also, that I was still striving for recognition in my songwriting and how

—

much pride I had when Keith would say in concert, "Melody and I wrote this song together." My prayer life and my time in the Word left so much to be desired, too. I also confessed that I took the best baby clothes for Josiah before sending some donated clothing off to Mexico. I knew I'd hurt people by not speaking the truth in love and by being judgmental. To be honest, I was even judging this revival. Actually, I was mad at Finney, and jealous of those who were starting to look happy while I was feeling totally miserable. I felt like such a mess.

Maybe I'm not repenting in the right way, I thought. As I sat in that car, I was devastated by the blackness of my heart. I thought I loved God. Maybe I didn't love him at all—maybe I never did. But the thing that scared me the most was the fear that I might be incapable of loving God. So why should he love me—or forgive me, for that matter? I started to question every motive of my heart and felt like I was tumbling down a dark shaft of despair.

After a while Keith came out to talk to me. As much as he wanted to see me have a breakthrough, he didn't think camping out in a parked car was the answer. "Mel, why don't you come back into the house now."

"I can't. I don't even know if I love God. How can I go to a prayer meeting?"

"Mel, you love God. I know you do. Maybe it's not gonna happen the same way for you. Come on back in."

I went back into the house, but I wasn't comforted. I saw the wickedness of my heart and I felt torn from the inside out. I didn't understand why I seemed to get "passed over" by the Lord.

There finally came a point, later, where I just had to let it go and go on—without the happy feelings and with the thought that maybe I wasn't a Christian. Perhaps God doesn't deal with everybody in the same way, I reasoned. But then, maybe I only felt like I'd been left behind in the darkness. I decided I would serve God in that darkness as fully as everyone else was serving him in the light—whether or not, I was really saved.

After several days, when the intensity of it all subsided, it seemed that the Lord had drawn near to our community in an incredible way. Later on, we would refer to this time as "The Revival". Charles Finney defined revival as "a new beginning of obedience to God", and that was definitely what happened. It was a life-changing time for all of us, myself included—even though my memories were a bit painful.

Keith also knew that his statements about "just getting saved" came from his black and white way of looking at things. It was just that he'd glimpsed a walk with God that required such a deeper

—

commitment, it was almost as if he'd never given his heart to the Lord before. He said, "It's like getting born again . . . *again!*"

Keith believed the Lord wanted the spirit of revival we'd just experienced to sweep the nation. It just happened that the very next concert Keith had scheduled was at the end of March in Tulsa at Oral Roberts University—in the 11,500 seat Mabee Center. Tulsa seemed like the perfect place to start, with its clusters of well-known ministries. And ORU was the best-known Christian university in America. When revival broke out there it would resound across the nation! Keith marveled at God's perfect planning.

It seemed that with "The Revival", Keith had also found his answer to our long-standing questions about finances.

One afternoon he bounced into the kitchen and said lightly, "Mel, we're just gonna go wherever God sends us and not worry about money."

"Well, usually you just go for offerings anyway." I wasn't sure why Keith was making this sound like it was so different from what we were already doing.

"Yeah, but we're not going to worry about how much of an offering or honorarium we get," he replied, "or even if we get one *at all*. In fact, I really feel like God is telling me we need to pay our own way into these cities—and not ask for anything from the churches!"

Now that *did* sound different.

Keith's new financial decision and his desire to see our revival spread had an immediate effect on his scheduled time at ORU. Since they didn't usually take offerings at the Mabee Center, they were going to bless Keith with $2,000 for one concert. But now the plans needed to change a bit. Keith didn't want the $2,000— and he wanted to go and minister for at least a week.

In Keith's thinking, when Finney went into a city it wasn't for a "one-night stand." He stayed until the Lord finished doing what he wanted to do. If revival broke out, Finney could be in the same town for months. With what had just happened to Keith and our community, it sure seemed like God was up to something big.

The first person Keith phoned in Tulsa was the ORU student body president who'd invited him in. Keith got the guy on the phone and explained to him what he felt God's new direction was—that we were to come for a week for free. The guy's jaw must have dropped.

A short time later, we received a return phone call from this brother, saying we had a green light. Instead of going to the Mabee Center, Keith could preach for a week—in the chapel! We were all so excited we could hardly see straight. So we made plans to go to Tulsa and had no idea when we'd be back.

Keith said, "If revival breaks out, we might even end up moving to Tulsa!" He wrote a prayer bulletin and sent it out to the 22,000 people who were now receiving our *Last Days Newsletter.* Keith asked them to pray because we were going to Tulsa and he believed God wanted to pour out his Spirit and bring repentance—and put a spirit of prayer and conviction upon the city.

Keith was also really excited about God picking ORU in particular as the place to begin. Like all ministries do, they'd been experiencing some financial difficulties. Keith really hoped that if the Lord birthed this spiritual re-awakening in this, the "cradle" of so many other ministries, it would open the door for fresh blessings to pour in. Keith said, "God is really going to bless ORU once this revival breaks out there!"

Keith sent Wayne Dillard and a few other guys to Tulsa two weeks ahead of the chapel meetings to meet with the local pastors so they could get ready and start praying. Keith had also planned a pastors' luncheon when he got to town so he could meet them and share his heart about the city-wide revival.

After Wayne had been in Tulsa for about a week though, Keith received an upsetting call from him.

"Keith, they don't want you to come."

Wayne explained that the student group that invited Keith had neglected one critical detail—they forgot to go through the proper channels with the change of plans. And the administration was surprised when they first found out about the upcoming revival on campus by reading about it in the school newspaper.

"I got a call from the ORU administration today and they said they didn't invite you in so you shouldn't come," Wayne told him.

Keith figured their concerns were understandable. After all, they didn't really know him or his ministry very well. From their point of view "uninviting" him probably seemed like the responsible thing to do.

Maybe the administration had heard about Keith's steamy message a year before at Oklahoma Baptist University. There was a tremendous response from the students—but it did cause some real shock waves when Keith told them:

"Going to church, or going to a Christian college, or going to cemetery—I mean seminary—doesn't make you a Christian any more than going to McDonalds makes you a hamburger! If there were that many on-fire people in all of Oklahoma, there'd be headlines all over the nation: 'Oklahoma Has Revival'!"

—

For whatever reasons, Keith's time in Tulsa was cancelled. Keith wasn't convinced however that the decision reflected the Lord's heart. He was going to pursue getting it reversed

Keith set up twenty-four-hour prayer chains at Last Days and everyone started fasting. Then the next day he was on the phone from 8:45 a.m. until dinner time, back and forth to Tulsa trying to work things out. But he was told, "We're sorry brother. We don't really know who you are. We're responsible to protect the students here. We can't let you come."

Keith finally told them he understood their position—but that he felt the Lord wanted him to come anyway. That day, he wrote:

MARCH 10, 1979

ORU is cancelled. We're going anyway. In my spirit I know it's right, but the rest of me is *scared!*

Had the best prayer/cry in a month. *Oh! did I cry!*

Keith did have some misgivings. He wondered if he'd really heard from God about going. He didn't want to be propelled by any false desire of his own to "bring a fiery message" to Tulsa. In the end, Keith received what he believed to be confirmation from the Lord. The Vineyard was going to send us out with their blessings, and there was a scripture passage that came to us, Jeremiah 23, that convinced Keith he should go "with the right motives". Keith struggled up to the very last minute. . . .

MARCH 11, 1979

In an hour and fifteen minutes, the Vineyard will lay hands on us to go to Tulsa and I'm not sure *totally* we're supposed to go! Oh, my pride, reputation and false faith all say "go". My mind and heart are divided. I can't find my spirit! . . . I must go for the right motives. God said, "Go!"

We loaded up "The Ark" with about twenty-five of our Last Days family and drove all the way to Tulsa. When we arrived we had no place to stay, but the student body president told us about a house for rent. It only had a few pieces of furniture and most of us slept on the floor, but it met our needs. We immediately started two things: A twenty-four-hour prayer chain and a series of meetings with the ORU administration, who were shocked that Keith actually came after being told not to.

At Keith's first meeting with the administration he told them about the mighty move of God we'd just experienced and how he believed God wanted it to spread across the nation—right from their chapel!

Keith was emphatic about what he felt God had told him. He even asked if he could rent the Mabee Center—though at $2,000 a night, that would mean taking out a loan. Though ORU had rented the arena in the past to secular artists like Billy Joel and Liza Minnelli, they'd continue to pray about it over the weekend before they gave Keith a final decision.

That night when Keith got back to our little rented house, he announced, "It's not over yet! But we need a miracle."

Twenty-four-hour prayer chains went on all through the weekend, and by now we were getting pretty good at it! Keith also called a fast. We wanted to do everything in our power to see God move.

In the meantime, some of the local pastors were very open to Keith. In fact when Keith sang and shared his vision for the city at a pastors' luncheon it turned into a prayer meeting, with many tears and heart-rending prayers. Keith had also scheduled meetings in some other churches and schools. He was determined to reach the city one way or another.

On Sunday morning, Keith preached at a local Baptist church in West Tulsa. The service usually ended like clockwork at noon, but because of the powerful move of God it didn't dismiss until 2:30 p.m.—and Keith was invited back for another service.

That night, Keith was given the evening service at Tulsa Christian Fellowship—the oldest charismatic fellowship in the city. His message and his songs centered on God's broken heart over the hypocrisy of lukewarm Christianity. Keith often said, "Christians don't like to talk about hypocrisy any more than turkeys like to talk about Thanksgiving!" This night he was driving the point home, and his preaching was even a bit abrasive. He'd come with a burden to shake the congregation into a confrontation with themselves and with God, and I knew he was about to pull out all the stops.

"You don't like it, do you?" he said. "You came to hear a concert, and you're getting cornered. The Christian walk is a bunch of squirming flesh getting nailed down to a cross. 'Hey man, I want a padded cross. You know, a Posture-Pedic Cross with nice springs in it. Something comfortable.' The gospel is a no compromise, absolute sell-out for Jesus, one hundred percent walk!"

Keith had been pacing the floor as he spoke, his piano long forgotten. "I hate to say this to you folks—I really love you but. . . ." I could feel it coming. Turning to the congregation, Keith pointed and said in a booming voice, "You brood of vipers and snakes! . . . Who call yourselves Christians and half-heartedly serve Him!"

Instant shock ran through the place. Some people in the congregation had obviously been going to church before Keith was born—let alone born-again. Even I couldn't believe my ears.

But suddenly, it didn't seem to matter. An overwhelming sense swept through the room. Keith had gone back to the piano and, as he began a song, he prayed, "Lord, these people can't know how much I love them. They've heard me yelling and screaming at them—but Lord, you know the heart you've put in me that hates sin and hypocrisy and compromising so much. You know how much I love these people and want to see them turn into blazing, glowing Christians. Oh God!—please bring a revival!"

Without hesitation, people started rushing forward to the altar rail, weeping and sobbing as they came and fell on their faces. The pastor joined Keith and they both led the congregation in a very powerful time of personal and corporate repentance. Keith recalled something the pastor had said in an earlier prayer and spoke it out like a battle cry—"Lord, let there be a revival and let it begin in me!"

It seemed like revival was, indeed, going to break out in Tulsa!

"I Want To Rain Upon You . . ."

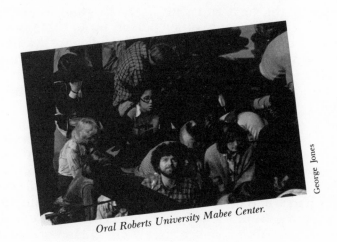

George Jones

Oral Roberts University Mabee Center.

O N MONDAY MORNING, WE WERE STILL WAITING TO GET WORD
on the Mabee Center. Keith rented a place called the Caravan
Ballroom, a country-western dance club, to use in the meantime.
It was only open on the weekends, so we rented it for Tuesday and
Wednesday nights, still hoping we could rent the Mabee Center
later in the week.

On Monday afternoon Keith got the final verdict from ORU. I waited
in the lounge and prayed we'd be able to rent it. Finally, he returned,
with an extra bounce in his springy step.

"Guess what?" Keith said with a gleam in his eye.

"They're going to let us rent it!" I said.

"Nope. We can't rent it. They're going to *give* it to us!"

"For *free?*"

"Yeah. This is it Mel. God did it!"

Not only was the administration going to let us have the Mabee Center for free, they were going to officially sponsor the concerts! We would have the Mabee Center on Thursday, Friday, and Saturday. After that it would be up to ORU if Keith carried on for more nights or not. Keith agreed that if they said "that's it" by Saturday night, he'd go home. They also told Keith he could give an altar call. The only other person up to that point who'd been allowed to give one at the Mabee Center was Katherine Kuhlman. On top of that, they were going to provide housing for us, and let us eat our meals in their cafeteria!

We were amazed by all of this—and very grateful to the Lord and to ORU. It was the miracle we'd been praying for.

Now we had five nights scheduled in Tulsa and started getting the word out—especially for the Caravan Ballroom since it was coming up fast! Keith was being careful not to presume upon the Lord, so he wasn't about to announce a revival. So Keith said, "Let's not call it anything. Let's just say it's a free concert!"

Keith had come to Tulsa with the attitude that he didn't want to take anything from the people of this city. He felt God had told him, "Freely you have received, freely give." He was beginning to have a strong conviction that the gospel was supposed to be free. Whether it was a gospel concert, recording, or tract, Keith felt he couldn't deny those things to anyone just because they might not have money.

So not only did we pay for everything ourselves, Keith determined not to take offerings at any of his meetings. At this point, according to the major Christian music surveys, Keith's *No Compromise* album had risen quickly to number one on the charts, and *For Him Who Has Ears To Hear* was now number four. But Keith had brought $8,000 worth of his albums to town, and they were not for sale—they were only to give away at the concerts. Another thing we brought to town was a little bit of Charles Finney. Keith and I had paraphrased the "Breaking Up The Fallow Ground" chapter in his book, and had it printed up to give to people at the concerts to take home as an outline for repentance.

On Tuesday and Wednesday evenings, the Caravan Ballroom, with a 1,100-person capacity, was packed out with people from churches and colleges in Tulsa. Keith's basic theme was the same—getting "Christians" saved.

"This country is full of unsaved 'Christians'," he said. "And this city is probably full of more of them than almost anywhere else in America." Both nights the dirty dance floor was filled with people on their knees, making commitments to Jesus Christ.

But I could sense that things were really just starting to build toward the coming ORU meetings.

During this time, Keith was really struggling with his own sense of weakness and inadequacy. He wanted to be "God's voice" and yet he saw how he didn't measure up to what it took to speak for God. In what few quiet moments Keith had in that very hectic week, he wrote a little in his journal:

The meetings have been good, but the Spirit is no heavier than last year, because I am not praying more than last year.

3:15 a.m.
Can't sleep. An angel wants to burn my lips with the coal. I _must_ count the cost. Isaiah 6:7,8—Here am I. Send me!

Prayer is the key. Make me a man of prayer!

I want to be God's voice, full of love, mercy and fire! But I must be dead!

I am ready for death! Kill _me_, destroy _me_, burn _me_ beyond recognition—I know now that you would never hurt or harm me. You only want me dead! Let it be done!

I don't want greatness. _I want you to be great!_

Lower me down, humble me. Teach me to _humble myself_, oh Lord! I love you _so much_—but not as _you_ love the Father. I want to love you that way!

Keith wanted to gather some elders around him so he phoned Leonard Ravenhill, who he hadn't even met yet, and offered to fly him up. He was unable to come. But on Wednesday afternoon, Winkie Pratney arrived with several other leaders we knew to give us moral support and prayer power.

I could see the mounting pressure of these days was taking its toll on Keith. He looked like the weight of the world had settled on his shoulders. He wasn't eating right, and he wasn't sleeping much either. Emotionally he was under tremendous strain. Now that the administration had given their okay, Keith felt he had to be on-target with God. He said, "If God didn't really tell me to come here, then I'm not a Christian and I've never heard God's voice at all." So, he paced and took long walks, wondering out loud, "Did I really hear God's voice?"

On Thursday afternoon, we went to the ORU campus to pray and prepare for the evening's meeting. The Mabee Center was the largest arena in Tulsa and probably one of the nicest. It had plush, folding theater-type seats and the whole arena sloped downward toward the stage which was the lowest part of the arena. There was a long beautiful floor-to-ceiling curtain that separated different-sized sections of the arena.

That evening, about 1,000 people showed up. Just before going out on-stage, Keith wrote:

MARCH 22, 1979, 6:15 Dressing Room
Here goes—burn me now, God—send a Pentecost!

That night, he talked about how *not* to grieve away the Holy Spirit. He centered on how often we ignore the things God wants us to do. "He doesn't *need* to use any of us," Keith said, "but he wants to use *all* of us—to our fullest potential. The greatest argument *against* Christianity is Christians! The world is tired of *hearing* 'Praise the Lord'. They want to *see* it!"

By the end of the evening, over half of the people responded to Keith's challenge to be totally sold-out for Jesus. Many were down on their knees in front for the altar call—weeping and repenting. Someone even got healed when Keith sang "Easter Song"—which often happened at Keith's concerts as the Lord would give him a word of knowledge about a particular disease or condition he was going to heal.

Afterward, though, Keith was really uncertain about how things went that night. He didn't *feel* anything. He didn't feel really good, and he didn't feel bad—he just felt kind of neutral. But Winkie and the others were very excited. Winkie told him, "God's presence was powerful tonight. These meetings could really break into something wonderful if they keep going like this!"

Winkie reminded Keith of a revival at Asbury, a Methodist college, a number of years ago. It broke out in a chapel service and went on for weeks. People would just walk onto the campus and the presence of the Lord was so strong they'd start weeping over things that weren't right in their lives. Classes were shut down while everyone was in the chapel weeping and repenting. It was a small college compared to ORU, but it affected Christian colleges across the nation. If revival broke out at ORU, its impact could be phenomenal

Friday night, there were twice as many people at the Mabee Center, and Keith was feeling more confident. He preached a powerful message on "faith without works is dead".

Keith said, "I'm not here to preach salvation by works. No such thing. God chose Abraham because Abraham had a godly heart. And then God gave him the grace to do godly works to prove his godliness." He used a simple analogy. "An apple tree *becomes* an apple tree as a gift of God. But it *proves* it's an apple tree by making apples."

Again there was a dramatic response at the end as over 1,000 people came forward to get right with God and quit playing "Christian" games.

Keith came away from that evening feeling terrific. But when he asked Winkie and the others what they thought he was surprised at their consensus. "Well, . . . it was great, Keith," Winkie said. "But to be honest, it didn't have the same touch of God on it as last night. It was *great* preaching, and the Holy Spirit moved . . . but it wasn't *revival* preaching."

Now Keith didn't know *what* to think. Thursday night he didn't feel anything and was surprised to hear how powerfully God was there. Then, the next night he felt wonderful, but the presence of the Lord was not as strong. Keith knew he couldn't trust his feelings, but he was really off-balance now—especially going into the third night. If God didn't move powerfully on Saturday night, it would be all over.

Keith fasted and prayed all day Saturday. He kept jotting things down on what seemed to be some kind of list he was making. And right up till the Saturday night meeting, he kept noting in his journal:

MARCH 24, 1979, 6 p.m. Dressing Room

I'm so tired.

My flesh is rebelling so hard. It doesn't want to have a prayer life. Help me, oh God.

Tonight, I either live gloriously, or die shamefully. Oh Lord, I'm so lazy, I don't see how I can handle this kind of life for very long! Help!

Please, Jesus, help me to do good *only* for your glory. Let me not entertain any other reasons, for they are not holy! I want *your* name to be great.

As Keith paced backstage, occasionally peeking through the stage curtains, it was obvious the crowd was going to be the biggest yet. The floor-to-ceiling curtain partitions were pulled back totally, to accommodate the surprise crowd of 4,500—mainly from ORU, but we learned there were many from local churches and colleges, as well.

When Keith walked out onto the stage he lost no time in getting to the heart of the matter.

"Tonight we're gonna speak about holiness.

"What is holiness? It means to be set apart. It doesn't mean you live in a monastery—it means you don't do worldly things. In

—

First John it says if any man loves the world he's an enemy of God."

Keith went on to talk about the importance of the law and why it needs to be preached—so that sin can be exposed for what it is. "I have a definition of sin that's pretty encompassing—anything that causes God pain."

I knew the concept of being able to hurt God would be new to a lot of people. I looked around to see how this audience was responding. Everyone seemed to be listening closely as Keith continued.

"God is the most loving person in the universe. That means he's also the most sensitive person in the universe. Love is making yourself vulnerable. The more you love, the more you can get hurt. How would you like to have eyes that saw every sin that was ever committed every single day? It says, 'The eyes of the Lord are in all places watching the good and the evil.' Our sin hurts God.

"God is the most patient person in the universe. But time is running out. The Bible says there will come a day called the Day of the Lord. It comes as a thief in the night. In that day no flesh will be justified or glorified before the Lord. That means, we'd better get out of the flesh quick!"

Keith reached for his Bible to pull out the list I'd seen him working on all day.

"Now I've got a list that the Lord gave me of sins on this campus. *Specific* sins."

My heart started to pound. The atmosphere made a noticeable shift—and a few people started to shift in their chairs, as well. Keith started reading:

"There is worldliness on this campus. How many people believe that?" A good number of hands went up—but not all. "Oh! Only half of you," Keith laughed. "What about the worldly half? Don't you think so?

"There is sexual immorality on this campus," he went on. "And there is *homosexuality* on this campus." Now the audience was as still as a roomful of tombstones.

"There are people that waste the time and the money God gives them. But the time is short. 'For we must work the works of Him who sent us while it is still day for night is coming when no man can work.' Nobody that believes the Bible would dare waste his precious time.

"And I'm telling you, there's dope being sold and smoked around here. There's people going out and drinking. And you know, there's an honor code here—right? No dope allowed.

—

People have to be in by a certain time. No one's allowed to lie or cheat and so forth. There's deception and self-deception among the students. Lying and cheating."

Keith went on to tell the story of Achan, from the book of Joshua, and what happens when there is "sin in the camp". When the walls of Jericho tumbled, a man named Achan got greedy and took a bit of the spoil for himself—some things devoted to idols, which God had forbid them to touch.

Keith explained that, in Joshua's very next battle, many men died, and God told Joshua why: "The sons of Israel cannot stand before their enemies. . . . For they have become accursed in my sight." Now Keith faced the audience squarely.

"There is *sin* in the camp! Oral Roberts has a dream, and it's of the Lord. His dream is to send out men and women of God from this campus all over the face of the earth. And every sin in your life produces a curse, because sin brings a curse. And I'm telling you, according to this principle, if there *is* sin in the camp—there's a curse upon the whole school!

"Tonight it's time for us to stare our sin in the eye with the light and the grace of God. God always speaks to us *specifically*, to heal us. We can't walk around with this spiritual-white-washed-hallelujah-praise-the-Lord, cover-up anymore!"

Keith went on to compare sin to venereal disease, saying people get v.d. having what they call "fun." The first symptoms are subtle and almost painless—then it incubates in their system and drives them mad, blind, and finally, dead. Keith told everyone, "Sin is fun to get, but it's like sugar-coated, long-acting cyanide!" He encouraged everyone to quit playing deadly games with God.

"Maybe if we get holy and put aside our sin, Oral's dream will come true. How many people here are guilty of mocking him? Gossiping about him and his family? I wonder how many of you prayed for him today or yesterday? I had to repent before I could come out and preach this because I've laughed at him and judged him, too. And I'm not saying there's nothing to repent of in the administration, or in Oral, or in me. But if there's something wrong with someone, the biblical way of changing it is to submit and pray. God can speak to them. I learned that last week."

Then Keith asked those who felt they needed to commit their life to Jesus to come forward. He also called forward those who God was dealing with about sin.

"Come and repent of your sexual sins. Your homosexuality. Your self-gratification. Your bitterness, cheating, lying, deceitfulness, gossip, rebellion, hypocrisy, disloyalty, vain glory, and pride—and your vain attempts at being religious.

"Let's come and return to the Lord. 'For He has torn us, but He will heal us.'" Keith quoted.

People from every part of the arena were starting to stream forward—filling the stage around Keith and pressing right up against the piano. As the stage area filled, people started lying in the aisles and across the front of the stage area. It looked like a bomb had gone off! There were bodies everywhere—people on their knees or on their faces—broken and weeping. It was an incredible sight.

Keith was softly playing the piano, not even looking at the people. His gaze was focused upward, on the Lord. And no one was focused on Keith, either. They were on their faces, calling out to God.

In a moment, Keith began to sob, too, with his head resting on the piano. The response had been tremendous—it looked like about 2,500 people came forward to get their lives right with God. But Keith's burden was for *more* than that. He believed God wanted to bring a *revival,* and suddenly he burst out with a tearful, pleading prayer.

"Lord Jesus, send your Holy Spirit and honor your Word. My preaching is garbage! I don't know what to say. The songs I've sung are all trash without your Spirit! God, send your Spirit, for without it we're all dead! Coming forward doesn't mean a hill of beans to you unless we've come forward in our hearts. God, send your Spirit upon us to break our hearts."

As Keith openly poured out his heart, the night seemed to ignite with an even stronger sense of God's presence. Then he said, "I feel there's somebody here that the Lord has told to share before this body. It might be a faculty member, administration, or a student. I don't know. But if the Lord's told you that you're to share, come now and do it. And make sure it's Jesus. And Holy Spirit, I ask that you'd control it. That you don't let this turn into soulishness."

As Keith opened up the microphone it was almost as if the very atmosphere caught its breath for a moment. There were already thousands of people lying on the floor, or on their knees with their faces buried in their chairs, and in the aisles. I could hear a few nervous coughs around the arena, and it seemed like an eternity until the first person made his way slowly to the microphone to say, "God has shown me tonight that I'm not really a Christian. I've gone to church all my life, but it's just been a farce. No real commitment. I had everyone fooled. Except God."

As this person was sharing, several more people made their way to the front, slowly picking their path over everyone on the floor. These people took their turn, repenting for things like gossiping, not supporting the faculty, lack of prayer, being lukewarm, or being a phony Christian. Most were weeping, and there was a very tender spirit moving through the whole place.

For the next half hour or more, the confessions started getting more serious and more personal. The weeping that accompanied these confessions was also getting more intense— maybe because the students realized they could be expelled for what they were sharing, especially the confessions about using drugs. Two or three people confessed to smoking grass or using drugs of various kinds. But these young people seemed more concerned about getting right with God than the possible consequences of their sin. Still, I wondered what the faculty members present were thinking.

Over and above all this, though, it felt like the Spirit of God had settled on us in a thick cloud. It was a brightness you could almost see—something gentle and tender, yet infinite. I knew something powerful was taking place.

So did Keith, apparently. He'd crawled under the nine-foot grand piano to pray and cry out to God. I sensed he was getting himself out of the way to let the Holy Spirit do his work. I could barely see Keith from where I was sitting. And people kept going up to the microphone, crawling over a sea of bodies to get there.

In a few more minutes, one young man got up and confessed an area of sexual immorality in his life. He was very broken, and extremely sorry. This threw us into an even deeper level of God's dealings.

Pretty soon, a clean-cut, neatly-dressed young guy took the microphone. He was trembling and weeping so much before he spoke, I just knew he was going to say something pretty heavy. He started off slowly. Haltingly.

"You . . . you all know who I am. You think I'm one of the most spiritual students on campus. Well, I'm not. I know what I have to say may get me kicked out of school, but I believe God wants me to share it anyway. . . .

"I don't know how to confess this, except to just come right out and say it. I've been involved in homosexuality here on campus . . . and God has broken my heart tonight. I see how much I've been hurting him, hurting you—and hurting the school. I really need God to forgive me. And with his help I'm going to change. . . ."

His confession sent shock waves across the arena. Many

people burst out into fresh waves of sobbing as this precious brother continued to share. It was apparent that we were just coming to the deep level of breaking we'd been praying for since God told Keith to preach revival in Tulsa. The Holy Spirit was so strongly present—he had been "raining" on us all night, first in a gentle sprinkle, and then in a steady shower. But now it felt like the very floodgates of heaven were about to burst wide open. Whatever was about to happen, we were all willing to do what was needed—even if it took hours, or all night, or even all week to walk it through. What Keith had seen in his spirit was starting to take shape before our eyes.

And then I saw one of the men in pastoral responsibility at ORU threading his way across the stage toward the young man who was still sharing. He came alongside of him and put his arm around his shoulder.

This man took the microphone and assured the student that he really appreciated his sharing and that his sin was forgiven by the Lord. He also told him that ORU would take no disciplinary action against him, which I thought was really neat, because he seemed so sorry. Then he gave some guidelines for the rest of the meeting, in essence, saying, "We feel things like this are to be confessed privately—and we don't think it's a good idea for any of you to share personal sins openly." It seemed like a good principle and it was given in a loving way.

But something happened at that moment.

The change in the atmosphere was so immediate, it was staggering. Keith crawled out from under the piano and looked around the arena with questioning eyes. I could tell he didn't know what to think. He talked a little bit and tried to encourage everyone, but he seemed at a bit of a loss. He even said, "I don't know what happened. Everything seems different. . . ."

Something had obviously changed—but it wasn't really clear what. There was a tangible sense of a loss of conviction, and nobody else got up to share. The Holy Spirit, it seemed, had been quenched in some way, and there was nothing you could do to whip it up or bring it back. It was over. Keith managed to close by leading everyone in a few songs of praise and worship.

As I stood to sing, "I Have Decided To Follow Jesus", my heart felt like a bag of cement. There was a sick feeling in the pit of my stomach. I felt a sense of terrible loss. Like something great had *almost* happened.

Keith closed with "Easter Song" and went straight to his dressing room. By the time I got there, he was on the floor—sobbing.

After a while, Winkie came in to talk.

"What did I do wrong?" Keith cried. "How did I grieve the Holy Spirit?" Keith was devastated. He told Winkie that he hadn't felt *anything* while he was ministering—that he had no sense of what God was doing. Then at the end, he knew something went wrong, but he didn't know what. He figured he must have blown it in some way.

Winkie tried to comfort him. "You're not to blame because you didn't *feel* anything. You preached, you sang, and then you got out of the way to let God do what he wanted to do. What happened was something totally out of your hands—the power of it and the disappointment of it. You were just a vessel God wanted to express revival through."

"Revival? Winkie . . . was it *revival?*"

Winkie had been in at least two real revivals. In answer to Keith's question, he nodded. "The exact same thing was starting to happen tonight that I've seen happen before, when whole communities were broken wide open to God in short periods of time. The same sense of the presence of God. The same conviction. Tonight was awesome—a sovereign move of God. I feel like it could have gone on—not just in time, but in effect—but something grieved the Spirit of God."

"I know," Keith said, "it seemed to change after people were told what to say and what not to. . . ."

Winkie interrupted him. "Keith, we need to be careful. We can't sin the sin of judgment. We just have to leave the whole thing in God's hands."

Winkie did say he had thought a bit of teaching as the confessions were going on probably would have been good. That perhaps *everyone* who needed to repent of sexually related sin could have been asked to stand along with the last guy. Then one person would not have had to stand alone to confess a sin others probably shared—and they all could have been prayed for together. Winkie thought the move of God would have continued then.

"But it was almost impossible to get to the stage," he said, "with all the bodies everywhere. And you were under the piano. I didn't feel a sense from the Lord to say or do anything, and neither did any of the other leaders I came with. It was God on the loose, and none of us wanted to interfere. When God moves like that you don't even want to breathe wrong. . . ."

There was a knock at the door. The ORU administration was ready to talk with Keith about the possibility of further meetings. Keith and Winkie met with them backstage. The administration expressed their appreciation for what they said were wonderful meetings. But they didn't think they should go on any further. They were right. It was over.

•

"Grace By Which I Stand"

Hawaii. 1979

OUR MOOD WAS A BIT GLUM AS WE LEFT TULSA AND HEADED toward east Texas. We'd decided to stop in and visit Winkie on our way back to California. We were in need of a little rest—and an encouraging word. Keith seemed especially "down", and I wondered what it would take to bring him out of it.

As we headed towards Lindale, eighty miles east of Dallas, the interstate highway was bordered on each side with huge vistas of open, green fields. There were enough truck-stop diners, backyard oil pumps, and herds of cattle to remind us every mile we drove that we were in the Lone Star State. When we turned off into Lindale, we were amazed that Texas was so lush. There were big beautiful oaks hung with clumps of mistletoe. There were piney woods and many little lakes.

There wasn't a tumble weed in sight!

Winkie had told us all about this unique little community out in the middle of nowhere. Several well-known ministries had chosen to put roots down in the area—Youth With A Mission, David Wilkerson and World Challenge, Dallas Holm and his band Praise, the Agape Force, and Calvary Commission. Even Leonard Ravenhill and Barry McGuire lived out here. We didn't know if God had some kind of "master plan" for the area, but we were interested in making the rounds.

One of the very first people Keith wanted to visit once we arrived was David Wilkerson, whose story was told in *The Cross and The Switchblade.* He was also known internationally for founding Teen Challenge, a successful rehabilitation ministry for teens. We'd read another of his books, *Debs, Dolls, and Dope,* and it had inspired us to keep helping difficult people at a time when we felt like giving up. He'd also just rocked the Christian world on its heels with his prophetic book, *The Vision,* about God's coming judgment of America and the Church.

As we drove through the iron gates of David Wilkerson's Twin Oaks Ranch, we were *very* impressed. Nestled on a few hundred acres of lush green pastures, with three lakes, there were over twenty ministry houses, several offices, and even a gymnasium. We met David Wilkerson in his office, quite a bit in awe that this man who was being so mightily used of God had agreed to meet with us.

David greeted us warmly. He was tall and thin, and his glasses had dark-to-light shading, which gave him a hip big city look. Keith got right to the point. He told him what had just happened at ORU and shared his concerns. Keith believed the Lord was brokenhearted over what happened on that last night—and he was confused over how to respond. David seemed to agree that God probably had much more in mind than actually happened.

Next, we went over to meet Leonard Ravenhill. After reading his books for two years, and talking to him on the phone from Tulsa, we couldn't wait to meet him face-to-face. I must admit I was a little apprehensive about meeting him. I thought, *This man is so spiritual he'll see right through me. He'll know every sin I've even thought about committing.*

When we met Leonard, however, my fears melted immediately. Leonard Ravenhill had such warm fatherly eyes! And he looked so distinguished, with a full head of thick gray hair and a friendly smile.

When he invited us into his living room, Keith stepped right up to him and gave him a big bear hug.

"I've wanted to meet you!" he said exuberantly.

"Well, I've wanted to meet *you!*" Leonard said, returning Keith's embrace.

When we met Leonard's wife, Martha, she was wearing a freshly-pressed, shirtwaist dress and her hair was pinned up in a neat little bun. She immediately offered us some English tea and an assortment of delicious, homemade cookies.

We sat on their sofa, and Keith began to pour out his heart right away. Keith's upset over what happened at ORU had been brewing, and he was very agitated now as he recounted all the details.

"Leonard, let's you and me drive back up to Tulsa and kneel before the Prayer Tower and ask God to throw it down!"

"Oh, no!" Leonard said, with a bit of a chuckle in his voice. "If we did that, it might fall on *us!*"

Leonard told Keith that, even though the move of God may actually have been hindered, the Bible clearly warns us not to raise our hand against God's anointed.

"When you were at ORU, you bared your heart to them, Keith. And the ones God was working on in that meeting—even if they live to be older than I am—will never forget that Saturday night when God spoke and men began to confess."

We must have stayed for well over an hour, and by the time we left we knew it wouldn't be our last visit with the Ravenhills.

Besides the personal turmoil Keith was feeling about his time at ORU, by now some "shock waves" from Keith's time there had started to fan out across the nation. In Tulsa itself, the secular newspaper, *Tulsa World,* ran a report on the last night of Keith's ministry—mentioning the way the confessions were suddenly stopped. Christian magazines would run reports too—and some were labeling Keith as a "fiery young prophet". But for now, all Keith wanted to do was put ORU behind him and enjoy the fellowship of all the wonderful people we were meeting in Lindale, Texas.

By this time, we'd found out that we really weren't in Lindale. That's just where the nearest post office happened to be. We were actually in an even smaller place called Garden Valley—a good ten miles from Lindale. Since we were still hoping to move out of the city, we decided to look around as long as we were in the area. But it was hard to imagine moving to Texas—of all places—when we'd grown up on the west coast.

Actually, we'd heard that an old friend of Keith's had a ranch in the area and decided to go see him. Keith first met him when he was a Hollywood hippie record company executive—and before either of them were Christians. After he became a Christian, he'd lived in his van in front of our house on Dolorosa Street for almost three months while we helped him pull his life together. Eventually he'd come here to get some training from the Agape Force and then he bought some land in the area.

Keith got directions to the property—but we got a little lost and just drove around enjoying the beautiful countryside. We came upon a large, sweeping field and out in the middle of it was a huge, wooden water wheel. Right behind it sat a log ranch house. What a picture! Keith and I both spotted it at the same time.

"Look at *that*," Keith exclaimed.

"Beautiful!"

Spontaneously, Keith prayed right out loud.

"Lord Jesus, that property needs to be used for you. We claim it for your kingdom!"

Then we had a good laugh, because we usually didn't run around "claiming" things—but that was how the prayer had sprung out of Keith's heart. As we drove on, we kept looking for his friend's property.

When we finally found the right driveway, we pulled in and his friend gave us a "tour". There was a beautiful ranch house with three bedrooms, sitting on 140 acres. As we walked around we found out it had a small chicken coop and two barns—one of them, two stories high. We came around the south side of the ranch house and were about to leave—when we saw it!

"Look at that!" Keith nearly shouted.

"It's the water wheel!" I laughed.

"Can you believe it? This is the land we prayed for a few minutes ago!"

Since the property bordered two highways, we didn't immediately see that side of it. We looked at each other, wondering if it was just an unusual coincidence, or if the Lord was trying to speak to us about moving into this area. Later Keith went back and told his friend he thought the Lord wanted us to buy his property. The only problem was, it wasn't for sale.

In the midst of all the intensity of this trip, one of the funniest moments we'd had in a long time just dropped on us out of nowhere. Maybe it was a little, humorous gift from the Lord. Keith and I were lying around in our hotel room talking about how Christians—ourselves included—could be so fickle in their faith. God miraculously delivers our souls from the jaws of destruction—and as soon as the going gets tough, we quickly forget how bad our pre-Christian life was! The first thing we do is look back to our old life with hungry eyes.

"It's just like the people of Israel," Keith said. "They're oppressed and dying in Egypt, so God sends Moses to deliver them. God even parts the Red Sea and feeds them manna from heaven every day. But all they do is grumble and complain!"

"Boy," I said, "that sure sounds like me sometimes."

"I can just hear them out there on their way to the Promised Land," Keith said, chuckling, "walking around and whining, 'I wanna go back to Egypt'!"

Then Keith put on his best Israeli accent and said, "So . . . you wanna go back to Egypt?"

That started it! We began throwing verses back and forth at each other, laughing ourselves silly over the trivial things that sometimes turn our hearts away from the Lord. . . .

So you wanna go back to Egypt,
Where it's warm and secure.
Are you sorry you bought the one-way ticket
When you thought you were sure?
You wanted to live in the Land of Promise,
But now it's getting so hard.
Are you sorry you're out here in the desert
'Stead of your own backyard?

Eating leeks and onions by the Nile.
Ooh, what breath! But dining out in style.
Ooh! My life's on the skids.
Give me the pyramids!

Well, there's nothing to do but travel.
And we sure travel a lot.
'Cause it's hard to keep your feet from moving
when
The sand gets so hot.
And in the morning it's manna hotcakes.
We snack on manna all day.
And they sure had a winner last night for dinner-
Flaming manna souffle.

Well, we once complained
For something new to munch.
The ground opened up
And had some of us for lunch.
Ooh! Such fire and smoke.
Can't God even take a joke? . . . Huh? . . . (No!)

We didn't know it at the time, but this song would play a very important part in Keith's next album—a subject that, in its own way, was starting to be a cause of real concern for him.

Once we got back to California, Keith was once again trying to sort through some major questions. Moving was one of them. We still had the dream of having a ranch in the country to help people get their lives together. Was it supposed to be in Texas?

Another big question for us was what to do about Keith's next record? Keith's contract with Sparrow had been fulfilled, and his ministry was soaring with huge record sales between his first two top-selling albums. He wasn't "unknown" anymore and could negotiate a very sweet deal with Sparrow or with another company if he wanted to. Only, now, he felt very strongly that the Lord wanted him to downplay money and not even charge for his ministry. Keith also had mounting questions about the Christian recording industry and what his involvement should be. Sparrow wanted him to sign on with them again and other record companies were vying for his next album, as well. Keith really needed to hear from the Lord because one thing seemed certain—he was going to be making more records.

In April, just a few weeks after the event at ORU, Keith decided to go away for a long weekend to fast and pray. He drove a few hours up to Big Bear, which was high up in the San Bernardino mountains. When he came home, he shared his journal with me and I could easily see in my mind's eye what the few days had been like for him. . . .

Keith had checked into the hotel and made a long prayer list. The core question was, "What is my calling and ministry?" The weight and responsibility of trying to be a full-time "pastor" to seventy people—many with great needs—and at the same time trying to fulfill his call to the Church at large was crushing him. Keith was wearing many hats at once and wanted to know what his priorities should be. He listed everything he was doing and asked God if he should scratch anything off: evangelist, revivalist, musician, singer, pastor, overseer, organizer. Keith also prayed about the future of the Last Days community, a possible move to Texas and who would go, the recording situation, and the motives and priorities of the ever-growing *Last Days Newsletter*.

Texas, somehow, was beginning to seem right. But would Keith's friend even sell us his ranch? And if he did, where would we get the money to buy it? We'd poured almost everything back into keeping everyone fed and paying the rent on all the houses.

Keith was also concerned about me. He prayed about my ministry and calling, and for a certainty of my salvation, since I'd never had a breakthrough during "The Revival".

It was a long, tough weekend since Keith was feeling more

bored and "cold" in spirit rather than "on fire" for the Lord, which he'd been preaching about.

APRIL 17, 1979

Here I am, waiting.

Scared, bored, hungry. Unbelieving, frustrated, even mad at God for making me go through this.

I preach against "Easy Grace" and then when it isn't easy I get mad at God for making it *just* the way I preach it!!! Oh! The total hypocrisy of it all!!

Please forgive me Daddy, break me and for Your sake, speak to me now please!!

Lord Jesus, please I want answers and help with these areas. I've never been a follower, I've been a leader all my life, but now I want to follow You.

Keith had to fight through it for a long while, but in the end, the sense of God's presence finally came:

I am helpless, more than since I first got saved. Even more so, because I have no Christian hope in myself!

I write, I can't pray. I scream inside, but not enough to cry. When I cry I get so excited I'm finally crying that I quit crying. Help! I'll try and pray again. Glory to Jesus . . .

Angels are here with me. The room is full . . .

What God really seemed to be after on this weekend was more of Keith himself. Was he willing to lay down everything for the Lord, including me? Including Josiah? What Keith had read several months ago, about Rees Howells giving up his own son, came back to him. Keith had to struggle with being willing not only to lay down his own life for the gospel, but also laying down his love for me and Josiah.

Another quote, by Joseph Parker, whom Leonard Ravenhill had written about in *Why Revival Tarries* came to him: "The man whose little sermon is 'repent' sets himself against his age and will, for the time being, be battered mercilessly by the age whose moral tone he challenges. There is but one end for such a man, 'Off with his head!' You had better not try to preach repentance until you have pledged your head to heaven."

Keith's retreat encompassed the day of Josiah's seven-month birthday. Keith wept for a long time about the question of his willingness to let the Lord have full rights to Josiah—no matter what. But when he finally came to the place of willingness, he wrote a song on his guitar in the form of a prayer—weeping the whole time.

The song lyrics were written in Keith's journal, but he didn't want me to read them. He took his journal back and opened it to the right page, then grabbed his guitar and sat cross-legged on the floor in front of me. He wept again as he sang:

Well, I pledge my head to heaven for the gospel.
And I ask no man on earth to fill my needs.
Like the sparrow up above,
I am enveloped in His love.
And I trust Him like those little ones
He feeds.

Well, I pledge my wife to heaven for the gospel.
Though our love each passing day
Just seems to grow. . . .

Tears were misting my vision now. And a hard lump tightened in my throat. He kept singing,

As I told her when we wed,
I'd surely rather be found dead,
Than to love her more than the One
Who saved my soul.

I'm your child,
And I wanna be in your family forever!
I'm your child, and I'm gonna follow you no matter
Whatever the cost,
Well I'm gonna count all things loss.

Well, I pledge my son to heaven for the gospel,
Though he's kicked and beaten,
Ridiculed and scorned.
I will teach him to rejoice
And lift a thankful, praising voice.
And to be like Him who bore the nails
And crown of thorns.

Well, I've had my chance to gain the world
And to live just like a king,
But without Your love
It doesn't mean a thing!

Well, I pledge my son . . . I pledge my wife . . .
I pledge my head to heaven.
I pledge my son . . . I pledge my wife . . .
I pledge my head to heaven for the gospel.

When Keith finished singing he looked at me waiting for my response. But how do you respond to a song like that? I was proud to be married to a man so committed to God that he would pay whatever price obedience might require—even if it cost him his wife and son. On the other hand, it wasn't some abstract ideal of commitment some stranger happened to be singing about. It was *my* husband, singing about me and our son. I told Keith, "The song is incredible."

But later, I prayed that God would give me the same grace to let go of Keith and Josiah, if I ever needed to.

One of the conclusions Keith announced when he came back from Big Bear was a surprise to everyone. Keith said he sensed that God had prepared some of our "family" to take their next step forward in their journey with the Lord. So Keith started meeting with each person to find out who was supposed to stay and who was being called out. Because of Keith's deep love for everyone, the process seemed to be more painful for him than anyone else. But Keith felt he was supposed to concentrate more on two things: *The Last Days Newsletter* and getting back out on the road to minister. The questions about Texas were still up in the air.

Keith also made a vow to the Lord to read ten chapters of the Bible, and spend one hour in prayer every day. He realized the spiritual foundation in his life had to be strengthened to support the weight of the ministry God was giving him.

APRIL 22, 1979

I'm not listening to my flesh which says, "Oh, you're becoming legal! God won't honor this forced prayer stuff!" Well, there are times when the Spirit's grieved by my "clock-watching" soul, but there are good times of prayer and I believe they will form into godly habits. Lord, please help your servant be consistent . . .

Lack of prayer is sin.
Legal prayer is sad.
***Freedom* is best.**

But over the next few weeks, with constant interruptions and distractions, Keith didn't always meet the required reading and prayer time he'd set for himself. When that happened he knew he was breaking his vow to God. That was too much for him to handle. He started slipping into depression.

One day, a good friend helped Keith see that, although God wanted him to spend time with him each day, the vows he made were keeping him under condemnation. He taught Keith about meditating on scripture as a way to focus in on the Word. Keith wrote, "My vows were too hard. . . . Please Jesus, let me out of them 'legally' and let me develop into a man of God through your discipline. My intentions . . . were to get to know you and I want to do that any way I can."

Even with this new bit of understanding, Keith seemed to alternate between feeling like he had no vision, and feeling like his vision was too big to really be of God. For my part, I was still stuck back at the place of wondering if I was *ever* going to have a breakthrough, or if I would ever feel confident that God accepted me. The beginning of our answers came totally unexpected.

In his typical way, Keith picked up the phone one night at about 11 p.m. and called Winkie just to say hi. It was 1 a.m. in Texas, but Winkie was up packing for a ministry trip to Hawaii. Keith immediately said, "Wow, can me and Mel come with you? Do you want me to sing?"

Winkie understood Keith's heart and knew he wasn't into dropping hints or trying to manipulate his way anywhere. Keith just really wanted to spend some time with Winkie—so, like a little kid, he kind of invited himself along. Somehow we managed to put together a few last-minute concerts to justify the trip, and within days we were off to Hawaii.

Once we landed in Hawaii things started happening quickly. At the Honolulu airport someone met us and, in true Hawaiian style, hung flowered leis around our necks. We went directly to a pastor's house to rest and catch up on our jet lag. Keith took a nap in the bedroom while I lay on the living room couch alone, amazed at the beauty of the Hawaiian scene just outside the window.

I could see tall, flowered palms and hear lots of birds chirping away at the crystal clear sky. I wasn't thinking about anything in particular, when a thought came to me. Actually, it seemed like more than a thought. It seemed like a still small voice, and it said, "I am going to give you the desire of your heart. You're going to have a little girl."

I didn't hear it audibly, but it was so clear I was taken aback. I wasn't even pregnant—nor was I even thinking about that subject. I thought it might be the Lord, but I wasn't sure. Recently I'd been wondering if I even knew how to hear him at all. It could have just been my own drifting thoughts. I figured time would tell.

Keith's last minute concert in Honolulu that night was packed with people. I decided to do a little exploring while Keith played, and I found a room upstairs in the back of the sanctuary. Actually, it was the singing that first drew me there.

As I peeked through the half-open door, I saw several

beautiful Hawaiian women in a time of worship and praise. As they sang, they were praising God with Hawaiian dance. The gentle flowing movements of their bodies and their delicate footwork seemed, to me, to be what God must have intended when he created dance. It was pure and sanctified for him. And their hands were speaking adoring words of worship like a beautiful, holy, sign language. I'd never seen anything like it.

Then they burst into a jubilant song of praise and celebration. I tore myself away, feeling a little guilty for sneaking off from the concert—but I could have stayed there all night.

It was ironic to me that I was "in ministry" and traveling all over the country with my husband who was a top Christian recording artist—and yet I wished I could break free and worship the Lord in joy and freedom like these ladies in the back room of a church.

Next, we went to Maui and then on to Kona to visit Youth With A Mission, which provided housing and hospitality for us on their base. They were in the process of starting a Christian university, and Loren Cunningham, the founder of YWAM, spent some time with us. We'd never met Loren before but we were immediately impressed with his gracious warmth and breadth of vision. He walked us around the "campus", which he saw more clearly in his mind at that moment, since everything was in the beginning stages.

Loren would point and say things like, "Over there will be the 'Plaza of the Nations'—representing every nation on earth!" It was actually a big rocky field, but he went on to paint such a vivid picture I could imagine it "finished" as he was talking. We were both excited about Loren's desire to equip Christians from around the world—spiritually, culturally, intellectually, and professionally—to use their God-given abilities to communicate the Good News in all nations.

Something in our hearts leapt just listening to Loren talk. Was it just that he had confidence in what God had shown him? Or was God stirring something else in our hearts? Before we left, Keith told Loren he'd been having trouble in some areas and knew he needed men of God to speak into his life.

"Loren, would you be open to me calling you sometimes, when I need counsel or advice?"

"I'd be glad to help you in any way I can," said Loren, with a warm smile.

In one way, Keith was crying out for somebody to come along and be a "father in the Lord" to him—and he sensed a father's heart in Loren.

Some friends of ours from California lived about twenty miles from the YWAM base, and we spent the last few days of our trip in their guest house. We'd first met Jimmy and Carol Owens through Buck and Annie Herring. They were the parents of our friend, Jamie Owens. At their home, we sat down to a big spaghetti dinner, and stayed up late talking. I really liked them and felt especially close to Carol. Her maturity in the Lord and spunky directness, laced with humor, made her easy to talk to. And I sure needed someone to talk to.

In the morning, I got up before Keith and slipped into the kitchen. Carol was there alone. She made some coffee and we sat at the kitchen table in the warm morning sun. Very quickly, I found myself pouring my heart out to her.

"I asked Jesus into my heart four years ago," I confided, "and even stood up at your musical, 'If My People', to make my first public declaration of faith. But, I don't know if I *really* love the Lord."

Then I just started crying. This was the first time I'd said out loud the words that often drove me crazy in the middle of the night: "Carol, I don't even know if I'm saved. . . ."

"Why would you feel that way?" she asked, evenly.

I told her that since the time of "The Revival", I'd been feeling more and more lost. That I knew my heart wasn't pure enough and that I was still undisciplined in many areas. I just wasn't living up to God's standards and I knew it.

"I usually mix sound for Keith at his concerts," I went on, "so I've heard his message over and over. Sometimes I just want to crawl under the soundboard and disappear. I've stood for so many of his altar calls I'm sure God must think I'm crazy by now. I just don't know what to do."

When I finished Carol reached over and laid her hand on mine, giving it a gentle squeeze. She said, "Melody, don't you hear what you're saying? This is so much *law*. Where's the grace?"

"Grace?"

Then she picked up her Bible, which had been lying on the kitchen table and turned to Galatians.

"Listen to this," she said. "'You have been severed from Christ, you who are seeking to be justified by *law*; you have fallen from grace.'"

"Yeah, but so many people just trample on God's grace—running around in sin and thinking it's okay."

"Maybe so, but that's not what *you're* doing. Melody, you need to receive God's grace—not deny it."

I knew that "easy believism" grieved the Lord. I certainly

didn't want to be too easy on myself. But on the other hand, I wondered if God was trying to tell me something through this trip—first, through the freedom of the beautiful worship dancers in Honolulu, and now through Carol.

Later in the day Jimmy and Carol talked with me and Keith, repeating much of what Carol had shared with me, and more. They listened to Keith's many difficult questions and patiently gave him answers from the scriptures. The spirit of it was kind of like "mom and dad" having a heart-to-heart talk with their kids.

Something was getting through.

We returned home with high hopes. Something had happened to us in Hawaii—meeting Loren, our special time with Winkie and the Owens. Just the beauty and grace of the islands helped put Keith a little more at ease from all the confusion he'd been trudging through. For a long time, I held onto the memory of the graceful, dark-haired women worshipping the Lord so openly.

A short time later, Keith wrote:

JULY 2, 1979

For the first time in months, I awoke with peace—*Real* Peace.

I can seek the Lord now, for an angel from God has come to minister to me. I love God so much, my heart overflows with quiet, gentle joy—my eyes water with tears for the peace in my soul. My faith is refreshed. My desire to commune with God and intercede for souls is renewed with power! My thirst for God's Word has greatly increased. The prison doors have swung open of themselves. The shackles have fallen off to the ground. My heart is bursting with joy and *hope! Oh! I can hope again.*

Jesus I'm so grateful that there was no formula—no secret way to regain my peace. No amount of Bible reading, or *forced* prayer time (on my part) brought this state on. But you in answer to the desperate crying out of my heart, came and rescued me from the bondage of works and self—spirituality of glorying in your presence. You want me to share your glory— but only as a gift, not as a result of *my* efforts, but as a result of your goodness, mercy, and love for me—

Thank you for helping me hang on!

1982

My mom moves to the ranch. 1981

Texas-style baptism. 1981

Keith at the piano.

In the studio with Bill Maxwell.

"I Want To Be More Like Jesus"

The big move. 1979

KEITH WROTE IN HIS JOURNAL ON AUGUST 3, 1979,
"We're moving in about a month to Texas!"

A quick phone call from Keith's friend in Texas set the wheels in motion. He prayed and felt he was to sell the ranch to Keith. Now the only problem was, where in the world would we get the money?

We needed a down payment of $31,500 in thirty days. But we knew if the Lord wanted us to move he would provide the money by the time we needed it.

Never in a million years would we have chosen to move to Texas. But besides the fact that we'd finally be able to move out of the suburbs of southern California, the main draw was the opportunity for relationships with others who understood the call on our lives. Keith felt like he'd finally found spiritual fellowship with men who were brothers in the Lord and some who were even "fathers in the faith". Even the small YWAM base, a few miles away, was neat because of the bonding Keith had felt with Loren Cunningham in Hawaii.

There were also many practical reasons to move to east Texas. We could get a lot more land for our money out there than we could in southern California. And Texas was centrally located, which meant all of our telephone and travel expenses would be much less. Most important, it seemed like God was leading us there.

But the question of the down payment remained.

To lighten the load for our move to Texas, plus make some much-needed money, Keith and I went back to our "financial roots". We had a big yard sale!

Actually, the sale spilled out over the whole lawn of our house and onto the lawn of the Harvey House next door. We went through everything we owned to see what we could do without— and so did the rest of our Last Days family. We ran ads in the newspapers and put signs up on all the nearby street corners. There was too much stuff to set up and tear down every weekend so we stayed "open" seven-days-a-week.

We had clothing, furniture, books, records—well, you name it, we had it. I sold my $200 rabbit coat for $75, and all of my silver and turquoise jewelry for almost nothing. We kept marking everything down until we were almost giving it away. It must have been one of the biggest and longest-running yard sales in history.

As Keith and I spent many hours talking to "customers" and making sales, Josiah was just learning how to walk. In his little cloth diaper, we'd send him back and forth between us on the front lawn with wild applause for every faltering step he took. We also spent a lot of time keeping him from eating the rocks he kept picking up. People never stopped commenting on how adorable he was, with his full head of flaxen blond curls and his big blue eyes. What they didn't know was that he had a little brother or sister on the way! I had now "officially" discovered I was pregnant with our second child. I couldn't help but wonder if what I thought the Lord had spoken to me in Hawaii would really come to pass.

While we were trying to raise money, we'd also been fasting and praying for a miracle. We'd even talked about getting a bank loan if we ended up needing one—and as the deadline day approached, it looked like we would.

One day, I noticed Keith was pacing much more than normal, so I finally asked him about it. "Keith, are you okay?"

"I'm going to have to apply for that loan. Today's Thursday and the money's due on Tuesday. We've only got five days left. But I don't *want* to get a loan. I seem to have lost my peace about it. I need to pray more today."

That night we had a special prayer meeting, and the Lord seemed to speak to Keith out of the book of Malachi. Keith was surprised but excited as he read: " . . . test me now in this . . . if I will not open for you the windows of heaven, and pour out for you a blessing until there is no more need."

"I think the Lord's telling us to forget the loan and trust him to supply the money by Tuesday."

Everyone was really excited, but I was apprehensive. How could we know for sure that scripture meant God was saying "no" on the loan? I wondered how Keith could feel so certain. I did my best to believe.

Over the next few days the Lord did fulfill his promise to provide. To our surprise, some of our good friends became part of the answer to our prayers. We were really blessed and humbled to receive $4,000 from Buck and Annie, $4,500 from Matthew Ward, and $1,000 from Sparrow Records. What generosity! Sure enough, by Tuesday the Lord had supplied the full $31,500.

The day the moving vans came, we were—as usual—in a frenzy of activity. What was left of seven households of furniture had to be moved, and there were mountains of large, cardboard boxes on our front lawn. It took two whole days for the vans to load everything up.

People-wise, we were a pared-down remnant of about twenty-five, including Wayne and Kathleen, who were now engaged to be married, Francine, Carol, Martin, Pam, Cindy and Kelly, and Michelle. A few newer people were moving with us, too—Sharon Madere from Arizona, and the twins Larry and Terry DeGraff. Larry and Terry were graphic artists who'd been doing a great job keeping *The Last Days Newsletter* looking good. Several people were scheduled to get training at another ministry including Jerry Bryant.

Finally, it was goodbye to the house on Dolorosa Street—and the other houses, too. In fact, we already had a buyer for Harvey House. They'd all served us well as we stretched their walls with people and activity.

I stood in the empty living room of our little yellow house and looked around with a twinge in my heart. We'd be renting it out now. I thought of all Keith and I were leaving behind—our families, many old friends, and all we'd known as a couple. And yet we had new hope and vision for the future. We also had our children—Josiah and Dawn and a new baby on the way—and there were all the beautiful people who wanted to come with us.

As I turned to walk out of our front door for the last time, I really wasn't sad after all. I felt ready for the future—whatever it might hold.

All twenty-five of us arrived in Texas, 1,500 miles later, and poured into the Ranch House on our new property. It was quite a change of style from California, with its high-pitched ceiling in the living room, the new bright red carpeting, and the exposed rustic logs all through the house. The kitchen was huge, with a long counter that would make a perfect serving line for all of us. And speaking of "all of us", it was going to be quite a squeeze after living in so many separate houses in California!

Fourteen single girls—two with babies—*all* shared a large bedroom at one end of the house. Right next to them, Keith and I shared our bedroom with Josiah and his crib. The single guys lived at the other end of the house, while the other married couple and their children shared "The Fish Room"—a small enclosed den with a huge built-in aquarium. It was a cozy beginning, to say the least.

Along with everyone else, Keith and I faced some new and interesting challenges. Behind the main wall on one side of our bedroom were fourteen girls—so we certainly couldn't talk very loud. And on the other side of another wall was some extremely loud bundling and mailing equipment that often ran all night. We shared "the blue bathroom" with the other couple—and whoever else needed it. It was across the hall from our bedroom, right off the main living room—which had become offices. In the morning, the trick was to slip into the bathroom without being stopped by someone in the office who had a question.

In the garage, we placed the Multi-1250 printing press we'd purchased to handle the ever-growing newsletter—and the collating machine Wayne had "invented" out of an egg-beater motor and some nylon line. It helped us gather all the pages of the newsletter together, instead of doing it by hand.

Ranch living was also light-years away from suburban living. As "city folks" we had a lot to learn. We quickly found that the neighbors didn't "take kindly" to people who don't tend their land—and mowing 140 acres was no small chore!

We quickly acquired some ranch machinery—tractors, a bush-hog and a few funky old trucks. Still a city boy at heart, Keith bought one tractor with an enclosed glass shell, which allowed for air-conditioning and a stereo! So we were off and running. The land was planted in hay and Keith loved to get out there and help cut and bale. There was always work to be done—keeping the fences mended and the fields fertilized. And the first time we burnt our fields, which is what they do in Texas, we nearly had a runaway fire!

And what was a farm without animals? Our long-standing dream of living off the land seemed to be on the verge of finally coming true. But over the months, lots of crazy things happened to show us just how inept we were at trying to become Texas ranchers.

Keith went to a local auction and bought thirty-five head of cattle, and in a short time we had over one hundred head. One day, a few of our guys tried to perform a simple surgery on one of the bulls. The bull died from shock. We didn't want this perfectly good bull to go to waste, but no one would come out to butcher it because it's illegal for them to cut up an animal that dies *before* the butcher gets there. We decided to do it ourselves.

The bull was hoisted upside down by the tractor, and soon the guys started carrying chunks of meat into the house. It was quite a scene! We had beef in the sinks and bathtubs—washing it and getting it ready to freeze.

But there was one other complication. Just before the bull died, he'd been given a shot of penicillin, which some of our people were allergic to. So we labeled the "penicillin leg" in a special way. For months, if we ate beef, we'd have two kinds! As you walked through the food line you'd see a little, hand-lettered sign that said, "Penicillin Meat", for those who needed to avoid it.

Then there was the Great Chicken Massacre. Keith bought a bunch of chickens so we could have fresh eggs. Everything was fine, until they got bad throat infections and couldn't swallow. We had two choices: kill them, or let them starve to death. Keith decided to make the slaughter a ministry event—sort of a cross-cultural experience for all of us city folks.

Keith gathered us in the kitchen to make the announcement: "Death is a reality on a ranch. If we want fried chicken, a chicken has to die. We've only seen the sanitized, supermarket version—covered in Saran Wrap with a price sticker on its belly. Someone else did the dirty work. If you're willing to eat a chicken you should be willing to kill one!"

All I can say is, I was glad I had to go see my baby doctor the morning of the slaughter! But I saw the pictures and heard the stories, and it went down in LDM history as the day the feathers flew!

We also did some crazy things "just for fun", since entertainment was limited out in the country. We bought a few riding horses, and one day Keith decided it would be "interesting" to bring one of them into the kitchen, just to see what would happen. We found out real quick. Everyone laughed themselves silly—even though we had a mess to clean up afterward.

Then there was the first tarantula Keith found. It was huge and hairy. He put it in a jar and wondered what to do with it. It wasn't poisonous, but it was big enough to seriously bite the kids, and needed to be disposed of. Keith decided to put the jar into the microwave. Everyone in the kitchen immediately took sides— the "that-would-be-a-horrible-yucky-thing-to-do" side consisted mostly of the girls, myself included. But "the boys" won, and Keith did the honors. Luckily the jar had a cover on it.

And once someone took a video camera into the barn all night to try and tape a calf being born. But "mom" refused to go into labor with the bright lights and gathering crowd. After having a baby myself—and feeling very big with this second pregnancy—I didn't blame her. I went home to bed!

We were having a great time living in the country, but we knew God had brought us here for greater purposes. One purpose, we'd thought, was to open another home to help people needing rehabilitation—and we intended to do that right away. But after praying, we just didn't have a sense of peace about it. In fact, God seemed to tell us specifically to go into a "holding pattern"—like an airplane circling a runway without landing.

That left us with a big question mark. Working in rehabilitation was our main reason for wanting to get out of the city. Now what were we supposed to do with all this land, besides farm it?

Since we weren't doing rehabilitation anymore, a lot of the rules we'd needed for people coming to us right off the streets were no longer necessary. In fact, right after the revival in California, we got rid of things like demerits and "buddies"—but relaxing things was a continual process as we grew in understanding. And in California, many people who decided to leave ended up back out on the streets taking drugs or just forsaking the Lord. So Keith's first instinct was to try to talk people into staying. But he came to a point in Texas where he told me, "The next time somebody wants to leave, I'm just gonna help them pack their bags. I won't even give my opinion unless they ask for it!"

Even if the ranch was a question mark, God's other purposes in bringing us to Texas became clear quickly. The fellowship with other Christians who had the same type of broad vision and drive was an enormous blessing to Keith. His friendship with Winkie Pratney made a big impact on him, especially in the area he had been having the hardest time with—his lack of self-discipline.

Once, when they were gone together for a few weeks on a long ministry trip, Keith voiced his concerns. "I just can't get my 'act' together. I feel so lazy sometimes. If I really loved God, I'd have more discipline, right?"

Winkie, who'd now had a chance to "observe" Keith up close, just smiled. But he gave him some serious advice. "There's nothing wrong with your spiritual life. But your physical laziness is bringing you down."

He pointed out that Keith had developed a "Bohemian", night-person lifestyle—up too late, in bed too long, not eating right, rarely making a bed or washing a dish.

"I can see how the enemy can attach a lot of lies to those areas of weakness—but your bad habits don't 'prove' you don't love the Lord," Winkie encouraged him. "But they're an open door for you to feel condemned. That's why you need to work at changing them."

When Winkie gave Keith his first "instructions"—to get up at a reasonable hour like 9 a.m., and to make his bed—Keith flinched. "That's what maids are for," he protested. After all, they were staying in hotels.

But Keith did it. And every morning Keith called Winkie in to "inspect" his room, to keep himself accountable.

At Winkie's advice, Keith also tried to eat a more balanced diet and pick up after himself. These were simple things. But as Winkie told him, "The grind of the road can be destructive to your spiritual life, Keith. It's important to be disciplined—and it's got to start with the basic areas—or else you burn-out. Or you'll 'shallow-out'."

All this went against Keith's natural grain. Keith didn't even practice the piano! Sometimes at the opening of a concert, he'd sit at the piano and let his fingers run all over the keys. People would clap, thinking, I guess, that he was being moved by the Spirit— but he was just loosening up his fingers! When it came to discipline, Keith was always trying to hit the "ultimate leap of faith"—but he'd miss the mark, of course, and crash. Winkie's advice to take "faith-sized bites" struck a chord, and Keith was willing to do whatever it took.

He wrote:

I used to think discipline and self-control was a natural by-product of a supernatural holiness and revival. But now I see that lack of self-discipline is keeping my holiness (which I already have in Jesus) from controlling my life and coming to the surface. This is a brand-new view, and I believe I've isolated the enemy's greatest stronghold in my life at this time. . . .

Discipline is not holiness—nor the way to holiness—it just helps you maintain it.

Keith and I were also continuing to write new songs and felt another album coming together. Besides the songs "So You Wanna Go Back To Egypt" and "I Pledge My Head To Heaven", there were songs like "Lies", "Unless The Lord Builds The House", and "I Want To Be More Like Jesus" which we wrote with Kelly Willard. It was time to go back into the studio.

Keith already knew that we were supposed to do something *very* different with this third album. But what? He had already decided not to charge anything for his concerts because that was ministry. But his recordings were being sold in bookstores all across the nation. Were they "products" or "ministry"? Keith could see where his recordings might be a bit of both, but his *reason* for doing them was definitely ministry. What if someone couldn't afford to buy one—wouldn't that exclude them from ministry because they couldn't pay for it?

Actually, one big decision about this album had been made just before the move to Texas. Keith was going to be producing it—and distributing it—*totally on his own*. It all came about in very unusual circumstances. . . .

Keith had came across some pretty strong scriptures that seemed to confirm what he was already feeling in his heart. He wrote them in his journal:

"Israel's priests instruct for a price and her prophets divine for money, yet they lean on the Lord saying, 'Is not the Lord in our midst'?" Micah 3:11

"For from the least to the greatest of them, everyone is greedy for gain." Jeremiah 6:13

On top of those scriptures, Keith came across another one in the book of Isaiah that really blew his mind. He excitedly read it to me. "'Ho! Every one who thirsts, come to the waters; And you who have no money come, buy and eat. Come, buy wine and milk without money and without cost.' Isn't that heavy?"

"Yes, but what do you want to do?"

"I really want to give the gift God gave me in music *freely* as Jesus has commanded, 'Freely you have received, now freely give.'"

Keith had been ordained by the Vineyard and, as an ordained minister of the gospel, he believed that his music was just a tool to present the ministry.

And then one day Keith came to me, looking as white as a sheet.

"Mel, I've been praying, and I believe God just told me I blew it! He was wanting me to start my own company so I could give my records away and I shouldn't have re-signed with Sparrow."

"Are you serious?" I said. "What are we going to do?"

Keith had just signed a new contract with Sparrow. He had done it mostly as a reaction to being "chased" by other companies. One record company was offering to set up a fund with $100,000 in it for each album Keith would do for them. The cost of making each album would come out of that, and whatever was left over from the $100,000 per album, he could take as a personal bonus. That meant if Keith could produce an album for, say, $40,000 he could put $60,000 in his pocket—for two, three, or five albums! On top of that, they would also give him a hefty cash bonus just for signing. This was an incredible offer and a major temptation for him, because we needed money for the vision and goals of Last Days.

But Keith had seen it as a temptation, and he reacted. Another company was pursuing him too—and, of course, Sparrow also wanted him with them. In response, he turned and ran back to Sparrow and re-signed with them for a $10,000 bonus. He figured it must be God, because it wasn't as good a deal.

After Keith chose Sparrow, Bill Maxwell also told him that one record company offered him cash under the table if he could persuade Keith to sign with them. Bill told them he didn't want any part of something like that—but that he'd be glad to set up an appointment for them to talk, for free.

Keith was really in a bind. He was legally and spiritually bound to fulfill the contract he signed with Sparrow. He'd been beside himself wondering how he could stay faithful to what God was asking him to do. Finally he phoned Billy Ray and asked if we could go over to see him.

Billy Ray lived in a large house in Northridge and he answered the door. With his sandy hair and freckles, he looked boyish. As we walked into his living room, he looked very relaxed, but we were nervous. Keith had a sense that his destiny was somehow going to be affected by this man's response. It would be crazy for Billy Ray to release his biggest artist from a legally signed contract. We had no way of knowing what would happen.

Billy Ray and his wife, who were both gifted with a sense of southern hospitality, invited us to take a seat on the huge semicircular couch in their spacious living room. I stared at the Chinese screens and shifted anxiously. Keith had come, not entirely sure what he would say. After a few moments of small talk, he launched in. "I guess you're wondering why I wanted to see you tonight . . ."

"I hope everything is okay. What's on your mind?"

Keith was never one to beat around the bush. "I need to ask you to let me out of my contract."

Billy Ray just looked at Keith, silently.

I focused on a small water lily down at the corner of one of the Chinese screens, wondering what was going to happen next. Keith went on to share his heart with Billy Ray.

" . . . I blew it. God just told me to start my own label and give my records away. I'm really sorry. I don't know what to do. I know I signed a contract and I'll honor it if I need to. But I'm asking you to release me from it. I'm not going to another company. I'm starting my own. I won't even be selling my records in the bookstores."

This definitely broke the ice. They talked back and forth for a few minutes and, finally, Billy Ray said, "If God doesn't want you at Sparrow, and I try to keep you, then I'd be fighting against God. That means God will be standing against me and the whole company."

We waited to see what more he'd say.

"Keith, if you want to be released from your contract I will not hold you to it. I'll let you go."

Keith was relieved. So was I. It couldn't have turned out better. Keith was very encouraged by Billy Ray's immediate willingness to release him.

Now Keith was ready to record his third album, and do whatever the Lord had in mind for it. As the February 1980 due date for our second child approached, so did the date Keith and I were scheduled to go to Los Angeles and work with Bill Maxwell.

We decided it would be easier—and much less expensive—for us to go to California to record than to fly Bill and all the musicians out to Texas.

Keith left the ministry in the capable hands of some of our upcoming leaders while we were gone and, a short time later, flew Michelle in to give him some much-needed administrative assistance. Michelle, who was a real wiz at pulling things together, had become a very close friend to both of us.

As it turned out, our second child arrived nine days early to very happy parents, who were right in the middle of making an album! Bethany Grace was born on February 5, 1980. A little girl—just as the Lord promised me in Honolulu! And her middle name symbolized some of the precious lessons the Lord had taught us during that time. Now I knew for sure that the Lord had really spoken to me, and I took it as a very special sign of his love for me.

My delivery was much easier than with Josiah. I left the hospital within a few hours, and that night Keith and I even went out to dinner. Amazingly, within days I felt good enough to go back in the studio—with Bethany Grace in my arms.

By this time, we'd decided to call the album, *So You Wanna Go Back To Egypt*. We were really excited about being able to give this album away—but it was an enormous step of faith. One day, Keith and I were talking about the money it was going to cost to do it.

"Do we have enough money to even produce this album?" I asked.

"We may have to mortgage our house back in Woodland Hills to get enough to press about 25,000 albums. If we give them all away and run out of money, we'll just consider the album a 'limited edition'. At least I'll know I've obeyed the Lord."

Even with the prospect of having to mortgage our house, we were still excited about the album. Nobody was going to be left out because of a lack of funds—and the messages of the songs were fresh and powerful to us. As Keith said, "I think I can sum up the theme of the whole album in one word—grace!"

"Grace?" I prodded him. "I can see that in some of the songs, but others are very convicting."

"Yeah, but look how patient God is. He doesn't give up on us, even when we grumble and complain, or give up on ourselves!"

Keith said he knew some people might think the album seemed a bit sad at times. But that it was completely honest.

One night at the studio, I was sitting in a beanbag chair, cuddling Bethany Grace. It was a fairly average night—until Bob Dylan showed up to play harmonica on "I Pledge My Head To

Heaven". It was, all at once, totally incredible and very normal. We'd spent some time getting to know Bob on various occasions before we'd moved to Texas.

We'd met Bob Dylan through an elder at the Vineyard sometime after "The Revival". After that, Bob came to our house for dinner, and another day we spent some time with him at his offices near Santa Monica. In fact, during the time he was writing the songs for his album, *Slow Train Coming,* Bob pulled out some lyric sheets and showed them to us. He wanted to know what we thought—and we told him. The lyrics were great. Then Keith and I exchanged glances as if to say, *Can you believe one of the world's greatest songwriters is asking our opinion?* Maybe it was his vulnerability that bonded our hearts to his in a special way.

Bob Dylan seemed to want to know what Keith thought in other areas besides music. Although he was one of the most well-known musicians in the world, he was the same as anyone who wanted to know more about God. He was full of eager questions and fresh excitement about his spiritual discoveries. Keith loved him deeply and they talked a lot. Once, however, Keith felt he went too far in trying to make a point. Later, in his journal, he wrote with regret, "Tried to be the Holy Spirit to Bob Dylan today. . . ."

One night, we took Bob over to Buck and Annie's house along with Bill Maxwell. We listened to one of Second Chapter's new albums and some rough mixes of Bob's latest album, *Saved.* Bob would tell us that he loved to pick up hitchhikers in his beat-up old car and talk to them about the Lord—without letting them know who he was. He said he was trying to read several chapters of the Bible a day. One of the things Keith counseled Bob to do was to try and get some time off the road so he could rest and study. He did attend a Bible school at the Vineyard for a while, but it seemed impossible for him to get much time "off". Nevertheless, Keith and Bob had kept in contact after we moved to Texas, and when Keith asked him to play on this album, we were thrilled that he said yes.

This night in the studio, as Bob got ready to play the harmonica, he talked with Bill for a few minutes. He told Bill that *For Him Who Has Ears To Hear* was one of his favorite albums of all time! And he hoped the production style of this album would be similar.

It did seem, as Keith said, that all the songs tied into the theme of grace in one way or another—especially grace when we are not doing as well as we would like in our walk with the Lord.

Keith wrote "You Love The World (And You're Avoiding Me)"

while we were in California working on the album. He told me, "This may sound like the happiest song on the whole album, but it's really the saddest, for me. I wrote it as if the Lord was talking to *me*!" It was all too easy for Keith to plop in front of the "tube" sometimes and get caught up in the program schedule. It's not that Keith was against TV or movies—but when those things got in the way of his relationship with the Lord, he knew it was no good. So he wrote:

> *I want you here with Me*
> *But you've been keeping other company.*
> *You can't sit still!*
> *It's plain to see, you love the world*
> *And you're avoiding Me.*
>
> *My Word sits there upon your desk,*
> *But you love your books and magazines the best.*
> *You prefer the light of your TV*
> *You love the world*
> *And you're avoiding Me!*
>
> *You used to pray. You were so brave.*
> *Now you can't keep even one*
> *Appointment we've made.*
> *Oh I gave My blood, to save your life.*
> *Tell me, tell me is it right?*
> *Will you leave Me here*
> *Alone again tonight?*

Another song, "Unless The Lord Builds The House", was all about being busy in ministry, which has its own special temptations—like doing things that seem "spiritual" but really aren't. Someone had written to Keith and told him, "Don't get so caught up in the work of the Lord, that you forget the Lord of the work!" Keith wrote this song:

> *Unless the Lord builds the house,*
> *They labor in vain who try at all,*
> *Building anything not according to His call.*
> *Unless the Lord wants it done,*
> *You better not work another day,*
> *Building anything that'll stand in His way.*
>
> *You love the Lord*
> *And it seems like He's been leading,*
> *You've asked Him to bless all your plans*
> *But are you so sure*
> *You're not just doing what you want to,*
> *Building your house on the sand . . .*
>
> *Working so hard at the things that you believe in,*
> *No one can tear you away.*

But don't you lose sight
Of the very One who calls you,
You may be sorry some day . . .
Some day.

For wood, hay and stubble,
Will all burn up in the fire.
But to love the Lord with all your heart,
Should be your one desire.

Keith started writing "O Lord, You're Beautiful" while we were on the road one time, but he didn't finish until a long time later. One morning, at our old house on Dolorosa Street, I woke up to the sound of Keith softly playing the piano which was in our bedroom then. I didn't know how long he'd been playing, but the presence of the Lord was strong as I lay there listening to the beautiful melody. Keith was weeping, and he told me, "The Lord brought me right into the throne room, and I sang to him and just worshipped." He hoped others would be drawn into worship when they heard this song:

O Lord, You're beautiful.
Your face is all I seek.
For when Your eyes are on this child,
Your grace abounds to me.

I wanna take Your Word
And shine it all around.
But first help me just to live it Lord!
And when I'm doing well,
Help me to never seek a crown,
For my reward is giving glory to You.

O Lord, please light the fire,
That once burned bright and clear.
Replace the lamp of my first love
That burns with holy fear!

Keith loved to write with other people and, just before we moved to Texas, Kelly Willard and her husband Dan came to visit us. Besides the great time we had just spending time together, Kelly had a little tune she played for Keith to see if he could add anything to it. It was beautiful! They worked on it a bit that night, and later Keith and I finished the lyrics to "I Want To Be More Like Jesus."

Kelly sang with Keith on the background vocals for the album, and when it came to this song she came up with some really beautiful "answer back" parts that seemed to give the song the perfect touch it needed.

As each day passes by, I feel my love run dry.
I get so weary worn and tossed 'round in the storm.
Well I'm blind to others' needs,
And I'm tired of planting seeds.
I seem to have a wealth of so many thoughts
About myself.

I want to
I need to
Be more like Jesus.
I want to
I need to
Be more like Him

Our Father's will was done,
By giving us His Son,
Who paid the highest cost,
To point us to the cross.
And when I think of Him
Taking on the whole world's sin,
I take one look at me, compared to
What I'm called to be.
Remember, there's no greater love
Than to lay down your life for a friend.

The end of all my prayers,
Is to care like my Lord cares.
My one and only goal-
His image in my soul.
Yes my weakness is revealed,
But by His stripes I'm healed!
He's faithful and He's true,
To complete the work He begins in you!

The first time I heard "Grace By Which I Stand", the hair stood up on my arms. I knew it was a song I needed to hear. I also knew that Keith wrote it to himself because he needed to hear it too. God had done powerful things in our lives in Hawaii, but the message of grace was still being transferred from our heads to our hearts.

When Keith first wrote this song, he was almost embarrassed. He knew most people thought he almost entirely ignored the subject of grace in his preaching and ministry. But for the liner notes Keith wrote, "The whole last year has been one endless lesson on the holy grace of God, and I praise him for the opportunity to share it with you!" In this song Keith points out that, apart from God, our *own* efforts for holiness are absolutely futile. As Keith sang this song in the studio, there was a hush as he poured out his emotions in a very personal and abandoned way:

225

Lord, the feelings are not the same,
I guess I'm older—I guess I've changed,
And how I wish it had been explained
That as you're growing, you must remember . . .

That nothing lasts—except the grace of God
By which I stand in Jesus!
I know that I would surely fall away,
Except for grace by which I'm saved.

Lord, I remember that special way
I vowed to serve You
When it was brand new.
But like Peter I can't even watch and pray
One hour with You, and I bet
I could deny You, too!

Well nothing lasts—except the grace of God
By which I stand in Jesus!
I know that I would surely fall away
Except for grace by which I'm saved . . .

After about two months in California, the album was finally
finished. We were all ready to go back to Texas. Francine and
Dawn, who were also with us, had changed about a million
diapers, and I was looking forward to getting back home and
adding Bethany's bassinet to our little bedroom in the Ranch
House. On the airplane back, Keith summarized our trip in his
own way. "I feel like we both just gave birth. You had a baby and I
had an album!"

"Hey, I've got an idea," I said with a laugh. "Next time *you*
can have the baby and I'll make the album!"

Keith looked at me with a silly, "you-know-I'd-never-survive-
childbirth" look and we settled in for the flight home. We were
excited to get back and show off our new little brown-eyed, dark-
haired baby girl—and play everybody a tape of the new album.

By May of 1980, the *Egypt* album had been mastered and
pressed and we were out on the road doing our first concerts with
our new price policy. We wondered if, after all our efforts, it was
really going to work.

At one of the first concerts we did, Keith had us keep the
record tables covered with drop cloths as usual until the evening's
ministry was over. This, in itself, was a very nontraditional
approach as far as Christian concerts went, since album sales really
helped cover the night's expenses. But Keith refused to sacrifice
the tone of the evening's ministry just so he could make more
money in sales. He went into each city with a burden to minister

to the people there. He didn't want to provide a diversion in back by giving them an excuse to go and "shop" while the ministry was going on. Now that we were giving albums away, Keith wanted to be even more careful about people getting drawn to the back before the evening had ended.

I was out in the hallway of a large arena, stacking albums and tapes as high as I could on the table. The only thing separating me from the throngs of people inside were a few sets of swinging doors. After the altar call and the last worship song, I could hear Keith starting to make our new price policy announcement from the stage:

"My records are in the back. We don't feel good about selling them or setting a price. You can give whatever you want for them, even nothing, if you don't have any money."

Suddenly, I heard the pounding of feet, as people started piling out of the bleachers. Then the swinging doors burst open, and masses of people charged toward me at the record tables.

"How much are these?"

"Wow, are they really free?"

I tried to respond as best I could to the many questions coming from a wall of unfamiliar faces.

"They're offered for whatever you can afford to give. You can take one for free if you don't have any money. . . ."

While I was answering one person, who was clearly wondering what to do, others just started grabbing albums. Some were handing me money, some weren't—and to my total amazement, some people were scooping up armloads of albums and taking off with them at a run. It was loud and crazy, and I couldn't answer everyone at once. I was surrounded by a sea of faces, reaching over and around each other to get to the records.

As the crowd of people pressed in, the record table kept inching its way backwards. Every few minutes, I would push it forward with all of my strength, but I was continually losing ground because of the press of bodies against it. I was slowly being backed up against the wall behind me until the inevitable happened.

I was literally pinned between the wall and the record table, wondering when Keith was going to show up to rescue me—and whether we were going to lose our shirts on our new way of "distributing" this record.

"Unless The Lord Builds The House"

Keith marrying Wayne and Kathleen.

A FTER OUR FIRST FEW CONCERTS—WHEN THE RECORD TABLES were wiped clean and I was nearly trampled in the rush—Keith knew he needed to define his price policy a little more clearly. From the beginning, he was aware that there would be some people who would take advantage—but he still wanted to provide a way for those who really couldn't afford to buy his records. Even though some of the responses were discouraging, Keith didn't want to give up.

Eventually, at the end of his concerts Keith would make his announcements a little more specific. "Those that don't have anything can get an album for nothing. And those that have little can get it for little. We believe the gospel's been getting a little too commercial. So, we wanted to *uncommercialize* our part of it. We just ask that you don't take more than one free album per household."

Keith was also offering the *Egypt* album through *The Last Days Newsletter* for whatever anyone could afford. He was letting the bookstores help distribute the album without actually selling it in their stores. If a store wanted to help distribute the album, we would send them a pad of order blanks with a place to stamp their store's name on them. Then, for every order that came in with the store's stamp on it, we would send the store one dollar as a thank you—even if the person ordering asked for the album for free.

Keith figured most people knew the "going price" of recordings in the bookstores and understood that making records was very expensive. What he actually set up was an honor system of payment—trusting that if someone could afford to buy one they would.

In an interview with *Contemporary Christian Music Magazine* about this, Keith said, "My whole reason for giving the album away is that I love people! Of course I don't want to see 50,000 people send in nothing. At the same time I don't want people to feel that I'm doing this to get a donation, or that they have to send in a donation."

In the same interview, they referred to a past comment of theirs that had a skeptical edge to it—if someone was too poor to buy an album, they were probably too poor to own something to play it on. The implied question being, just *how* committed was Keith to helping people receive ministry? Keith told them he *would* respond to a sincere request from someone who needed something to listen to ministry on.

That was just the beginning of misunderstandings over his new price policy. Keith was being viewed, skeptically, as a nontraditionalist. But Keith pressed on throughout the rest of 1980, doing what he felt the Lord was telling him to do— continually clarifying his position.

Keith also started taking some rather nontraditional steps with his concerts that summer too. Concerts were usually sponsored by a local church in a given area, but Keith started running into some boundaries that concerned him. Sometimes he'd receive a phone call from the church he was about to go to and he'd be questioned about where he stood on certain doctrinal issues. And quite often, before a concert, Keith would be approached by someone in authority who would tell him things like, "We invited you in to sing, but we don't want you to preach," or "Don't give an altar call," or "Don't talk about the Holy Spirit, or speaking in tongues, or healing." Keith wanted to respect their wishes, yet he found it difficult to limit what he felt God had sent him there to accomplish.

And when Keith went into a city he wanted to reach the "church at large" there. But if his concert was at one church, the other denominations in town usually would not get the word out to their congregations. There didn't seem to be much cooperation between the different bodies of believers. If different churches did get together, there was this problem: If Keith gave an altar call, who got the new converts? Keith wanted everyone to come—but there seemed to be several different "camps" of believers, and they didn't fellowship together much.

In fact, the way the churches were separated by doctrinal issues was very difficult to deal with, since Keith might be in seven different churches in the same number of days. It was mind-boggling really. It wasn't just fulfilling an itinerary of concerts, it was having to go out and face a whole nation full of Christians who emphasized different things in their teachings. Sometimes he didn't know which "camp" he was walking into—the faith camp, the evangelicals, or the charismatics—just to name a few. Every Christian should be full of faith and charismatically evangelistic— but it wasn't that simple. It could wear you out just trying to figure out where people were at, so you didn't offend them. Keith did try—but diplomacy did not always come easy for him.

All of these things started adding up—the limitations on what to say and do, the tone of the meetings, and the frustration of trying to get several denominations together at any one church. Keith was remembering his unhindered time of ministry at the Caravan Ballroom in Tulsa. We'd just rented a hall and invited the city. Keith began to get the idea to use what he called "neutral auditoriums"—a place every church in town could feel comfortable sending their people to, where no one would feel they had their "toes stepped on".

From then on, whenever it seemed right, we paid our own way into different cities. There, we'd rent an arena and take an offering to cover our expenses. However, there was still one thing that kept bothering Keith about his ministry—his growing celebrity status.

Most nights, after pouring his heart out—almost begging people to get right with God—there would be long lines of people waiting to meet him at the foot of the stage. Some wanted counsel and prayer. But the majority just wanted to get close to him. Some wanted to talk about sound equipment, how they could break into the music ministry, or get a record deal. Keith saw the same shine he used to have in his eyes—the hunger to be popular and be up in front of people.

For a long time Keith just disappeared after his concerts and didn't talk to anyone, because he was so upset by the hero-worship he saw in people's eyes. And not wanting to encourage anyone in idolatry, or be stumbled himself, Keith simply slipped backstage. Keith was so concerned over this issue that a few years earlier he'd even written an article called, "Music or Missions". It talked about churches full of "star-struck" Christians—what it did to the Lord and the ministers themselves:

Can't you see that you are hurting these ministers? They try desperately to tell you that they don't deserve to be praised, and because of this, you squeal with delight and praise them all the more.

How come no one idolizes or praises the missionaries who give up everything and live in poverty, endangering their lives and their families with every danger that the American dream has almost completely eliminated? How come no one lifts up and exalts the ghetto and prison ministers and preachers? Because we are taught early on 1) that comfort is our goal and security and 2) that we should always seek for a lot of people to like us. . . .

There had just been a terrible slaughter of some women missionaries in Africa and Keith made the comparison between the lives they lived and the life the average music minister lives.

Who lives more comfortably and has more "fans" than the latest bright and shining gospel star? Who lived less comfortably, and had less friends and supporters than the selfless missionaries who were raped, mutilated, and butchered to the glory of God recently in Africa?

Quit trying to make gods out of music ministers, and quit trying to become like those gods. The Lord commands you to "Deny yourself, take up your cross daily, and follow Me." My piano is not my cross. It is my tool. I'd never play the thing again if God would show me a more effective tool for proclaiming His totally-demanding gospel. . . .

One big area Keith felt he needed to focus on was the Christian music industry itself. Now that he had made a break from the usual way of doing things, he felt he could speak to those involved in every aspect of Christian music.

Sometime before this, Keith had gone to a meeting of the Fellowship of Contemporary Christian Ministries (FCCM), which consisted of artists, promoters, producers, and record company people. At one point, Keith stood up and, with a broken heart, told everyone that they were making too many demands on each other and on the concert-goers—demands that were not holy and not blameless. Keith said they all looked too much like the world and not enough like Jesus—himself included. Keith ended up on his knees before them all, weeping and saying, "From now on, I will not come into any of your communities unless I come as a servant." He stayed on his knees pledging himself to be a servant to the body of Christ and repenting for wrong attitudes that he'd held. There was a very powerful move of God and everyone ended up taking communion together.

The next time Keith went to an FCCM meeting, it was with something different in mind—ticket sales. Keith felt like selling tickets to a night of ministry was equal to a pastor who would only come pray for the sick if you promised to pay him in advance. This FCCM meeting didn't end as sweetly as the last one.

Keith had been pressing Buck Herring pretty hard about the fact that the Second Chapter of Acts was selling tickets to their concerts. Buck felt they had clear direction from the Lord to ask people to pay $3 to help with the expenses. Keith kept challenging him, and they went 'round on this issue a lot. Buck ended up going back to God to ask him if there was a better way to do it, and after a long process he felt the Lord did show him another way.

Keith felt the Lord wanted him to go the FCCM and confront the whole Christian music industry with the concept of accepting offerings instead of selling tickets. And he wanted Buck to tell everyone what the Lord had shown him. So at the next FCCM meeting, Keith presented a clear challenge to everyone present and told them he felt it was wrong to sell tickets.

"The ticket prices for concerts are a nail in Jesus' hand. Unbelievers aren't going to pay to hear about Jesus because deep in their hearts they know shouldn't have to. The gospel is free!"

Keith knew they could well ask, "What's the difference between a Christian plumber charging for his services, and a singer or speaker charging for theirs? Didn't the Apostle Paul charge for his tents?" Keith said, "There's a difference between a man's vocation or skill and his ministry gift. If I was just an *entertainer*, I'd have no problem charging for concerts—but ministry is different.

"In fact, Paul made tents for a living so he wouldn't *have* to charge for the gospel. After all, tents are tents and ministry is ministry!"

Then Keith quoted from Paul out of First Corinthians, "What then is my reward? That, when I preach the gospel, I may offer the gospel without charge, so as not to make full use of my right in the gospel."

Buck stood up at that point and told how the Lord had led him. He said he'd finally made a list of all the reasons to sell tickets at a concert—and a list of all the reasons to do offering concerts.

Buck told the group, which was pretty somber by now, "All the reasons to do ticketed concerts were logistical. There wasn't one spiritual reason there. But all the reasons to do offering concerts were spiritual. The Lord told me if we would take this step of faith, we'd be able to minister to the body in deeper ways because they'd trust us. They'd know ministry was our only motive for being there."

When Buck sat down, the atmosphere heated up immediately. There was quite a bit of open and rather animated discussion. Some people seemed receptive to Keith and Buck. Others were wondering who Keith thought he was to come and challenge them in such an absolute way. A few of the sponsors were worried, too. Second Chapter and Keith were doing some of the largest Christian concerts in America at that time.

One sponsor said, "If the high-profile artists start doing concerts for free it will make everybody else look bad."

The meeting ended with sharply divided positions. But Keith came away feeling that he'd poured out his heart, and that was all he could do.

Besides the selling of Christian music, Keith was also grieved by all the Christian merchandising going on. Everyday items like clocks, coasters, drinking mugs, and wallets were selling for twice their usual price just because some enterprising Christian—or non-Christian—stamped a dove or a fish on them. We'd actually seen ads for Christian doggie sweaters—and even Christian ashtrays!

Then one day, we saw what we felt was the ultimate slap in the face to Jesus. Browsing in a large Christian bookstore, we came across a hand-made ceramic piggy bank. Engraved on the side of this plump little pig were the words, "Jesus Saves". We felt sick at heart.

It seemed that selling Christian products was very big business—not only in Christian bookstores, but at festivals as well. I was with Keith the day someone told us that at one Jesus festival they sold over $98,000 worth of "Jesus Junk" in just a few days! Keith nearly fell over from hearing those two words casually linked together.

"Jesus—and junk?" He said angrily. "Those must be the two most opposite words in the English language!"

On one hand, Keith saw Christian ashtrays, doggie sweaters and piggy banks. And on the other hand he saw Jesus—like a pure, white, rose—crushed beneath tons of garbage and debris, his sacrifice and his heart cry sinking from view.

Keith decided to write an article for *The Last Days Newsletter*, called, "The Selling of Jesus". In it, he wrote about his feelings when he saw the "Jesus Saves" piggy bank, quoting The Book of Revelation:

I could hear the echoes of " . . . those who had been slain because of the Word of God, and because of the testimony which they had maintained; and they cried out with a loud voice, saying, 'How long, Oh Lord, holy and true, wilt thou refrain from judging and avenging our blood on those who dwell on the earth?'"

How do you think the Lord feels, after giving His life for the sins of the world, to be reduced to something that helps sell merchandise? I'm certain He would make a whip and cleanse the Church of such garbage if He were on the earth today, but a more permanent remedy is planned. It's called Judgment Day. . . .

It seemed that Keith had an unending and, for some, an unnerving jealousy for God to be honored. Maybe it was because of all the years he'd spent lost in a spiritual maze that he couldn't bear to see the truth taken for granted or compromised in any way.

As Keith kept studying the Bible, he continually examined every doctrine he came across against the Word of God. He was also avidly reading many Christian books on a broad range of topics—some issues that he felt needed to be addressed in the body of Christ. In Keith's zeal, both the Protestant Church and the Catholic Church got caught in his line of fire.

One day, Keith was reading a book about the Catholic Church. He came flying into the kitchen looking very upset. "Mel, can you imagine this? Catholics are really *devoted* to Jesus—right? They build big churches, with beautiful statues and everything. But this book claims that some of them don't realize they can really *know* Jesus. Imagine—loving Jesus, but having no assurance of heaven."

Keith read more books about Catholic doctrines, and as he did he started to feel that he should write something about it. He prayed for a long time—and got counsel from Christian leaders. But the counsel was divided.

Some of the leaders Keith talked to said, "Yes, the Lord is leading you to do this." But others counseled Keith not to write anything, saying, "It's not the Lord. What you're reading in those books isn't totally accurate." Keith was torn, but in the end he believed the Lord wanted him to go ahead and write something. When Keith launched into the series he called "The Catholic Chronicles", he wrote a forward to clarify what he was trying to accomplish:

I want to make it completely understood that neither I nor anyone else at Last Days Ministries have anything at all personally against Catholics. We know of many loving, committed and sincere believers among their ranks. In fact, there are quite a few who receive our newsletter, even a priest in New England who corresponds with me regularly (and if you're reading this now—I love you!)

While Keith was concerned about the Catholic Church making God too mysterious, distant, and unknowable—it seemed like the Protestant Church had almost the opposite problem. Many Protestants seemed to be too familiar with God—taking him for granted. If it seemed "too hard" for Catholics to get saved, it seemed "too easy" for Protestants. So, in the same issue of the newsletter that Keith concluded writing "The Catholic Chronicles", he began another series called, "What's Wrong With The Gospel?" At home, Keith called this series "The Protestant Chronicles".

From what we'd seen while traveling in born-again circles for six years now, many things were all coming to a head in Keith's thinking. Some of the writings of A.W. Tozer were having a strong influence on Keith, as well. At one of our Bible studies, Keith picked up Tozer's book and read us a quote:

"The cross of Roman times knew no compromise, it never made concessions. It won all its arguments by killing its opponent and silencing him for good. It spared not Christ, but slew Him the same as the rest . . . With perfect knowledge of all this, Christ said, 'If any man will come after Me, let him deny himself, take up his cross and follow Me.' So the cross not only brought Christ's life to an end, it also ends the first life, the old life of every one of His true followers. . . . this and nothing less is true Christianity. We must do something about the cross, and there's only one of two things we can do—*flee it or die upon it!*"

In his introduction to the two part series "What's Wrong With The Gospel?" Keith said:

What's wrong with the Gospel? Absolutely nothing! That is, of course, if you're talking about the gospel of the Bible—the very message that Jesus preached. . . . But what about the stuff that's being preached today? Is it truly "gospel-preaching?" . . . I believe with all my heart that Jesus would be ashamed of most of the "gospel" messages that are being preached today, mainly because they lack almost every major point He Himself preached on. How dare we try to change the gospel! We remove most of its vital parts, and replace them with artificial limbs of our own. Isn't Jesus the master evangelist? Shouldn't we judge our evangelism by His example?

Keith's two-part article ran in the same issue of *The Last Days Newsletter*. Section One was called, "The Missing Parts," or the parts that have been "surgically removed in most of today's preaching". The first thing Keith talked about was how Jesus shed his blood so we could have the power to be set free:

It's a fact that the very word blood scares people. It's also a fact that the blood of Christ scares the devil, because it is the only cleansing agent for a sin-sick soul. What we have now is a bloodless gospel! . . . Remove the blood from the preaching of the gospel, and you remove the power to conquer the devil for the souls of men!

Next, Keith talked about removing the cross from the gospel:

Paul said, "I determined to know nothing among you except Jesus Christ, and Him crucified." Nowadays it's "Jesus Christ and what He can do for you!" You cannot have more exact opposites than the Bible's Christ-centered gospel and our modern, cross-less, "Me-centered gospel." . . . Today the Lord is presented as a sort of "ice-cream man/Santa Claus." And the Church is the "candy store" where you can get "every goodie your heart desires."

Keith summed up this first section by saying:

First and foremost, today's gospel appeals to the selfish. If people come to Jesus mainly to get a blessing, or only to get forgiveness, they will ultimately be disappointed. But if they come to give Him their lives in honor and worship, then they will truly have forgiveness and joy—more than they could ever imagine!

In Section Two, Keith talked about what he called "The Added Parts". This time he talked about the dangers of the traditions of men.

—
237

Then Keith listed some of the tools, methods, and concepts that have become so much a part of presenting the modern gospel, that they have become almost inseparable from it. Sometimes those practices even distort the gospel. Among those things, Keith felt, were the altar call and the easy assurance of salvation just because someone "came forward". He also examined the idea of the "sinner's prayer":

It is obvious that there is no "set" sinner's prayer. The words are not important, it's the state of heart of the one saying it. I believe that a true "sinner's prayer" will gush out of anyone who truly is seeking God, and is tired of being enslaved to sin.

Then Keith took a risky look at the term and concept of Jesus being our "personal Savior":

I find it very disturbing, when something unnecessary is added to the gospel. The term "personal Savior" isn't very harmful in itself, but it shows a kind of mind-set that is willing to "invent" terms, and then allow these terms to be preached as if they were actually found in the Bible. Would you ever introduce your sister like this, "This is Sheila, my personal sister?" Ridiculous! But nevertheless, people solemnly speak of Christ as their personal Savior, as if when He returns He will not have two, but three titles written across His thigh, "King of Kings! Lord of Lords! and Personal Savior!"

One of the things that really bothered Keith was seeing bumper stickers with what he called, "cheap cliches and 'Christian' slogans". He wanted to call attention to what some of these slogans were really projecting.

"Please be patient, God isn't finished with me yet." This can really be a horrible replacement for "I'm sorry!" . . . It puts the blame on the wrong person—"The reason I'm such a creep is because God isn't finished with me yet!"
Then there is that other fabulous excuse that absolutely ends all quests or expectations for holiness: "Christians aren't perfect . . . just forgiven!" What we're saying by this fabulous piece of prose is, "Madam, you cannot trust your teenage daughter with my Christian son, you'd better keep your eye on him . . . he's not safe . . . he's just forgiven!"

In summary, Keith pleaded with Christians to examine what they were doing:

Don't you see what fools we are! We preach a man-made, plastic gospel. We get people to "come forward" to the altar by bringing psychological pressures that have nothing to do with God. We "lead them" in a prayer that they are not yet convinced they need to say. And then to top it all off, we give them "counseling" . . . telling them it is a sin to doubt that they're saved!

Beloved family, the world around us is going to hell. Not because of communism, television, drugs, sex, alcohol, or the devil himself. It is because of the Church! We are to blame! We alone have the commission, the power, and the truth of God at our constant disposal to deliver sinner after sinner from eternal death. And even though some are willing to go . . . they are taking a watered-down, distorted version of God's message which God has not promised to anoint. That is why we are failing.

When Keith wrote all of these articles, it was with an overwhelming desire to see the Church free of compromise and counterfeit conversions. He knew he said some strong things, but he hoped the body of Christ would be all the stronger for it. As these articles appeared in the newsletter over a period of months, Keith had no idea how strong a storm of controversy his writings would cause.

Meanwhile . . . "back at the ranch" . . . Keith and I had made some big changes in our living arrangements. Every available space had been seized by one "department" or another. One of my biggest concerns while living at the Ranch House had been finding Josiah a safe place to play. Almost two years old now, he was curious and into everything. One day, I'd noticed his little mouth "working" on something, and when I got him to spit it out, my heart almost stopped. He'd been sucking on a push-pin that must have fallen off one of the bulletin boards! I was afraid to think of what would have happened if he'd swallowed it.

Also, living in a "fishbowl" did have its challenges. You have to develop certain techniques within a marriage when you're surrounded with people all the time. When Keith and I had differing opinions, we learned to have "soft disagreements". Keith and I had learned how to flash each other those "let's go talk in the other room" looks without anyone else noticing.

Living with so many people was also taking a toll on me— especially because things always moved so fast. Sometimes it seemed like I was the last one to know about important decisions, and I felt like I was often lost in the shuffle. Maybe the hardest times were when I needed to talk to Keith, but he was so worn out from counseling or from being in a long meeting, and he just didn't have enough energy left to give me "equal time".

At those times, I'd count my blessings, which were many. Still, it seemed like the "grace" was starting to lift.

The long and short of it was, we'd begun to feel like we needed our own place. Because we lived out in the country, there wasn't much housing available without building it yourself. There was, however, one small, white house right across the road from our ranch. Keith had even thought of making them an offer—but it wasn't for sale.

Then one day, while we were cooking dinner in the kitchen of the Ranch House, one of the girls casually said, "Oh, guess what? I was over looking at that house across the road today. It's for sale."

I couldn't believe my ears. "The white house?"

"Yes. They just put the sign out."

Keith and I lost no time.

We walked right across the road to ask if we could look at the place. The owners told us the house was over one hundred years old and, needless to say, it needed a lot of work! It had three bedrooms and one bathroom, but not one level floor—a can placed at one side of the kitchen linoleum rolled across to the other wall. The rooms were covered in dark paneling and the rug was matted and—well, everything was old. But it was available and fixable—and it looked like a palace to us!

Keith bought it on the spot as a parsonage and we moved right in. Within weeks I'd discovered I was pregnant with our third child. So it was perfect timing.

So we spent the winter building fires in the fireplace of our new little home, and then watching the wildflowers start to pop up in our fields at the beginning of spring. By summer Josiah was almost three, running around the yard in his shorts, grabbing grasshoppers and playing with his dump trucks. We'd taken him on his first missionary trip to Mexico and he came home praying for the children who "don't have a house over their bed". While Josiah was like a blond lightning-flash, Bethany was like a deep well of serene waters—peaceful, pensive, and starting to take her first steps. Dawn had turned sixteen and was growing into a beautiful young woman with a real servant's heart—helping with the children at home and on the road. For us as a family things were starting to settle down a little bit—just before the storm hit.

In the beginning of 1981—even with our moving out—the Ranch House continued to stretch at the seams. The garage had become the print shop, the living room became the office and literature distribution department, the laundry room (besides housing the washer and dryer) was crammed with artists and drafting tables, and the kitchen and dining room were used for album packing and mailing, as well as eating. The ministry also needed more space—and quickly!

Keith decided we needed a real office building and, just before the slab was poured, he made it twice as big as he originally intended. At first we wondered what we would do with all the space. But before the building was even completed, we not only knew we could fill it, we knew it would not be our last. We now had real offices, a print shop, and a guys' dorm in one large, two-story metal building.

We were excited about some of our new neighbors, too. Buck and Annie, Steve and Nelly, and Matt had bought some land right next to us! And my mom, who'd become a Christian a few years before, moved a mobile home about one hundred yards away from our back door to be a hands-on grandma to our growing family.

The one sad note was that Michelle, our longtime friend and secretary, had abruptly left us by this time. Tension had built between Keith and Michelle for a little while. There were some disagreements on how to do things. Michelle was burned-out from the long hours of endless work and the intensity of everyday life at Last Days. And Keith wasn't always the easiest person to serve, either. Besides, Michelle felt her experiences as a Christian were very limited—the only thing she'd known was being with me and Keith. She felt she needed more room to grow and that it might be best if she left.

Both Keith and I tried to talk Michelle out of leaving. We felt really miserable and let our feelings get the best of us. Toward the end it got very emotional and, in a room full of people, Keith said some things that wounded Michelle. When she left she was extremely hurt. And Michelle wasn't the last one to leave. Over time, probably a dozen people left feeling like some of our old rules weren't changing quickly enough, or that Keith wasn't hearing their viewpoint as well as he should have. For the most part they were probably right.

Summer of 1981 brought the birth of our beautiful third child, Rebekah Joy—on July 17th. The summer also brought something not so pleasant.

In response to Keith's controversial series of articles, an avalanche of mail hit Last Days. It came from all quarters—bookstore owners and patrons, recording artists and record companies, Protestants and Catholics, pastors and priests. Some of it was positive, some negative. In sheer numbers, however, nothing topped the negative response Keith received from "What's Wrong With The Gospel?" Some of it was really fiery. We always liked to get mail—the pros and the cons—and did our best to answer everyone who had a question. And there were a lot of questions.

One seemingly insignificant event that summer was to have an impact we had no way of anticipating.

Since Keith was gearing up to spend a lot more time out on the road, he was very interested in some news he'd picked up. The YWAM base down the road was thinking about putting in an airstrip. Not too long after we'd moved here, YWAM had bought Twin Oaks Ranch from David Wilkerson. Keith jumped on the airstrip idea and he went right over to see YWAM's National Director, Leland Paris.

When Keith returned, he said excitedly, "Boy, an airstrip would save a lot of time and hassle. Maybe I can even get a pilot's license!"

To his dismay, that idea wasn't well received by anyone. Least of all me.

"I don't think you should even *consider* becoming a pilot."

"Come on, Mel, you know I could do it."

"Of course you *could*—I just don't think you should."

A short time later, Keith talked to Wayne about it and he had a very strong reaction too.

"Keith, I don't feel good about it," Wayne was saying.

Keith got irritated. "Oh, come on. What's the big deal?"

"I don't want any part of it. Don't do it."

Everyone who knew Keith seemed to "see red" when the subject came up. We all knew the stress and intense pressures he faced every day. Flying an airplane seemed like the last thing he needed to be doing.

While we were on the road just at the end of summer Keith brought the subject up with the pastor who had invited us in.

"It's too dangerous," the pastor replied immediately. "A pastor friend of mine just died because he took off in bad weather. He said he was going to 'trust God' to get him to his destination safely."

He made some other strong points, too.

"Keith, do you know why ministers have the highest rate of pilot's insurance?"

"Why?" he asked, a bit impatiently.

"Because they take the most risks. They think they're indestructible. They have the most accidents."

I could tell Keith was getting upset. Why wouldn't anyone get excited about his idea to be a pilot? He just stood up and shrugged his shoulders.

"Well, I don't know what everybody's so worried about. I'm not gonna take any risks."

"Open Your Eyes"

With Rebekah, Josiah and Bethany. 1982

NE DAY, A MAN NAMED JOHN DAWSON ACCIDENTALLY STRAYED into Keith's line of fire. He'd invited Keith to minister at a large concert at the Anaheim Stadium to raise money for refugees from Thailand and Cambodia. A coalition of various groups was working together to pull it off—Episcopalians, Charismatics, Catholics, Evangelicals and Pentecostals. John, who was directing the YWAM work in Los Angeles, California, had seen Keith in concert and believed he would be a key person for the program, so he sent an invitation.

At that time, unknown to John, Keith was very concerned about Christians reducing biblical truth to the lowest common denominator for the sake of unity. So when Keith got the invitation, he shot back a strong but earnest letter turning down the invitation. He really wanted to help the Boat People, but he felt ecumenical gatherings were a compromise and that John was in error for taking part in it.

When Keith received another letter from John Dawson, he was impressed. John had written a thoughtful letter, saying, "Brother, the cooperative effort to raise money for six different relief agencies to help the Boat People is an expression of concern and compassion—not compromise."

John assured Keith the gathering was not some kind of conspiracy against the truth. He even gave Keith a word of correction. "Keith, in saying some of the things you did, you were entering into the sin of judgment."

To John's surprise, he immediately received a letter from Keith that had a repentant tone—and a plea for understanding. "I'm in a very dark time in my life right now," he wrote. "I'm just trying to sort a lot of thoughts. I'm sorry for coming on so strong. Please forgive me."

Keith did not wind up at the Anaheim benefit, but a friendship between Keith and John rooted and grew throughout 1981—which gave us another link to YWAM.

The newest struggle Keith was referring to had grown out of the backlash from his series of articles and the continued misunderstanding about Keith's opposition to merchandising the gospel. Not that he felt the ideas were wrong—but his "prophetic calling" left him with many questions that turned like screws in his soul.

If others in the body of Christ were "hands" or "feet", Keith always felt like he was an elbow.

"If I had my choice," he lamented to me one day, "I'd much rather be the mercy shower than the prophetic voice. Everybody tells me I'm a prophet. What if I'm not? And if I am, what does one look like?"

Keith and his new friend, John Dawson, who by now had been to Texas to visit us, had constant discussions about Keith's giftings and calling.

"Why can't I just relax and be the guy that always has something nice to say?" Keith asked him.

"God has given you an intense, prophetic personality," John answered. "You see things in black and white. That's a strength—and a weakness. But you have a very definite place on God's leadership team for this generation."

"What kind of place?"

"You're like a John the Baptist. Your role is to prepare the way of the Lord. But like everyone else, prophets have a certain test to pass."

"Great, what is it?"

"The test of every prophet is to take the wide circle of influence that God has given them and, instead of capturing it for themselves, turn it over to One who's greater—for greater purposes in the kingdom."

"Boy, that's right," said Keith. "When John the Baptist announced Jesus to the crowd, he knew he was giving his own ministry away!"

John also helped us see that, just as every individual has a destiny to fulfill, every *nation* has a destiny to fulfill too. "America is a leader among nations. But what are we leading people *to*? America is here to bless the nations, and your message—whatever it is—has got to include a call to turn from sin to *that*."

John, was about Keith's age and originally from New Zealand. He talked to us about being a teenager 6,000 miles away from the States, but being heavily influenced by what was going on in our youth culture. Our blue jeans and music had made it all the way to Red Square, but when God made America such a strong world influence, he must have had more in mind than blue jeans and music. "We're already 'discipling' nations, in a very broad sense— but what are we *discipling* them to?"

Keith was really starting to expand his scope of thinking. John's challenge stuck with him. "America is here to bless the nations, Keith. It's one thing to call people to turn from sin—but I think your message needs to somehow include a call for Christians to get involved in being part of that blessing."

Keith was moved by John—and at the same time perplexed. He was already doing more thinking about his message about holiness. What did holiness mean? He'd been encouraging people to hear from the Lord and then be obedient to what they were called to do. But now, with John's voice echoing in his ears, he wondered, was there an even bigger picture? Was God painting on a larger canvas than we'd even imagined?

Keith was totally impressed with YWAM and the way their thousands of volunteers served in mission bases all over the world. And he was intrigued by the things YWAM had learned from cooperating with people from different cultures to get the gospel out to the lost—to some who had never heard of Jesus ever before. I could tell that, through this time of questioning, things were stirring in his heart again.

Keith wrote about these stirrings in his journal that summer:

. . . the Lord has been doing a work in our hearts. . . . We are being led into evangelism. It's amazing. The freedom and peace of my heart is what's so surprising. . . . I have a leading from the Lord to do an evangelistic album. . . . Please, holy Lord, give me the secret of winning souls. I want to put it to music. . . .

Keith's new questions about the "prophetic calling" were taking some shape, and opening up new possibilities.

Several months later, in October 1981, Keith did a family night concert at YWAM's Twin Oaks Ranch. That night, Keith talked with a strange sense of urgency. Even on the way over there, he remarked about how fast time was flying by for him.

And at the concert, he kept talking about heaven—and hell.

"I want to use my music to draw the lost," he told the YWAM audience. "That's one of the things I want to do until God takes me home. Life is short. The Bible calls it a vapor. . . . William Booth, from the Salvation Army, wished that every graduate from his training school could be suspended by a rope over hell for twenty-four hours! Then they could see what they were saving men from. I want to have a vision of heaven in my mind and the stench of hell in my nostrils as I go to preach the gospel!"

Some of the things he said that night startled even me. There were huge changes going on inside this dear, loving, intense man I'd been married to for almost eight years.

"As as far as I know," Keith said, "I'm not a prophet. And I don't want to be. In fact, since I've been a Christian I've had hundreds of people tell me I'm a prophet. Except I've never had God tell me I'm a prophet. And I figure that he's the one that ought to know. So I decided I want to be just a plain-old Christian. If I could just stand before the Lord and hear him say, 'Well done. You were a good and faithful Christian,' I'd be really happy."

On January 17, 1982, in Keith's first journal entry of the year, he did the usual "taking stock" of his life, his family, and his spiritual state. Along with a growing sense of wanting to get on with a deeper walk with God, he wrote:

. . . I have found much approval in men's eyes, but what about God's eyes? It seems He accepts me and loves me! I know He is not impressed with my works anymore than He was with Solomon's. But I think He likes my heart. And if I will be judged on the motive and intent of my heart, then I'm OK. . . .

For out of a good heart, must come good fruit. . . . Oh, Lord, help me accept myself as I am. Or help me change. . . .

He also wrote:

JANUARY 29, 1982

God has been so kind and patient with me. . . . He showed me that my vision was far too small and that I had lost my pioneer spirit. . . .

That "other-worldy" tone kept cropping up—just a thread or hint of it—even in our conversation.

One day early in the year, Keith and I were working together in the new office we shared, making song selections for Keith's fourth album. He'd been thinking about doing an album for the lost—a fulfillment of the dream he'd had ever since he was a teenager and wanted to record his *Revelations* collection, about "a family for God". But now, he felt God was telling him to do an album of worship songs instead, a recording that would inspire people to worship instead of another "hard message" album! Keith was elated.

But while we were discussing the songs, I was surprised to hear him say, out of the blue, "Melody, for the first time in my life I feel like I'm ready to go and be with the Lord."

"What do you mean?" I said lightly. "Has the Lord told you something I need to know?"

"No. I just mean that I have a real peace in my heart. I've finally come to a place of rest. I have a total asurance that if the Lord took me home I would go to heaven to be with him."

I'd never heard Keith say something like that before. And he sounded so confident and peaceful. I was so blessed to know that Keith had finally come to that place of inner rest.

There was another evidence of Keith's new feeling of "settled-ness" and it had to do with me. Keith had commissioned me in the past to write some articles in the newsletter. A few—like "Children, Things We Throw Away?", a pro-life article—had been reprinted as tracts and had several million in circulation. But even though Keith and I had worked side by side to lay the foundation of Last Days, I'd always kept a low profile—especially in the recording studio.

On this new worship album, however, Keith wanted to record a song I'd written from Psalm 95. And, amazingly, he wanted *me* to sing the lead on it while he sang harmony. I was thrilled! I had totally let go of the idea of ever singing with Keith. That question had been settled long ago, except for a few background parts I'd done. Now Keith even told me I could start taking voice lessons if I wanted. Even though the song would end up getting cut in the final selection, I felt so encouraged, I could have burst.

Keith decided to name this album, *Songs For The Shepherd,* and we arrived in Los Angeles to record it with all the children in tow. Once again, we would be working with Bill Maxwell.

One song I'd written five years earlier did make it on the album—it was called, "There Is A Redeemer". Keith loved it, but he thought it might be a little too short:

> *There is a Redeemer,*
> *Jesus God's own Son!*
> *Precious Lamb of God,*
> *Messiah,*
> *Oh, Holy One!*

The chorus offered a simple thanks to the Father for giving us his Son. Keith wanted to add another verse. I was amazed at the way he could pull words out of the air. In a few minutes of work, he sang them for me:

> *When I stand in glory*
> *I will see His face.*
> *There, I'll serve my King forever*
> *In that holy place. . . .*

I liked it—but the verse seemed slightly out of place with the rest of the song. It even seemed a little odd that Keith took the song in that direction, going from thanking God to meeting him face-to-face.

And in the studio, the presence of the Lord seemed to flood all over Keith as he sang that song. Goose bumps raced up my arms. During certain parts Keith wept so much it was hard for him to sing at all. This was no performance. It was some kind of very real experience, just between him and the Lord.

We decided to record three songs that the Lord gave us during the time of revival in 1979. On two of them—"Draw Me" and "The Promise Song"—Keith wrote the music and we wrote the lyrics together. "Draw Me" is a song of desperation—knowing that it takes the grace of God even for us to be drawn into his presence.

"The Promise Song" was very happy and upbeat, talking about the many promises the Lord has said he'll keep, if we obey him.

"Until That Final Day" was another song Keith wrote during the revival. Once again, there was a sense of finality in these words—not so much of the end of earthly life, but of finally breaking through to be an overcomer:

> *My flesh is tired of seeking God*
> *But on my knees I'll stay.*
> *I want to be a pleasing child*
> *Until that final day . . .*
>
> *One sleepless night of anguished prayer,*
> *I triumph over sin.*
> *One battle in the Holy War*
> *God's promised me to win!*

During our time in Los Angeles, we did the photo session in Hollywood for the cover. It was the most fun we'd ever had doing a photo session—mainly because an animal handler came to the studio with several lambs. We tried the shot various ways—with Keith holding two and three lambs and, finally, with just one draped around his shoulders.

As usual, Keith did not like having his picture taken. It was hard for him to relax. I needed to stand behind the photographer and talk to Keith continually. The best way to get him looking natural was to tell him a funny story or a joke. I tried to remember every humorous thing I'd heard in the last year while Keith smiled and kept saying through his teeth, "Come on, Mel, think of something *really* funny!"

Sometime during the session we got the idea for Keith to hold all of the children in his arms. After all, they were *his* little lambs! It was quite a feat to get Josiah on his shoulders and Rebekah and Bethany in his arms. Then they all needed to look good at the same time the picture was snapped. We were cooing, shaking baby rattles, and trying to get the kids to laugh.

In the midst of the shoot, I had such a great sense of satisfaction rush into my heart. God was so good to us. It was obvious that Keith felt the same way—his face just lit up as soon as the children were placed in his arms. He was such a proud and happy daddy. What a beautiful family we had!

At the end of the session we all gathered together to take one big family portrait with Dawn. The make-up artist did a fantastic number on Dawn. With her long straight hair and high cheekbones, she looked like a model—all grown up and beautiful at seventeen. With Keith's determination to avoid cameras, even at home, it was hard to even get him in a casual shot. So getting this family portrait done was a blessing—in more ways than I knew just then.

Immediately after the album was finished, Keith had some spring concert crusades planned. We'd be flying to them from our own backyard this time, because the much talked about airstrip had become a reality—and since we had a longer stretch of straight flat land on our property than YWAM, we built it. We were really excited about this new, timesaving way to travel.

These crusades were planned to be different from any other concert series Keith had ever done. Keith's new twist was inspired by Charles Finney. Finney would preach, then have separate meetings where those who were under conviction could come to find out more about becoming a Christian. Keith decided he would also have "Inquirers Meetings" the day after the concert, for those who wanted to make serious commitments to the Lord. Keith wanted to take some time with the new converts to carefully instruct them in the ways of the Lord, and there wasn't much time in a concert setting to do that. Winkie Pratney and John Dawson were scheduled to teach at the Inquirers Meetings in different cities.

On the first round of concerts, however, most people were not interested in returning the next day for another meeting. Keith was frustrated:

APRIL 5, 1982

I've been mostly disappointed by the so-called crusades. Mainly because I feel like I have no anointing. The worst part is that the audience doesn't even seem to notice. . . .There's nothing more sickening than to turn around and have to use the same methods you've despised for years. The silly "altar call" is all that seems to separate "the sheep from the audience." The inquirers meeting is a total failure. . . .

At the next concert city, Keith realized that his heart was crusted over from the "too-busy-to-seek-God-enough" months in Los Angeles while we were making the album. After a long time of prayer the day of the concert, things changed.

APRIL 12, 1982

One thing I asked God for in that prayer time was His heart. That's the only thing I needed from Him. . . . that night's concert was one of the best I've ever had. The Word of God flowed out of my mouth in the smoothest way ever. I worshipped God and it didn't matter that there were even people there—it was God that I wanted to impress and bless and that's all! . . .

He also wrote, two days later:

I sure hope the Lord saves me from the fate of another concert without an anointing. I'll just die if I have to go out in front of a crowd again without His love and presence.

It was as if, during these crusades, the Lord was calling Keith to a deeper level of understanding and a higher vision of what it would take, in the Spirit, to accomplish God's next major move in the world. And the first glimpse came during the second set of crusades, while John Dawson was with us.

The key discussions between Keith and John centered on spiritual warfare. Keith was fascinated by the idea John presented, based on Ephesians 6 and other scriptures, that every city has a specific ruling principality assigned to it by Satan. If whole cities were going to be stirred by the Lord, the "strongman" in each city needed to be bound by entering into spiritual warfare.

At dinner, the night of the Houston concert, Keith said to John, "Let's do all the stuff you've been talking about for tonight's concert!" And so we left the restaurant to pray spiritual warfare prayers over Houston. When we got to the house where we were staying, Keith had another concern. "I feel really weak and nervous tonight," he said.

"Do you always feel this way?" John asked.

"Yeah, I do. I don't have this great big confidence, but somehow God comes through. We really need to pray."

As Keith and John bowed to pray, the Spirit of God seemed to come in a very strong way—not for the city of Houston, but for Keith. Keith was kneeling down, head on his knees like a little boy. John laid his hand on Keith's back and began to pray over him. But when John spoke, it was like God the Father speaking to his child, telling of his unconditional, accepting love for Keith. He also spoke of Keith's destiny—that he was going to be used to pull down strongholds. That when he spoke, he was to speak as the mouthpiece of God and the Word would be sharp and two-edged with authority. Then the power of the enemy would be broken.

Keith and John then began to pray, and felt they were shown that there was a certain principality over the city of Houston. The Lord gave them a whole strategy of how to bind this "strongman" and plunder his goods.

Keith had a powerful night of ministry that night and God blessed in every way. There were two hundred inquirers that night and the $10,000 of expenses were met even though the arena was only one-quarter full!

There were other highlights of our spring tours.

There was St. Louis, Missouri, where the Market Square Arena was packed with 10,000 people loudly chanting, "Jesus! Jesus!" an hour before the concert. In fact, far more people had come to hear Keith that night than to see the Russian ballet dancer, Rudolf Nureyev, who was appearing in the smaller arena behind us. About 650 came to the "Inquirers Meeting" after the concert.

And there was the concert in Indianapolis, where Keith sang and preached to his largest crowd ever—12,000 people.

Things were suddenly starting to mushroom. Keith and I had just met with a radio consultant and we were planning to start a syndicated program together in the fall.

But perhaps the greatest "expansion" was the broadening of our spiritual perspective. We weren't just caught up in personal struggles, or even in challenges to Keith's ministry. We were starting to see that we were caught up in frontline spiritual warfare that could affect a generation.

As Keith wrote, just after returning by private airplane to our ranch:

We flew home in about 3 hours to our own strip. I flew up in the cockpit for a while and got even more of a desire to learn how to fly. Please Jesus, do not let me even start pilot's lessons unless you want me to. I realize that my own fleshly nature is not conducive to being a pilot, and that the devil would like to kill me if he could. . . .

After the album and the spring crusades, Keith and I were exhausted. We'd never really taken a regular vacation before and when the idea came up now, it sounded wonderful. Keith still joked about delivering pizzas on our honeymoon, so he wanted to bless me with a trip to Europe. We decided to go for two weeks, and to leave the kids at home so we could have our very first, bonafide vacation ever.

Or so I thought.

The week before we were planning to leave for Europe, God brought a "chance" meeting Keith's way. Keith dropped in to see Leland Paris at YWAM and Don Stephens, YWAM's Director for Europe, was sitting in Leland's office. Don immediately set up an itinerary so that Keith and I could see the YWAM bases in Europe and even teach in one or two of their schools.

When we left at the end of May, our first visit was to the base called Holmstead Manor, in southern England. On our drive there we found out why so many of the early masters of art loved to paint the English countryside. It was absolutely beautiful—blue skies, billowy white clouds, and rolling hills of various shades of green. I just sat back enjoying the peaceful ride. When we arrived at the base, Keith and I were both stunned. It was a huge castle! A real one, sitting on a gentle knoll and looking like a picture postcard.

Operating a missions base out of a castle—including a training school and ministry outreaches throughout the area—looked like fun. But it was obviously a sacrificial lifestyle. Castles don't come with many modern conveniences. We'd seen a big swimming pool on the grounds but it was cracked, empty, and growing moss. Even if they had extra money—which they didn't—we knew fixing the pool would be considered a luxury. As we left that day, Keith left a large gift designated specifically to fix the pool.

Already, our vacation was becoming a lot of fun, seeing neat places and meeting wonderful people.

But it was in Amsterdam that we first realized there might be a different purpose for this trip.

When we hit the streets of Amsterdam, it was light-years away from the quiet English countryside. The narrow streets were bustling with people, bicycles, and what seemed like wandering young people from all over the world.

Amsterdam is considered the drug capital of Europe, and there is open prostitution. In fact, the YWAM base sits right on the corner of a world famous "red light" district, where they have an amazing outreach to the people in the city—including the prostitutes, drug addicts, and runaways that gravitate there because of its wild reputation.

It was hard to miss the YWAM base. It was in a massive, five-story building across from the train station near the center of town. Across the top, in lights, were the words "Jesus Loves You" in both English and Dutch.

Floyd McClung, the leader of this center, was like a "gentle giant", standing six-foot-seven. And Sally, his wife, was a pretty blond who was very involved in the ministry as well as raising their two children, Matthew and Misha. I was very impressed at their trust in God, taking their children to live in a neighborhood few people would even choose to walk in. Their commitment impressed me, too. They were building for the long haul, and praying for the people of Amsterdam with an intensity that moved me.

Something about Amsterdam gave you the impression of two worlds existing side by side. Floyd took Keith and me on a walking tour after dark, and I have to confess that, even in this modern, European city, lit by street lights, I felt very uncomfortable. It was not the same city we had seen by daylight.

During the day, there had been bright blue skies and sunlight sparkling on the famous canals. Now, the dark canals only reflected the streetlamps and the glare of neon signs from the "red light" district, with row after row of nightclubs and bars. Each one advertised naked women, live sex acts, or some other type of perversion. Their doors were open and blaring music spilled out into the streets. As we passed, hustlers called out, wanting us to come inside. Everybody was hustling somebody. The streets were full of strange men wearing dark glasses, and women. Lots of women.

"Prostitution is legally licensed in Amsterdam," Floyd told us. "It's a way of life for many women. Some of them are even married."

"You mean their husbands don't care?" I said in shock.

"Nope. Some women just work an eight-hour shift like a regular job. Especially the ones who sit in the windows."

The windows. That was probably the thing that separated this "red light" district from those in the States. Here, many women would display themselves in the windows of regular houses, while men—from pimply-faced boys to grandfathers—went "shopping". It was sick. It was also heartbreaking.

Just when I thought we'd seen the worst of it, I glanced down a dark, narrow little side street. Standing right out in the street were several women—almost totally naked. Even from a distance, one woman in particular caught my eye. There was something about her. Maybe it was the slouch of her shoulders as she stood there waiting for her next customer. She seemed so lost and dejected. I wondered what incredible wounding had taken place in her life to get her to this point. Any minute, someone might walk up and pay money for her and take her off to do God knows what. I knew all of her human dignity and self-esteem must be destroyed for her to sell herself on the street like a piece of meat.

Later that night, I was haunted by her image. I could lie there in a nice warm bed, with my husband who loved me and was committed to me. But who knew where that woman was right now, or how she was being treated. I knew prostitutes were often brutalized and even murdered. I would soon return to America, to my happy children and a nice ministry filled with nice people. But what was the future for this woman? My heart ached over the memory.

"Keith, are you asleep?"

"No. I'm not."

"Do you think it's the jet lag?"

"No." What we had seen had shaken him up too. "All this stuff has blown me away. I want to help, but I don't know how."

The next day, Floyd and Sally took us out shopping so I could buy a few things—chocolates and toys for the kids and a few dresses for me. Keith and I were planning our fourth child, so I looked for something pretty, but with room to grow. In the daylight, I could again see the Amsterdam of the postcards—the flowers, canals, streetcars, and skinny buildings with graceful, gable tops. But the darker world of the night was somehow still present, like the shadow of a double-exposure on a picture. I couldn't shake the sense. Once you've seen the darkness, how can you pretend it's not there?

We wound up buying ice cream cones and strolling for a while. I caught myself thinking, *Wow, I'm eating ice cream with missionaries.* Then I felt foolish. What did I think missionaries were like, anyway? I guess I wasn't prepared to meet such incredible people. To me, the word missionary sometimes conjured the image of a person who couldn't make it in the "real world", so they retreated to the mission field. But I looked at Floyd—who Keith was pumping with questions just now—and Sally, and I thought, *These people could land on the top of the heap in whatever they chose to do.* And I wondered if it was the Greens who'd somehow forgotten what the "real world" was really like.

Keith asked Floyd, "What are your greatest needs?"

"We've got so many. . . ."

"If you could pick one, what would it be?" Keith had blessed one YWAM base with money to fix their pool, and I thought maybe Keith was wanting to bless Floyd and Sally too.

"People," Floyd said. "More people who have a heart to reach the lost for Jesus."

By now, we'd reached "The Cleft", a quaint little pancake house YWAM had opened—right in the middle of the "red light" district, two doors down from an official Satanic church! Talk about facing spiritual warfare!

We sat at a table in "The Cleft", and Floyd and Sally told us the strategy the Lord had given them for winning this warfare, one soul at a time.

One of their many stories gripped me the most. The story of Magriet, who'd been a prostitute and heroin addict for twenty-one years. Besides the ministry at "The Cleft", YWAM did a lot of "friendship evangelism". Magriet was a "street prostitute", which the locals considered to be a step down from "working the windows". The YWAMers visited Magriet regularly on the streets

—

255

and kept asking her to come to the base for a meal. Touched by their persistence and obvious love, she finally gave in. Magriet stayed for an evangelistic meeting, and gave her heart to the Lord. Eventually, she left Amsterdam to attend a church in another city, where she was still growing in the Lord.

So there *was* real light in the midst of this real darkness. Bright light.

As we left and headed south, Keith and I talked for a long time. We'd been moved by the people who had dedicated their lives to serve, but also overwhelmed by seeing so many lost people—with so few to help them. It wasn't like America where there was a vibrant church on every corner. As we traveled through Germany, Austria, and Italy, it was the same. We kept asking the same questions. How could there ever be a big enough movement to meet all the needs we were seeing? And what were the systems for getting the people that did want to go onto the front lines and into the action? You can't just tell people to "go" without heping them get there. In Lausanne, Switzerland, we met up with Don Stephens again. He had something on his mind.

"I want you to pray about flying to Greece with me tomorrow. I want you to see the ship."

Don was launching the YWAM Mercy Ship Ministries, and the chosen vessel of honor was docked in Greece getting renovated and made seaworthy. It had been a passenger liner. But Don wanted to sail it around the world under the banner of Jesus.

Don went on to tell us that the first time he heard Keith's recording of the "Easter Song" he got choked up with both joy and tears. He'd named the ship the M/V Anastasis, which means resurrection in Greek, and the Lord used the song to help encourage him not to give up in launching the ship ministry.

Later that night, Keith and I felt a go-ahead from the Lord to go to Greece.

Once on board the M/V Anastasis we were shocked—this was more than a ship, it was a floating city for the Lord! The ship was staffed with 120 people from thirty nations. It was two football fields long, eight stories high, seventy feet wide, with huge cargo-holds to take donated food, medicine, and clothing to people with little or nothing—evangelizing at every port. And *everybody* was a volunteer, raising their own support—including Don and his wife, Deyon, and the Captain, Ben Applegate, who'd worked for thirty years at a shipping company.

Don said there would also be a hospital on board, so they could perform surgery right at the docks. And they'd have a training school—only this one would be a traveling one!

But the impact from this part of the trip didn't come so much from seeing a first-class ship, or the scope of their mission, as much as it came from being touched by the lives of Don and Deyon Stephens.

On the outside they looked like a typical southern California family—good-looking enough to have their pictures in an ad! Don was tall and dark-haired, and Deyon and their three children were all blonds. With Don's giftings, he could have been a corporate president somewhere, bringing home a hefty paycheck. But instead, they were living in a small ship's cabin that made our old bedroom in the Ranch House look like a palace! It was decorated nicely—but it was *tiny*.

Being a mom, I focused in on their children—Heidi, Luke, and John Paul. John Paul, their youngest, was handicapped. At six he couldn't speak, feed himself, or walk without assistance. But he was a beautiful child and had obviously received much love. He was surrounded by a big loving family, including the staff family on board. I remembered the times I'd thought (with great relief) that God wouldn't ask me to go to the mission field because I had children—as if that automatically disqualified me. Well, my thinking was getting turned around. By this time I'd seen many children on the mission field with their parents, and they were some of the greatest kids I'd ever met.

The circumstances were hard on the ship—and they didn't have enough money to fix everything or put fuel in the tanks, let alone pay for the planned voyage to the States. But everyone had such a joyful spirit. We didn't hear any grumbling or complaining anywhere. It was an obvious sacrifice—but they'd transcended that. They were on a mission for God. We instantly loved them and loved what they were doing.

When we saw how they were living, Keith said to Don, "Could we pay for you and your family, and two or three other couples that you choose, to go to the beach and enjoy yourselves for a few days?"

So the next day, we wound up at Kinetta Beach, halfway between Athens and Corinth. This particular beach had real significance for our YWAM guests because it was where their "fish miracle" happened.

Just a few months before, the whole crew was in the middle of a rotating commitment to forty days of fasting and prayer. They wanted to launch the public ministry of the ship and, at that time, the government wouldn't allow the crew to live on the ship. So some of them had to rent these little beach bungalows at Kinetta. One day, while a crew member was walking at the shore, twelve fish literally jumped out of the water and onto the beach. A few days later, 210 fish did the same thing while another crew member was sitting on the sand. And then a few days after that, on the 38th day of the fast, in the middle of a time of intercession, the fish started jumping again. In all, a total of 8,301 fish jumped onto the beach in those few days! And in full view of many local residents, who had never seen anything like it.

Don said, "As soon as we began to see what was happening, we took a very accurate account, and the total is not exaggerated by even one fish."

For Don, it was a modern-day parable, a sign from the Lord that he was hearing their prayers and would provide the necessary finances, bring in a harvest of souls, and release a fresh wave of people into world missions. After the fish were counted and cleaned, the crew ate them for months. In fact, we even had a taste.

I sat on the white sand with Deyon one afternoon at the edge of the blue, Aegean Sea. She was holding John Paul and letting him splash in the water. We were talking about the Lord and his goodness. She told me one of the ways the Lord revealed himself to her through this child. She told me about a day when she went to the Lord in tears of disappointment at the lack of relationship she was experiencing with her young son.

"Lord, he doesn't even know me. If I didn't feed him, love him, and clothe him, he would die. Yet he doesn't even acknowledge my presence."

She asked the Lord it if would be possible for John Paul to respond even a little to the tremendous love she felt for him. A glimmer of recognition. A turning of the head. A smile.

"But in that moment, instead, I had a revelation of how God longs for relationship with his children. John Paul could not respond. Men often will not respond to God."

Deyon loved her son deeply—you couldn't miss that. She wouldn't have chosen the hardships of his handicap but she understood in a deep measure how, "God works all things together for good to those that love him."

"Our family has learned lessons of acceptance, service, compassion, and patience that apply far beyond John Paul. We've learned that God loves us for who we are and not solely for what we can do."

"Grace," I responded quickly.

"Yes. Grace."

Meanwhile Keith was excited about the ship's practical expression of Christianity to the needy—feeding, clothing, and giving medical aid from the ship hospital—which went hand-in-hand with proclaiming the gospel.

Keith told Don, "You'll need other ships in the future. We'll help get the word out for staff and filling the cargo bay. That's one of the reasons for our friendship!"

By the time we left Greece, we were overwhelmed by all we'd seen on the ship, in Amsterdam, and across Europe. The need was tremendous. But we were also excited about the vision, commitment, and sacrifice we saw in all the leaders we'd just met. Now we knew why Loren Cunningham had given almost twenty years of his life, building YWAM to lay a foundation to reach the world.

I could already see what was going on in Keith's mind. John Dawson's counsel was coming back: "What are you telling people to repent *to*?"—"America has a destiny. . . ." Keith could see there were systems, like YWAM, in place to reach the lost. And there were Christians who were called to go. He wanted to bridge the gap between the two.

By this time, about 230,000 people were getting our newsletter and Keith was already planning ways to reach all of them—and everyone who came to his concerts, too.

I thought of the lady I'd seen down that little side street in Amsterdam. One lost person on her way toward eternal separation from God. The world was full of people like her.

We wanted to go home and sound a trumpet while the message was hot and burning in our hearts—to call together an army of people to rescue those who were perishing. An army marching against the enemy in the power of God!

On a final stopover in England, words and messages were already forming in our heads.

One night, over dinner in an English steakhouse, I felt an urgency to get this new message into a song for Keith as quickly as possible. Maybe it was the pained reflection in his eyes. Here were fields of souls ripe for harvest—but there were so few workers. We usually wrote songs about our personal experiences, but this time I sensed I needed to capture our feelings right away. I grabbed a paper napkin and started writing down some words:

Jesus commands us to go!
It should be an exception if we stay. . . .

Shortly after returning from Europe, Keith moved into action! He planned three large benefit concerts to help the M/V Anastasis and a fall concert tour to bring a missions challenge to the Christians in America. Keith also had a few previous commitments—two festivals in southern California. The perfect place to try out his new message. And as it turned out, Keith would be ministering with Loren Cunningham! Keith wanted to talk to him about everything the Lord had shown us in Europe.

The concerts were at Devonshire Downs and there was room for several thousand people in the bleachers and in the field. Keith sang in the afternoon under the blazing sun, but at his evening concert his message came across most powerfully.

There was a new kind of excitement in Keith when he walked onto the stage that night in June.

Keith sat down purposely at the piano and took a moment to talk about our international God. "God is not an American, or even a Republican as some of us like to think! He loves everybody the same, and his heart goes out to the masses whether they're known or forgotten."

Then he picked up his Bible. "There's a little command found in the Bible that says, 'Go ye into all the nations and preach the gospel unto every creature, and make disciples of men.' And we like to think that was for the disciples. That's for old ladies that can't find husbands and need to bury their troubles on the mission field. That's for humanitarians. Or that's for *real* Christians who are so spiritual they can't stay in society, so they gotta go overseas and bury themselves in some tribe somewhere down in the Amazon!"

Keith was really starting to warm up now, and he had everyone's attention.

"I'll tell you what, folks, the world isn't being won today because we're not doing it! It's *our* fault! This generation of Christians is responsible for this generation of souls on the earth. Nowhere in the world is the gospel so plentiful as in the United States. Nowhere! And I don't want to see us stand before God on that day and say, 'But God, I didn't *hear* you call me!' Here's something for all of you to chew on—you don't need to hear a call. You're *already* called!"

Besides our recent trip, Keith was being fueled by the shocking statistics we'd heard. They were hard to believe, but they were true. There were only 85,000 people on the mission field in the whole world! And only a small percentage were trying to reach the 2.7 billion who'd never even heard the Gospel *once* or about one for every 450,000. While in America there were over one million full-time workers which is one worker for every 230 people! And to top it off, ninety-four percent of all ordained preachers worldwide ministered to only nine percent of the world's population—those who spoke English.

"It's either God's will that the world's going to hell or it's the Church's fault because they're not being obedient to what the Bible says about going into all nations and preaching the gospel. If you stay home from going into all the nations, you'd better be able to say to God, 'You called me to stay home. I know that as a fact'!"

Like all outdoor events there's always a little shuffling around the fringes, but the crowd was riveted by Keith's direct message. Keith asked everybody who knew they had a definite call from God to stay home to raise their hands. Then he counted!

"One . . . two. Two. Might be three or four that I missed. Well, the rest of you are called unless God tells you otherwise. Now don't go out and sell everything and leave tomorrow! Get some training.

"There's a rule in the armed forces: Always obey the last order you got, until you get new orders from command headquarters. The last order I got in my Bible was 'Go'!"

Then Keith played two of our new songs. We'd finished "Jesus Commands Us To Go" together, and I'd just written one that was so new Keith had to pull a lyric sheet out of his Bible to read as he sang. Even from the side of the stage, I could see his eyes fill with compassion as he sang "Open Your Eyes":

> *Open your eyes to the world all around you,*
> *Open your eyes . . . open your eyes.*
> *This world is much more than the things*
> *That surround you.*
> *You must arise and open your eyes.*
> *Sometimes we're too busy to share.*
> *But Jesus wants us to care.*
>
> *Open your arms to the naked and shivering.*
> *Open your arms . . . open your arms.*
> *We need a little less taking,*
> *A whole lot more giving.*
> *We're so safe and warm, we can open our arms*
> *And love a little bit stronger*
> *And pray a lttle bit longer!*
>
> *Jesus says*
> *When we love someone in His name*
> *We're loving Him.*
> *And Jesus says*
> *When we touch someone in His name*
> *We're touching Him.*
> *And we need to show them the light,*
> *We've got to pour out our lives!*

Open your hearts to the ones who are desperate.
Open your hearts . . . open your hearts.
They may never repay you,
But their souls are worth it!
New life you impart, when you open your heart.
Jesus loves all men the same
So we've got to go out in His name. . . .

Unknown to any of us, Sparrow had a cameraman to videotape all of their artists that night. Keith was no longer with Sparrow, but when he sat down at the piano this fellow had a sense that he was "supposed to" tape him anyway. So he turned the video camera on.

Keith would have objected. He didn't like having cameras rolling during his ministry. This would be one of the *only* videos of Keith in concert.

After the concert, we had a late night meal at a coffee shop with John Dawson, who was also at the festival. Keith figured John would be excited about his strong missions message.

"Keith," John said, "God is getting ready to use you in a big way to challenge a multitude of young people into missions. But if you keep overstating the point, you'll disqualify the whole message."

"Well, that's how strong I feel it! God's heart is broken because his people refuse to *go* when the need is so great!"

"That's true! But it's up to God to tell each person *where* to go. Keith, I know your heart is right, but you can't say 99.99 per cent are called to leave America and everybody else is in sin."

Keith realized that in his urgency, he did overstate the point.

"Well how would you say it then?" he asked John.

They had quite a lengthy discussion about presenting the truth of missions in a way that wouldn't put guilt on those who are genuinely called to serve the Lord in America.

Keith saw John's point and realized he could still present a strong challenge, but in a slightly different way. And as we got up to leave the coffee shop, Keith said, "Next time, I'll say it differently."

We had asked Loren and his wife, Darlene, to join us at a beach house we'd rented for a week in Oxnard. On the first evening, we sat up talking a long time—sharing visions and dreams in the Lord. And the next morning, some new ideas crystalized.

Keith and Loren had ministered together a few times now, and Keith thought they made a great team.

"Loren, let's keep doing this!" he said. "Let's go across the nation together and get the word out about missions and challenge people to go! I'll have big concerts and you can come and share the vision."

"That sounds wonderful," Loren agreed. "And let's have a faith goal of seeing 100,000 people raised up for world missions."

One hundred thousand! That number jumped out at me. While in Greece, Keith and I sat on the beach under the stars with Don and Deyon Stephens and prayed for the lost. Keith looked up into the clear sky of countless, twinkling lights and asked God for 100,000 short-term missionaries. We all agreed in prayer. Now, on another continent, and at another beach, Loren had come out with the same number to pray for.

A beautiful sense of God's presence filled the room. We all felt it was a special moment, and knew we needed to pray together and seal everything in the Spirit. Like old friends, we moved almost effortlessly into deep levels of prayer.

Loren prayed about the vision.

"Lord, you see the whole world and all the needs in it. Show us how to get more laborers to the field. We're asking for 100,000, Lord."

Keith was lying on the floor—face down before the Lord.

"Oh, God," Keith said, choked with emotion, "help me be a vessel to carry this message to your people. I want to do my part. Give people hearts to hear."

"And God," said Darlene, "we ask that you would especially speak to the Christian youth. Show us how to stir them with a vision to reach the lost."

I'd felt a prayer building up in my heart as well, and I jumped in after Darlene. "Lord, please let your people see that being a missionary is not 'weird' but that it's the most exciting way to live on the face of the earth!"

By the time we were done praying, our hearts were bonded together. We knew the Lord had knit our hearts for ministry purposes as well as the joy of friendship. But for Keith, it was even deeper. In a way, his heart had found a home. Loren was so full of grace, and Keith's high intensity didn't rattle him. Loren loved and accepted Keith. And Keith knew it. As they embraced to say goodbye, there was a very tender spirit between them. There were tears in Keith's eyes.

"You're like a father to me," Keith whispered.

It was an awareness in both of their hearts—a rare and special relationship. A gift from the Lord.

As we watched the Cunninghams drive off, we had such a rush of excitement in our hearts. Keith was going to travel all across America with Loren, stirring people toward missions!

How could any of us have known it was not to be?

Our happy family. 1981

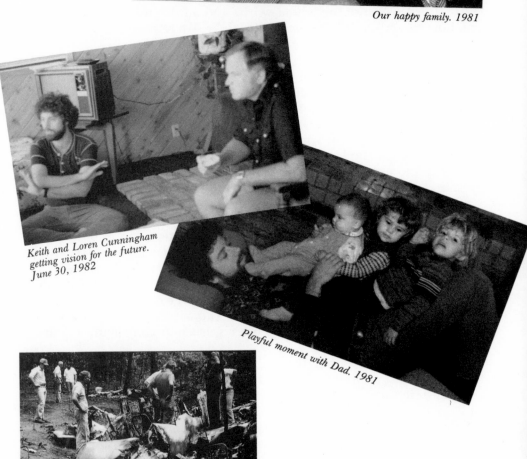

Keith and Loren Cunningham getting vision for the future. June 30, 1982

Playful moment with Dad. 1981

Cessna 414.

"Unless A Grain Of Wheat . . ."

Gary Null

A STRING OF STRANGE EVENTS, HAPPENING AROUND THE SAME time, left us with an unsettled feeling after we returned to Texas. First, the dog we'd had ever since we'd lived in California had started acting strange. When Keith took her to the vet, he discovered she had cancer. She was headed toward a slow painful death and we had two options. We could put her to sleep, or Keith could bring her home and shoot her. The vet said that would be quicker and more humane.

"Shoot her? I don't even own a gun," Keith objected.

When Keith came home and told me the news he was visibly upset.

Nevertheless, he borrowed a gun and walked out into the fields, with our dog walking painfully at his side. Totally unsuspecting. I choked up as I watched them go.

When Keith came back, he told me he took Cy to the edge of the grave he'd dug and told her to sit. She was wagging her tail and looking at him with her big liquid-brown eyes. Keith closed his eyes and pulled the trigger. He returned home spattered with her blood and very upset by the whole thing.

Next, a freak fire started in the storage closet of the new family room we'd built on our home. We were up after midnight having a meeting with some of the ministry leaders when we smelled smoke. At first we couldn't figure out where the smell was coming from, but we sniffed our way over to the closet. Somehow a feather comforter stored on the top shelf had gotten too close to a bare lightbulb which might have been left on for days. When we opened the door it was smouldering and smoking, ready to ignite. Only the fact that we'd been awake and in that part of the house saved us from a more disastrous fire.

Then, Keith and I were talking in the family room one day when we heard a crash! We jumped from the impact of it and rushed into the kitchen. Part of the ceiling had fallen in—a huge chunk, about six feet by four feet, was laying on the floor right in front of the sink. It was soaking wet and felt like it weighed a ton. There must have been a slow leak in the roof. My first instinct was to be sure one of the kids wasn't trapped underneath. But they were in another room—Josiah playing with his little men and Bethany with her "babies". I sent up a prayer of gratitude, knowing that if either one of them had been playing on the floor there, the weight of the ceiling could have caused severe injury—or worse.

And then there was this other, more vague feeling. Keith was the one who voiced it. "I just don't know what it is. Things are going too good. I feel it's the calm before the storm. Like something bad's going to happen."

Just hearing him gave me an uneasy feeling, too.

The truth of the matter was things really were going good. Very good. Even Keith's journal entries reflected the mood:

We have so much to be grateful for. The only thing we need is a closer walk with God. We have everything else a Christian couple could ever want, and for this I'm eternally grateful, Jesus.

Earlier in the year, we had started a ten-week, Intensive Christian Training School for believers interested in learning more about the character of God and about Christian service. We were also just raising the beams on our new, half-million dollar cafeteria and worship center with classrooms, bookstore, guest rooms, and plenty of space to fellowship.

At one of those early ICT classes, still being held in the Ranch House, Keith said, "I've been going back through our tracts and rewriting them a little bit. Taking out some of the rough edges and barbs. Keeping what's from Jesus, and taking out a lot of what's from Keith. There are even a couple of them I'm just going to take out of print. Our message, as you will see, will be to strengthen, encourage, and build up believers—not so much to shoot at things that are wrong but to build up the areas that are right. I'm not saying that what I wrote or preached in the past was wrong. It's just that some of it could have been said a little differently—and with a lot more grace."

Grace. That was the operative word in Keith's life these days.

Keith had already decided to quit distributing "The Selling of Jesus," and he was in the process of reevaluating "The Catholic Chronicles". He believed he'd been too harsh in places and told me, "There's too much of me in them." He had also edited, "What's Wrong With The Gospel?"

Keith had even come to a place of believing that God *could* direct some Christian artists to do ticketed concerts. In his heart, I think he hoped they'd make a way for those who could not afford the price of a ticket to be able to attend—but he was no longer willing to say someone who sold tickets was automatically in sin. Keith knew the Lord had led him in a totally different way, but he also knew God might tell someone else to do things differently.

I was seeing a new kind of thoughtful maturity coming into Keith's life. In part, I could attribute it to some of the relationships Keith had developed with people like Winkie, Leonard, John, Leland and now with Loren. The grace, wisdom and patience of these men was starting to rub off on Keith. And Keith, hungering for more contentment in his own life, soaked it up.

One day, Leland came to him in regard to some strong statements Keith had made.

"Keith, God is preparing you to become a strong voice. I have no doubt about it. But as a friend I want to tell you that if you strike out at everyone and turn them off, you might lose your ability to speak into their lives. When God is ready for you to speak to leaders, the doors might not be open."

Keith looked at him for a moment and simply said, "Thank you. I need that. I need people speaking into my life."

Keith was coming into a lot of new light. And at each glimpse of higher ground he took action. Several months before, he'd begun to realize that his own humanity had crept into his leadership style at Last Days, and he wrote a letter to those who might have been offended. He acknowledged that we had erred in the past with some of our rules and policies and let them know how things had changed. To those that had been hurt Keith said, "I am totally, completely, and utterly sorry."

Keith was also in the midst of writing letters of apology and making phone calls to different individuals whenever the Lord showed him there was something he needed to make right. It was a beautiful thing to watch, because Keith was so excited about seeing relationships restored that had been strained. He went at it with urgency.

Keith wrote a letter to a huge listing of Christian bookstore owners across America, saying that when he decided to pull his recordings from the bookstores, he'd said some things too strongly, offending a lot of good people who really did love the Lord. He said he was only trying to be obedient to what God wanted *him* to do, but that bookstores were also a God-ordained way of distribution. "My desire to not exclude anyone has not decreased at all," he wrote. "I hope you can understand that I am a man of principle, and yet, like a pendulum, I have a tendency to go too far to make a point. I fear that in the past I have done just that."

Keith wanted the bookstores to go ahead and sell his albums, but he wanted to have a sticker on each one that said, "If you cannot afford the retail price of this album, write to Last Days Ministries and we'll send you information on how you can get it for whatever you can afford."

On all fronts, Keith was feeling like he might have been too absolute in some areas. There could have been another way to say some of the same things—an approach that would not compromise his beliefs, but at the same time make it easier for others to hear the *spirit* of what he was saying.

Keith also knew there were many others out there with strong personalities who might "be trapped" in their giftings, like he had been. Using himself as an example, he wrote an article in the newsletter called "For Prophets Only". Keith knew there was a prophetic gifting from the Lord, but this article was a balancing word for those who liked to think of themselves as "prophets".

Keith wrote:

. . . *young people (usually men) who believe that God has raised them up to tell people what is wrong with their ministry or their lives, or both. [A common problem in the church today,] these people are usually hurt,*

*independent, talkative, stubborn, unteachable, and unyielding. I know,
because I have been one of them!*

*They don't beat around the bush, but say exactly what's on their mind
. . . aren't very popular, but don't care because they believe they're "being
persecuted for righteousness' sake". They find fault with almost everything
and . . . say to be "kind" would be phoney for them. They know that the
fruit of the Holy Spirit includes kindness, gentleness, self-control, and
long-suffering, but say most people misinterpret those Scriptures, and
besides, there's a lot more in the Bible about zeal and judgment and the
wrath of God. . . .deep inside, most of them really do want to please God,
but they're so insulated from criticism (because they think they're a rejected
"prophet") that no one can reach them. And unless God intervenes in their
lives, they cannot truly be used in any long-term way because of their
unteachable, uncorrectable spirit.*

*So many people told me I was a "prophet" over the years I believed
"they must be right." . . . It's not that I no longer believe I'm called to do
that, it's just that now I see that every believer is called to do that.*

*I'm not called to be a prophet, I'm called to be a CHRISTIAN—a
servant of the living God! That is the highest calling that anyone can
realize. . . .*

At first, when I saw all the changes Keith was going through,
I found myself thinking, *I hope Keith doesn't lose his edge.*

No chance. As remarkable as his changes were, Keith was still
unmistakably Keith. He was intense in his faith, outspoken in his
opinions, and very strong in his convictions. Only he wasn't quite
as driven. He still got impatient and on edge sometimes, but he
had more peace than ever before. And as Keith received the grace
God had given him, he could extend more grace to others.

In early July, John Dawson invited us up to the YWAM base
in Cimmaron, Colorado. Keith and the kids and I flew up in the
Cessna 414, with one of the pilots from the YWAM Twin Oaks
base. Keith went mainly to spend more time with John but it
ended up being the restful vacation we'd envisioned for Europe.

Keith was at rest and loving life when he wrote:

JULY 22, 1982

**We went to Colorado and had a great time. The family and I
caught about 120 trout. We had some good family fellowship
and I can definitely say that I had my vacation. . . .**

**We have found out that Melody is pregnant! Thank You
Father, I truly pray this child is healthy. . . . Please, Father, I
need your help. I am in great need of wisdom beyond my years
and ability. . . . Today I went to work on my missions article.
Please help me redeem my time!**

Others noticed the inner change in Keith, too.

A few days after I found out I was pregnant, all of Second Chapter came over to the Ranch House for dinner. They were leaving for New York the next day to do some concerts on the inner city streets with David Wilkerson.

After dinner Keith took Josiah outside with Annie and Nelly. There was a storm blowing up in the distance and the thunderous black sky was dramatic. They stood at the top of a sloping field and Josiah, his blond curls popping out from under his cowboy hat, was jumping up and down in excitement as they watched the colors change and the clouds roll by. "Wow, Daddy look!" he shouted.

Annie sensed such a big difference in Keith. For him, everything usually needed a purpose. But now he wasn't saying, "This meadow would be prettier if there was an orphanage for the Lord in it." He was enjoying the simple beauty of God's creation. Watching Keith hold Josiah, in this relaxed moment, it occurred to Annie how different Keith was now, in the summer of 1982, from the way he'd been just a year before.

One night, Annie and Buck went out to dinner with us. On the drive home, she'd said, "I'm so grateful that God loves me. That's the first thing I knew about God, and it's gotten me through every bit of misery and every bit of joy."

But Keith had replied, "Sometimes I'm not sure if God loves me. I know he's right. I know he's God. But as far as really *feeling* his love for me—well, I don't know it like you do."

Annie's heart hurt when Keith had said that—but tonight for many reasons she was sure he'd discovered that love. She'd seen it in him. One afternoon recently, Keith caught her eye in a chance moment and simply said, "I love you." He said it in such a free yet forever kind of way—just like the love of the Father.

Now he was so relaxed, like a happy daddy sharing the colors of the deepening sky with his little boy. They were all wondering if we'd get hit with any rain this time. Typical of the weather in Texas, your neighbor can get rained on and you won't.

Sometimes storms just blow up out of nowhere.

On July 28th, I stepped out onto our back porch, and a blast of furnace-hot humid air hit me in the face. It was so stifling I could hardly breathe. It had to be the most oppressive day we'd had this year.

I hoped the air conditioning would be working in the Ranch House, where I was headed for our regular prayer meeting. The whole ministry fasted one day a week, from after dinner Tuesday until dinner on Wednesday. Today, Wednesday, we'd all stopped to gather for worship and prayer.

Keith sat cross-legged with his guitar on the living room floor of the Ranch House and led us in worship. He seemed particularly peaceful as he gazed around the room at everyone lovingly. He was also visibly excited about our missions vision—and about me.

Keith surprised me totally when he announced, "God is going to raise my wife up! She is going to speak out against abortion—but that's not all."

Where was this coming from? Why now—just when I was pregnant again?

"The Lord is going to use Melody in a mighty way," Keith was saying, "and she's going to speak about many different things, in many different places!"

It was news to me. But I was willing, if that's what the Lord wanted.

Once the meeting broke, I eventually ended up in the office. Keith had already been there and had typed in his journal, which he was now keeping on computer. I caught Michelle's name on what looked like a very long entry, and figured Keith must have been talking about her expected visit the next day. They were on the verge of a reconciliation.

I started to "save" his entry so I could use the terminal to work on an article. But in the middle of the normal process I lost confidence. What if I erased it by accident? I went and found Keith and he came in to finish the process. However, as usual, he was moving fast. He hit the wrong button and blipped out his own entry. Keith knew it was his fault, but he was upset with me for even messing with the computer while he was using it. I felt terrible. But luckily, he only lost that one entry.

One of the highlights of this blistering hot day was that John and DeDe Smalley were coming for a quick visit. We'd met them years ago when we first started going to the Vineyard. They had six children, and they were all on their way to Connecticut to start a home fellowship and eventually a church.

The Smalley's arrived shortly before dinner. Keith took them on a quick tour of the offices, and then we sat talking at the dinner table in the Ranch House living room as we broke our fast.

DeDe and I were comparing notes on motherhood while Keith and John talked excitedly about the new work in Connecticut. John was enthusiastic about the move and the new opportunities for ministry. Keith wanted him to lead one of our

"New Believers Meetings" after our fall tour on the east coast. We already had some arenas booked for it.

Josiah and Bethany came in just then. They were dressed in matching, light-blue bib shorts, looking adorable. They had just returned from their swimming lessons, and their hair hung in damp ringlets around their sun-kissed faces. They both looked like little angels. I was proud, to say the least, of these two sweet little children.

After dinner, Keith lost no time because it was getting late. Even though we were all tired they wanted to see the rest of the ranch, including a quick, sightseeing flight in our leased Cessna 414. Our pilot Don Burmeister, who'd flown in the military, would take them up. Apparently, John had promised one of their children a plane ride, and Keith was excited to give them a bird's-eye view of the area.

I took all the small children to our house to play, while the rest went off in a station wagon to see more of the ranch.

Just a little while later, Keith rushed into the house. I was standing at the sink, and Keith wanted me to come with them on the flight. I didn't want to go, so Keith dashed back out the front door.

I was struck by the sudden silence. The living room was empty. Were all the kids going, too? No, Rebekah was still playing in her bedroom.

I ran to the front door. Keith was standing on the far side of the station wagon. He was just about to get in. John and DeDe were inside with all their kids. Josiah was already inside, too. I couldn't even see him amidst all the other heads. All I could see was Bethany. She was standing by the gate and in her sweet little girl voice, she was calling, "I want to go too!"

Keith said, "Let her in the car."

The door swung open and Bethany took a few steps toward the car. I stood on the porch and thought, "No! Not her too. I, at least, want to keep Bethany!" It seemed like a crazy thought. But Bethany was lifted into the car. It was all happening so fast. I didn't expect *all* the kids to go.

Something didn't seem right. I wanted to run out and call my children back, but I didn't want to be a spoilsport. I knew they'd cry if I tried to separate them from the other kids, but I couldn't understand where these awful feelings were coming from. I felt stupid for being a "worried mother", and I told myself they'd be back in a few minutes all safe and sound.

Just as Bethany was lifted into the car, Keith hesitated. He called across the yard to me in an offhanded way.

"If I don't come back, raise Rebekah to be a woman of God."

With Keith traveling so much we'd talked about the possibility of death before. But this seemed like an odd time to bring up the subject. Of course, he was kidding.

"What about this one?" I said with a slight laugh, patting my just-pregnant tummy.

"If it's a boy, name him Daniel!"

"You mean you don't want me to name him after you?"

I said it playfully, but the conversation was starting to take on serious tones.

"Okay. If it's a boy, you can name him after me."

Keith jumped in, and the car drove off. As I walked back into the house, it felt so empty. I really didn't like Keith taking the kids on the airplane any more than necessary. I felt so uneasy I figured I'd better pass the time constructively. So I sat down at the computer terminal and started to write. I knew I was going to feel silly about my fears when they all got back . . . in a few minutes.

But in a few minutes the phone rang.

It was one of the girls from the office. "Our plane just went down! I'm going to call an ambulance, but I wanted to tell Keith first. Will you tell him?"

It was like getting socked in the stomach.

"Sure. . . .", I said, numbly. I didn't want to take even a moment to explain that Keith already knew.

I grabbed the car keys and ran out the door, leaving Rebekah with one of the girls who was staying with us to help me with the kids.

It took me less than a minute to get to the mile-long runway, but try as I might to find our plane at the far end, I couldn't see anything. I drove down the airstrip, and there were people running. I quickly picked up a few as I went along. At the far end of the runway there was a large field, owned by someone else. And beyond that there were woods. From the end of the airstrip I could now see a thin column of smoke rising out of the woods in the distance.

I remembered the phone message, "Our plane just went down. . . ." What did that mean? I'd thought maybe it just "went down" at the end of the airstrip. Malfunctioned, or skid on its side after an aborted take-off. But it had obviously meant the plane was in the air and "went down" from there.

Every breath I drew became a prayer. *Jesus . . . Jesus . . . Jesus . . . this can't be happening.*

I couldn't drive through our neighbor's field to the woods, because it was fenced off. People were jumping the fence and going on foot but it was a big field and I thought I'd get there quicker by driving. One of the guys I'd picked up said he knew how to get there on another road. But when we got onto the highway that bordered the south end of our property we couldn't get where we needed to go. There was a locked gate across that road.

I waited in the car while he ran to the nearest house to see if they could let us through. I was getting angry now. Did anyone know where we were going? I kept thinking I should have been there already. A numb feeling was covering me—only my stomach was turning. *Please God, let them be alive.*

The property owner came running out and we jumped in his pickup truck. Unlocking the gate, he drove us across the field and onto a road that wound through the woods. Finally, it looked like we were close. It had taken so long, an ambulance was already parked at the edge of the woods by a barbed-wire fence.

I jumped out of the pickup and someone lifted me over the fence. Then I took off through the thick, uncleared woods, my thin, cotton gauze skirt catching on the sharp branches and underbrush, not really knowing what direction I should even go in. Other people were running through the woods, too, and I was very frustrated because they all seemed to be passing me by.

I stopped a few times, totally out of breath, and feeling like I might pass out. But I had to keep going. My husband and children needed me.

I kept running, listening for their screams or cries. It was totally quiet, except for the sound of people running through the woods. Since I didn't hear anyone crying out in pain I told myself that everyone was probably fine. Maybe a little shook up—but fine. *Keith might even be amused when he sees how distraught I am.*

After what seemed like an eternity, I finally broke into a clearing.

Instantly, I was overwhelmed by the awesome silence that just hung in the air. Everyone there was just standing still. No one said a word. I felt something warm beneath my feet. The ground I was standing on was black and smoldering. Hopefully, I peered through the smoky haze—but I didn't see Keith, or the children, or anyone else who was on the airplane. I didn't even see the plane.

One girl I knew walked toward me. Tears were slipping down her face. She looked at me as if to say something—then quietly passed by. I didn't understand. Walking forward into the silence, I headed toward what seemed to be the center of the charred area. Some trees were broken off halfway up, and the ground was littered with downed limbs, like there had been a big explosion. Everything was totally calm—and hushed.

I finally got in sight of a blackened, smoking metal shell. Where were my babies? Where was Keith? One of the men walked up and hugged me—wrapped his arms around my shoulders and almost hung on me, sobbing out loud. I started crying too, but I wasn't sure why. I thought, *Maybe this isn't even our plane! Maybe another plane crashed and we only thought it was ours.* I asked someone, but it *was* our Cessna. Maybe someone had been thrown from the plane. They had already searched, and found no one.

I got as close as I could to what was left of the airplane and looked right inside, because the top was completely gone. I couldn't see anyone. Then I said to myself, *What are you looking for, Melody? What do you want to see? Do you want to see your husband and children burnt to a crisp? Is that the way you want to remember them?*

I quickly turned and walked away and didn't look again. In a few minutes, Janet, our pilot's wife, arrived. She was stunned, but calm as we spoke.

"Where's Keith?" she asked.

"Keith was in the plane with Josiah and Bethany and the Smalley's."

"Oh, no!" she exclaimed.

Then Janet said, "Do you know for sure who was flying the plane?"

"As far as I know, Keith said Don was the one taking them up," I replied.

Some rescue workers arrived. They were asking how many people were in the plane, and I was the only person who knew exactly who was on board. I started counting. "There were the Smalley's with their six kids—that's eight. And Keith and our kids, and Don. Twelve."

The rescue workers just looked at me when I told them. Then it hit me, too. Why on earth did *twelve* people go up in that plane?

Now I felt so weak I wanted to lie down, but there wasn't any place there in the woods. I felt so very vulnerable suddenly. There was no point in staying around, so I turned and started back out of the woods. Janet came, too.

When we were almost out of the woods, we passed a fireman on his way in. He must have thought I was a survivor, because I'm sure I looked a mess.

He smiled. "Everybody okay?"

I simply said, "There are no survivors." What that meant to him, and what that meant to me, were two different things.

As Janet and I, and a few others, were driving back through the field, the strangest thing started happening. It had been a totally clear day, but suddenly dark clouds seemed to gather out of nowhere. The odd thing was, they were only over our property. Now, large lightning bolts shot from the clouds—all the way to the ground. And it suddenly started to rain. The drops were huge, like fifty-cent pieces as they spattered against the windshield.

As we turned onto the highway and drove along our property line, it was easy to see that the clouds and lightning were only over our land! The raindrops looked like huge heavenly tears. We felt the distinct presence of the Lord in those moments. He *wanted* us to know he was there. What happened was not *apart* from his knowing or caring. Most definitely, what we were seeing was a demonstration of his power—and his presence.

When I got home I headed straight for the phone and called Leonard before doing anything else.

"Leonard, this is Melody," I said, still numb. "Keith and Josiah and Bethany have gone to be with the Lord."

"I'll be right over!"

Then, I fell on my knees beside my bed and started sobbing.

Later I was hit with every emotion imaginable. I felt like my insides had been ripped out but, by some mistake, I didn't die. Waves of numbness and intense sorrow washed over me again and again. Sometimes I cried my heart out to the Lord. And sometimes I could talk about the crash like I was talking about something that happened to someone else.

My last conversation with Keith kept coming back. What prompted him to talk about not coming back? Why didn't I say something about my concerns? Why didn't I grab Bethany when I had the chance? I felt so guilty. Maybe the plane wouldn't have crashed if there had been one or two less children in it. Maybe it was my fault.

One of the hardest things was not having Keith to talk to, especially about the children. Keith was the only other human being who could possibly understand my anguish over losing Josiah and Bethany, the only one who loved them as much as I did. I'd think things like, *Keith, you won't believe what happened,* or, *Keith, our babies are dead. . . .* I wanted him to hold me while I cried. To tell me we could make it—that he understood. But I was on my own with God for the first time. I wondered if I could make it.

And besides my personal loss, I thought of the others on the plane—they were gone as well. They were such wonderful people who were totally committed to helping others and serving God with all their hearts. And all the children! None of it made any sense.

I also grieved over losing Keith's ministry to the world. What a terrible loss. We so desperately need people like Keith, people who love us enough to tell us the truth. With all that the Lord had been showing Keith recently, I knew his ministry would have been more powerful than ever.

I knew God was ultimately in control. He didn't intervene when the plane started to go down. He could have, but he didn't. That must mean the crash was his will. Or was it? Maybe it was a strategy of the enemy to get rid of Keith. Even if it was, God *allowed* it. I had a million questions, but knowing *why* wouldn't change anything.

The only thing that kept me going was a sense of the presence of God. I was blanketed in his grace. I felt his presence like I'd never felt it before. Buffering the blows. Holding me. Comforting me. It didn't erase the pain. But I felt God's tender heart for me. The pain was real and it was constant. When I wanted to lie down and not get up he helped me to my feet. When I didn't want to eat he reminded me of the new life inside me that he'd given me to take care of. And my precious little Rebekah needed me, too.

Some things I had to just "put on hold". In the meantime, the loss of my husband, two children and nine others was enough to deal with. The reality of the situation demanded my immediate attention.

People needed to be notified. Arrangements needed to be made. The word about the crash traveled quickly through our quiet little community of Garden Valley, and my home was filled with activity—especially the coming and going of friends. Leonard and Martha Ravenhill, Leland Paris, Jimmy and Carol Owens who had moved here from Hawaii, and many others. I was comforted by so many people who loved me and showed it by their caring presence. They brought me food, cried with me, and dropped their lives to help me pick up and go on with mine.

On the night of the crash, John Dawson phoned. His first words to me were, "What we need right now is just to hear from Jesus. Get a pencil."

I grabbed one immediately, and wrote swiftly as John spoke the heart of the Lord to me:
"They are with Me.
My glory is revealed to them.
They are in my arms,

———

In My presence,
Not far from you, for I am with you, also.
Nothing has been in vain,
I will build on this foundation.
In gentleness I will lead you
And a multitude will enter my presence.
But a little while, my daughter,
And you, too, shall enter my presence—
For life in the body is as a passing shadow.
In that day I will wipe away every tear,
For you will all sit at My table."

Then John said, "Melody, your own healing comes from entering into their joy." That really spoke to me. I knew it was right.

But it was easier said than done. I did rejoice that they were with the Lord. I knew I would see them again in heaven, which made heaven all the sweeter to me. It was deeply comforting to know that my loved ones were in the presence of the Lord. I knew *they* were fine. But *I* was miserable. *I missed them.*

On the morning following the crash, I opened my eyes and for a split second it felt like any other morning. That was the only relief of the day as reality came quickly crashing in. I had a scheduled doctor's appointment that day to go in and have my pregnancy "officially" confirmed. I decided to keep it. I had to spend my time doing *something*.

My pregnancy was confirmed, but being in town was terrible. The plane crash was headline news. Complete with pictures. I saw newspapers in the drug store, and outside the restaurant where I stopped to eat. I wanted to stop and scream out loud to everyone— "That's my *family*. My husband. My children. How can you act like everything is normal? How can you be smiling today?"

For a few days, my friends Chris and Carole Beatty slept in the family room by the front door to provide a sense of security for the household. It was a good thing, because as news of the crash broke, the media came out in full force. It got crazy. News helicopters circled overhead, and we were swamped with reporters and camera crews wanting statements. A blockade was finally set up at the Last Days driveway to maintain some sense of privacy. So the news teams camped out there, just a few hundred yards from my door. Reporters knocked on my door, too. And Chris was there to talk to them.

As word got out to friends they began arriving for the Memorial Service scheduled for Saturday July 31st at the Agape Force ranch. Among them were Bill Maxwell, Don Stephens, Billy

Ray Hearn, Todd Fishkind, and many other friends and relatives from around the nation. Michelle came, too. It wasn't the reunion we'd expected, but just being together sealed the healing that had already begun.

Word also started to fan out all over the nation and literally around the world. Loren Cunningham was in Okinawa, Japan, when the news came over the U.S. Armed Forces radio station. Don Stephens was in Finland when he heard. Keith's grandmother in southern California unfortunately found out when she saw Keith's picture flashed across her television screen on the early morning news. Phone calls, letters, flowers, and telegrams poured in from people of all walks of life who had been touched by Keith and his music. But the majority of messages came from Christians out on the frontlines somewhere, who had been encouraged to serve Jesus in a deeper way because of Keith's ministry.

One of the important details I wanted to take care of was to write a letter to everyone who received our newsletter. On Friday, July 30th, I sat at a computer terminal up in the building. I wanted to tell them what happened in case they hadn't heard over the news, and to let them know that I was all right. And that God was faithful. With all my heart I believed God was sovereign and I held fast to that truth. I wanted everyone else to hang onto it, too.

As I sat there thinking, praying and crying, a phrase came into my mind out of nowhere: *A grain of wheat.*

I thought, *Isn't there something in the Bible about "a grain of wheat?"* I looked it up. It was John 12:24: "Unless a grain of wheat falls to the ground and dies it remains alone, but if it dies it bears much fruit."

I caught my breath as I read it. It was the first time I'd ever received a scripture in that way. And it was so specific. Was this the Lord speaking his heart to me regarding Keith's death? One of the things I was troubled about was the loss of Keith's ministry to the world. Was this God giving me a promise? Could he redeem even *this* disaster? The verse seemed to be a promise. But how on earth could it be fulfilled?

On Saturday, we had a Memorial Service for Keith, Don, Josiah, and Bethany. Several people were going to speak, and I decided I wanted to say something if I could get through it. The Memorial Service was open to anyone—but I was shocked to see all the cars lining the highway as we approached. Thousands of people had come from all over. Inside, it was standing room only.

Wayne Dillard, in his opening prayer, brought a very personal and sweet remembrance . . .

"Lord, I see today that we're not the ones to have suffered the greatest loss—but those who never knew Don and Keith and the Smalleys and the kids. Who were never touched by their lives and never drawn closer to you because of their love and their commitment to you."

Bill Maxwell reflected on meeting Keith and on those who had been impacted by his life.

"I met Keith before he did his first album. Billy Ray Hearn said, 'I have an artist who would like to talk to you about producing his album.' My first question was, 'Does he love Jesus?' Billy Ray said, 'You're gonna be in for a shock!'

"Keith was the kind of person that pricked you! He would arouse something in you. Sometimes it wasn't pleasant, but it all worked for good. Keith said we were like two rough edges working together. But something smooth came out of it."

John Dawson brought a word of comfort, encouraging us not to look at the situation from our own perspective. "Our friends who are departed from us are in a greater place of joy and contentment and fulfillment than they have ever known—or we could ever understand. And this, which we regard as a tragedy, prematurely put them in a position of receiving their hearts' desire."

I was planning to speak after John, but my heart was pounding so hard I thought I'd pass out. I decided to try, and when I did, I felt the grace of the Lord bathe me.

"I know that Keith is where he wanted to be most. His heart was so with the Lord—he just had such a desire and burning to be close to Jesus. And he really didn't care about this life!

"The children were unexpected. I was not prepared for Jesus to take Josiah and Bethany. But I think maybe they needed to be with their dad and God knew that. He took them on an airplane ride—and they just kept going. I don't understand, but I trust the Lord and I know that he has my best, and everyone's best, in mind.

"For those of you that don't already know, I'm pregnant and I'm due in March. And I am so grateful. I think this pregnancy is God's mercy to me. I am not empty. Jesus gave Keith two babies, and he's given me two. We're gonna share them. I'm really rejoicing in that."

Next, Tracey Hansen shared about Don. Tracey had worked closely with Don at Last Days. "I really loved Don. . . . Don has two strong sons who know the Lord and Savior, Jesus Christ, and they desire to serve him with their whole heart. That's the mark of a successful father. . . . the desire of Don's life was to serve the Lord God with all that he had."

One of the keynotes from Leonard Ravenhill's message was that this tragedy was making people all over the world respond to a sermon that none of us could have preached more powerfully. Somehow the Holy Spirit was saying to people all over, "Are you living too much for time and not enough for eternity?"

"Hundreds of phone calls came to me. Nobody said they loved Keith's preaching. Everybody said, 'We loved *Keith*.' David Wilkerson called from New York. He recently went into a town after Keith had been there. He said, 'That boy's got a message! Some of the churches were shaken in that town and the pastors rang home to do a bit of adjusting!'

"The Salvation Army never spoke about dying—they always talked about being promoted. The embarrassment is if you get to heaven without any blood on you—without any notches on your sword. You'll have to go back to the junior class, I'm sure. . . .

"Supposing Keith had just relaxed and said 'Let somebody else do it'. No, we're not going to be saved by works . . . but we're going to be rewarded for them!

"Someone once said, 'Any road will do if you're going nowhere.' I thought, 'Wait a minute! There are only two roads.' Either you're marching to Zion on the narrow way that leads to life eternal, or you're in the jazz band going to a lost eternity!

"There are three kinds of people in the world this afternoon—those who are afraid, those who don't know enough to be afraid, and those who know their Bibles.

"The only people entering are those whose names are written in the Lamb's Book of Life—isn't that wonderful? Is your name written there? . . . Nobody has ever cheated their way into eternity, into the presence of God. We preachers have the most serious job in the world. It's not to be popular, not to be nice—it's to get people to step out of darkness into the light. Life is short, eternity is long."

On Sunday we had the burial, open only to personal friends. I buried the children in the same coffin with Keith, in the arms of their daddy.

The only consolation I had in the terrible way everyone died was to hear that it was almost certain that they were all knocked unconscious from the impact of the crash and that they didn't suffer in the fire. Leonard spoke again at the funeral, and when it was over, I picked up the first handful of dirt, in Jewish tradition, and threw it into the grave. My mother followed suit, and so did several others as the small crowd dispersed.

Just ten days after Keith and the others went to be with the Lord, the M/V Anastasis was due to dock in southern California after its voyage from Greece. Keith loved the vision of the mercy ship so much that he'd sent them $28,000 to pay for their Panama Canal crossing and provide food for the six-week voyage. Keith planned to greet the ship. I went instead. Leland Paris just "happened" to be on the same flight so we sat together and talked about the future of Last Days.

At the docking ceremony I spoke for about ten minutes along with several others. And as the Anastasis pulled into the docks, Keith's recording of "Holy Holy Holy" was playing over the sound system. It was a very moving moment for everyone.

In the coming days and weeks, talk centered around the impact of Keith's ministry and what it might continue to be. But when the visitors slowed down, in my quiet moments many questions remained. I knew the Lord could tell me anything he wanted me to know. I didn't know if he would. I wasn't going to demand anything from him—but I did ask for any understanding he could give me. Trust was made for the darkness. I resolved to trust God's character, whether I got any insights or not. I knew I'd never have all the answers until I stood before God. Still, I knew people were wondering, why?

Probably one of the biggest questions people asked was, "Why did the plane crash?" Months later after long investigations, the FAA would conclude that the crash occurred because of human error rather than some type of equipment failure. Thinking back, it *had* been a very hot and hectic day. Really, only God knows *exactly* what happened. For me, the question wasn't so much "why?"—because I knew I'd never have a complete answer to that this side of heaven. The question was, what would God do with Keith's ministry now? Would the Lord fulfill the promise of the scripture he had given me?

The scripture that had come to me about the grain of wheat turned out to be very significant. At the same time I'd gotten that scripture at my desk in Texas, God was speaking to someone else on the other side of the world. In Japan, when Loren Cunningham heard the news about Keith, a scripture immediately leapt into his mind, "Unless a grain of wheat falls to the ground and dies. . . ."

It turned out to be far more than a poetic note of comfort. In the months following Keith's death, remarkable reports came from across the country and around the world. Almost at once I was beginning to see how the falling of this one grain of wheat was indeed going to bear fruit.

The Lord touched millions of lives through Keith, and he would be missed. There was a deep grieving that swept through the body of Christ when he died. There was a sobering, too. God took one of his choice servants home at the age of twenty-eight, and it spoke reality to all of us. We have no time guarantees. I wondered if I would have been ready to stand in front of God with no advance warning. A lot of people asked themselves the same question.

Winkie spoke at several summer festivals that year. And every night after he spoke, it was the same. Crowds of young people gathered around him and opened their hearts. Most of them were weeping as they told Winkie, "I've gotten serious with God since Keith died!" . . . "God told me He wanted *me* to shine his light in the darkness!" Lives were being turned around everywhere.

And of course, many told me their reactions when they heard about the crash. One guy I'd never met before told me he was driving in his car when he heard the news on the radio. Stunned, he pulled off to the side of the road and wept. Another fellow I hadn't known told me he took three days off work and grieved as if someone in his family had died. Both said they'd cried out to God, saying, "Lord, who's going to speak to our generation now?" Both got the same answer, "You are."

God was using the pain people were feeling over losing Keith to call them forth. Not to "replace" Keith, because no one can ever be replaced. Keith's unique expression of Jesus was gone. But the void was used to point believers to Jesus. Many realized they'd been cheering Keith on, but the things he was doing or saying could never replace what God wanted *them* to do. Who was going to speak out now? The answer was in Keith's "For Prophets Only" article; "*Every* Christian is called to speak to their generation."

One day, I was sitting in a Dallas coffee shop with our good friend, John Dawson. John brought up the conversation he'd had with Keith about the prophet's test of taking their wide circle of influence and using it for God's bigger purposes.

"John, do you think Keith passed the test?" I asked.

It was quiet for a moment as John studied his hands. Then his face brightened.

"Oh yeah! Of course he did."

"How?"

"Keith was really well known and many people were willing to follow him. But he wasn't going to amass all that power for himself or even for Last Days! He wanted to raise up 100,000 people for short-term missions, and millions of dollars for missions service. And not just for YWAM, but for missions groups everywhere."

"Wow, Keith really did pass the test! He was submitting his ministry to God's larger purposes for reaching the world. I'm so proud of him!"

"I am too," said John. "I am too."

Over the years, I kept hearing wonderful things about Keith from people who knew him and loved him. Of them all, perhaps one of the most precious experiences came one day, almost by accident.

It was the summer of 1987. I was on the east coast to make a guest appearance on a Christian television program. Right next to my waterfront hotel was a little mall with lots of specialty shops. In a few stray moments, I decided to wander over and look around. I ended up in a tiny, little import store.

There was a young girl working there who patiently helped me look at some imported jewelry. She was very thin and delicate looking, which might be why the cross around her neck looked so huge. I wondered if she was a Christian. Then I noticed her faded, blue-jean purse and jacket behind the counter, with several slogan-buttons pinned on them. One of them read "I Love Jesus."

"I'm looking at that cross around your neck," I said. "Are you a Christian?"

Her eyes lit up. "Yes, I am. Are you?"

"Yes. I'm part of a ministry out in Texas."

"Really? What one?"

"Have you ever heard of Last Days Ministries?"

"Last Days? . . . It sounds kind of familiar, but I can't really place it."

"Well, have you ever heard of Keith Green?"

"Keith Green? Oh yes! I love his music. I listen to it all the time."

"Well, I'm Melody. I was married to Keith."

She looked at me in surprise. Then her eyes immediately brimmed with tears.

"*You're* Melody Green? What are you doing out here?"

I told her, and then asked her how long she'd know the Lord.

"I've been a Christian for a year-and-a-half. Keith's music is just about the only music I listen to. I *love* his music. It's changed my life and drawn me closer to the Lord. I sit my friends down who don't know the Lord and say, 'You *have* to hear this song!' I give his tapes away all the time and keep having to buy new ones."

—
284

As we talked I could tell she'd been through some rough times. I could also tell that she was sold out to Jesus. She was new in her faith, but she'd already helped many friends and strangers come into a relationship with the Lord. She had a fire burning in her soul for God—and apparently Keith played, and continued to play, a big part in lighting the flame. As I saw the way her life had been touched by Keith's life, I saw how his ministry continued on. Not before thousands, but in one life.

One precious life.

And wasn't that what it was all about? She thought I was someone special but she had no way of knowing how special she was to me.

Before I left we held hands and prayed while a few customers browsed. As I walked back out into the sunshine and later caught my airplane home, my heart was filled to overflowing with thoughts of the goodness and mercy of God. He had just given me another glimpse of what loving him was all about.

Jesus West Coast. 1982

Rebekah Joy and Rachel Hope. 1988

A S I SIT WRITING THIS IT'S BEEN ALMOST SEVEN YEARS TO THE day since Keith, our children, and the others went to be with the Lord. I started to write this book a few times through those years, but something—or Someone perhaps—always intervened.

Maybe I needed time to heal before I could intentionally reopen the wounds. There was no way around it, my season of grieving was long and painful. But the grace of God carried me through. For me, gratitude helped keep bitterness from my door. The time I had with Keith, Josiah, and Bethany was a precious gift from God, and I'm grateful. I'm also grateful to know the Lord. I can't imagine walking through such a valley without Him.

God looks at death differently than we do. Especially the death of the righteous. The Lord sees it from the other side of the veil. Those who get left behind have one experience—but for those who enter into the presence of the Lord it's a new beginning. It took awhile to see, but God had a new beginning for me, too.

Today, Rachel is six and Rebekah is almost eight. They're happy, bright, and joyful. And they keep me on my toes! Dawn is all grown up and married. Having a family to raise and being part of a busy ministry helped me look to the future. When I focused on what "could have been" I got stuck. But the Lord kept telling me He *still* had a call on my life, even though Keith was gone.

And so, my children have done some of their growing up on "the road". Rachel had her first birthday in Canada, during our two years of Keith Green Memorial Concerts. And Rebekah lost her first tooth in New Jersey while we were at a conference. But recently we've spent the majority of our time in Texas, where we still live in the same hundred-year-old house, and serve the same wonderful Lord.

Now for my "regrets". This book just wasn't big enough to tell all the stories I wanted to tell, or talk about all the great people I wanted to. I was told, "Melody, no one will read a book *that* thick!" So hard choices were made.

It was also hard to pick entries from Keith's volumes of journals. Keith told me I could "do something" with them if anything ever happened to him. "*Edited* of course," Keith said. Some editing was needed either for length of entry, clarity, or privacy. However, no meanings or intents were altered. I believe Keith would have been comfortable with what was printed, since he shared his testimony freely. Keith's family asked to remain unnamed for privacy sake, and I changed some names to protect the privacy of others when "their stories" crossed paths with "ours".

Keith's story is really a reflection of the ongoing message and ministry of Last Days. A lot has happened at LDM, and I'm excited about where the Lord is taking us from here. But I'm getting ahead of myself. Let me fill in the gap between July of 1982 to July of 1989.

During the Memorial Concerts we traveled to 110 cities and spoke to over 300,000 people. Loren Cunningham said, "I don't know of a time in history when more youth were presented a missionary challenge." Operation Mobilization said scores of people came to serve with them as a result. The YWAM training schools were jammed with students (up to fifty percent per class) from 1982 to 1984—and they're still coming. Don Stephens recently told me of a girl who was thirteen when she heard Keith's missions challenge. At twenty, she's now serving on the M/V Anastasis. Only eternity will show the fruit that is still being yielded for the kingdom.

On the home front, we have more people who've come to Texas to serve at Last Days (about 130 currently), more buildings for them to serve in and a bigger more colorful printing press. Americans Against Abortion, the sister ministry we founded in June 1985, continues to educate the public, save babies' lives and spare women the trauma of abortion. But our growth has not just been physical. More importantly, we've continued to grow spiritually.

In 1987, I told Rebekah LDM was going to have a big party to celebrate our tenth birthday. I made a big deal out of it, the way moms do, because I wanted her to get excited. She simply said, "Mom . . . ten years old isn't *that* old." She was only six. She was also right. We're twelve now, but that's hardly all grown up. I'm grateful for how far we've come—and I'm excited as we head forward to some new beginnings!

In order for there to be a "new" beginning, something has to be completed. Completing this book in the seventh year after Keith's death is significant for me and Last Days. In the Bible, the number "seven" symbolizes completion. There are seven notes in a musical scale, seven days in a week, and seven colors in the spectrum. In fact, my actual deadline for this book was July 7th— which is the seventh day of the seventh month of the seventh year. And I'm now reading the final proof on the seven year anniversary of the crash. I didn't plan it that way. It just "happened", and I believe it's a confirmation of God's perfect timing. My hunch is that the Lord has something He wants this generation to gain from Keith's story at this particular time. I hope it will encourage many, not to look to Keith, but to see the call God has on *their* life.

One of the larger messages of this book is this: What God did in Keiths life, He can do in yours! Keith had been a Christian for seven years when he went home. Because of his high profile as a new believer, he did a lot of his growing in the public eye. He didn't have the luxury of years of obscure service so he could emerge in a more "tidy" way. Keith hit like a bombshell. Then left just as suddenly. Perhaps there's something precious to glean from closely observing the strengths and weaknesses of a fellow struggler in the faith. Maybe it's the simple fact that we all have areas of weakness, but God is faithful to use us in the fullest way if we give ourselves totally to Him.

The Lord has already given you gifts to use for Him. Keith's pattern of gifting was easy to see even as a tiny child. That's because some of his gifts were so public. Your giftings may be different than Keith's, but they're just as important. Whether they're "up-front" or "behind-the-scenes" gifts, God wants you to use them for Him! You have an important part to play in this generation. That's why you're living in this time of history.

You have a call on your life and a destiny to fulfill! But to find your purpose for living you first need to be sure you're plugged into the Source of *all* life. That's the most important thing. If you don't already have a relationship with Jesus, I encourage you to open your heart as Keith did. God is knowable. And He is real. God will be faithful to reveal Himself to all who sincerely seek Him. There's not a life that can't be transformed. A heart that cannot be mended. A wound that cannot be healed. I know from personal experience. When we give ourselves to the Lord, He is faithful in all things. And if you already know the Lord, then do what He is calling you to do, with all your heart!

My prayer is that this book will be a part of a new beginning for you in some way. It is for me in several ways. "Seven" is the number of completion but, biblically, "eight" symbolizes the first in a series, or new beginnings. Most immediately, as I enter the eighth year after Keith's death I'll be taking a two-month journey to gain a fresh perspective on the world around us. I'll be going into Asia, Africa, Europe, and the USSR. I hope to return with a fresh missions vision and new ways for LDM to work with others to carry the message of God's love around the world. Please pray that LDM will fulfill our destiny as we approach the year 2000 and beyond. I'll pray that you fulfill yours, too!

May the Lord bless you as you press on to know Him. My address is in the following "we'd like to hear from you" section. I really would love to hear any comments you may have or any ways the Lord touched you through this book. I love you!

Melody Green
July 28, 1989

Memories of Keith
by *Leonard Ravenhill*

William Booth, founder of the Salvation Army, and Keith Green had one thing in common. They both saw the gates of hell. Booth saw them from the outside. Keith saw them from the inside. Keith had been to the bottom of the barrel. He'd felt the horror and the misery. He was a prisoner and nobody could break the chains. But God rescued him! "Religion" couldn't do it. Vows couldn't do it. Psychology couldn't do it. But Jesus did it!

Keith had a radical New Birth experience plus a Baptism of Fire and became a spiritual revolutionary. God took him, cleansed him, occupied him, and anointed him.

Keith hungered to know about those heroes who moved their generation for God and he followed in their steps. He had a holy zeal and a purity I've seen in very few. I don't think Keith was preoccupied with the gospel of Christ as much as he was with the *person* of Christ. I think *that* was his consuming passion. He wasn't just a preacher. He was a crusader. And he poured out the inner passion of his soul through the vibrant lyrics of his songs.

In that great Final Day, many will rise up and call Keith blessed. He bowed his whole being before the One who said, "To bring fire on earth I come," and by Him he was ignited—his heart an altar and God's love the flame.

I'm in my 83rd year, but it doesn't necessarily mean I'm wiser or stronger. It doesn't mean I've done more. It's not the stretch of life that matters. It's the depth of life. It's not how long we live. It's *how* we live. Keith was a man who seemed to live on the edge of eternity. And he was ready to step into it.

It can truly be said of Keith that, "He being dead, yet speaketh." And he will speak right on to the generations beyond us. I wish we had ten thousand people like him. I pray that many will catch a vision from his life—and trust and obey.

The words of my favorite hymn paint a portrait of my dear friend Keith. I thank God Keith ever came my way.

I would the precious time redeem,
And longer live for this alone,
To spend, and to be spent, for them
Who have not yet my Saviour known:
Fully on these my mission prove.
And only breathe, to breathe Thy love.

My talents, gifts, and graces, Lord,
Into Thy blessed hands receive;
And let me live to preach Thy word,
And let me to Thy glory live;
My every sacred moment spend
In publishing the sinners' Friend.

Enlarge, inflame, and fill my heart
With boundless charity divine;
So shall I all my strength exert,
And love them with a zeal like Thine;
And lead them to Thy open side,
The sheep for whom their Shepherd died.

Charles Wesley, 1707-1788

When I sat down to write this book, I had no idea I'd spend nearly a thousand hours typing at my computer. Still, this book was not written alone. Many others played vital roles in making it a reality. Without them, something important would have been missing or left undone. I want to give thanks for the greatest gift on earth besides having a relationship with Jesus Christ—the joy of serving the Lord with family and friends.

With Deep Gratitude To

My mom—*for years of prayer and for loving me through thick and thin as only a mother could.*

Keith's parents—*for your continued love for me and the children. Thanks too for filling in so many details about Keith's childhood.*

Rebekah and Rachel—*for your hugs, kisses, and prayers. And for giving up many fun times "with mommy" while I wrote.*

David Hazard—*for "walking me through" my first book. It was a blessing to collaborate with such an experienced writer and editor extraordinaire. I couldn't have done it without you!*

My faithful family at Last Days Ministries—*for standing with me in love, encouragement, and support. And for your long days and nights of "storming the Throne" for me and this book project. I am also grateful to all my friends across the nation who prayed, including those I won't meet this side of eternity. I believe God answered your prayers.*

Debbie Schneider—*for having such a servant's heart and helping to keep me and the household "in running order!" And to Pat Strumsky, Jill Bryant, Lori Andrews, and Kim Basinger—for keeping me and the kids "fed, warm, and alive!" during various stages of this book.*

Bob Ayala, Wayne Dillard, and Del Tucker—*for your friendship, love, and support. I appreciate your willingness to carry so many extra responsibilities while I "disappeared to write."*

Leonard and Martha Ravenhill, and Winkie and Fae Pratney—*for pouring your lives, your prayers, and your hearts into Keith and me and Last Days Ministries. You have made a difference in my life! Thank you too, Leonard and Winkie for your powerful and moving reflections about Keith.*

Loren and Darlene Cunningham, Leland and Fran Paris, Don and Deyon Stephens, Floyd and Sally McClung, John and Julie Dawson, and the rest of my Youth With A Mission family—*for your input on this book and for years of steadfast support and encouragement.*

Kathleen Dillard—*for stacks of encouraging notes.*

Bill Maxwell—*for your friendship and your continued care in stewarding "the sounds" of Keith's music.*

Kim Basinger, Cynthia Brown, Brian Byrd, Carol DeGraff, Margaret Farmer, Brenda Gadd, Kim Geiger, Chloe Lovejoy, Mark Handel, Janine Newman, Steve Quinn, Rose Tucker, Francine Weisberg, and Randy Welch—*for countless hours of typing, transcribing, fact finding, photo sorting, computer expertise, and practical assistance.*

Bill Hearn, Barbara Hearn, Billy Ray Hearn and the rest of the folks at Sparrow Press—*for having a big vision for this book and for your commitment to quality. Thanks too, for living on "the edge of the unknown" with me while I raced toward the deadline.*

Michelle Brandes, Todd Fishkind, Peter and Cag Granet, Steve and Nelly Greisen, Kenn Gulliksen, Buck and Annie Herring, Janet Stabler, Randy Stonehill, and many others—*for graciously allowing me to mix a tiny part of your story in with Keith's.*

Rich Boyer and Mark Lanier—*for giving so freely of yourselves to work through details and contract matters. I appreciate your generous hearts to serve.*

Ed and Cathi Basler—*for "flowers from the moon" and other assorted goodies. You kept me laughing!*

Erik Burmeister, Carol Campbell, Betty Daffin, Matthew Porter, Pam Warren, and Randy Welch—*for tackling the whole manuscript on short notice to give me your comments from a reader's perspective.*

Larry DeGraff—*for such a powerful portrait of Keith.*

And special gratitude to Fred Markert—*for constant encouragement, support, and sacrifice—above and beyond the call of duty! Your contributions spanned so many areas it would be impossible to list them all—but I am exceedingly grateful for your servant's heart and all you did to help make this book a reality.*

And most importantly, I want to thank the Lord Jesus Christ for His goodness and mercy to me. Without the grace of God, His resurrection power, and His faithfulness, this book would not have been possible.

ALL ABOUT LAST DAYS MINISTRIES

Just as Keith's music continues as an inheritance to this generation, so does Last Days Ministries and its many areas of outreach. Today, Melody Green is president of Last Days Ministries and director of its pro-life arm, Americans Against Abortion.

We at LDM are committed to the Lord Jesus, to each other, and to reaching the world with God's love. We try to use the most effective means available to communicate the Lord's heart to a hurting world.

The Last Days Magazine is published quarterly and sent to hundreds of thousands worldwide. It's filled with colorful articles to encourage believers in their faith. We've heard many stories of changed lives because of the ministry received from articles written by people like—Keith Green, Leonard Ravenhill, Loren Cunningham, David Wilkerson, Brother Andrew, Winkie Pratney, John Dawson, George Verwer, Melody Green, and others. Tracts, audio, and video teachings by these and other Christian leaders are available in our Ministry Materials Catalog. And the Lord has really blessed our literature ministry—to date we've printed and mailed over 59 million tracts!

In 1985 we produced the *Keith Green Memorial Concert Video*. It includes a 25-minute excerpt from one of Keith's last concerts, plus Melody's account of the crash and God's mercy since then. Over 5,000 have been distributed all over the world.

Last Days Ministries also plays a vital pro-life role. In 1978 Keith asked Melody to write about abortion. The article was entitled *Children, Things We Throw Away?* Over 14 million have been distributed world-wide and it laid the foundation for LDM's pro-life arm—Americans Against Abortion, founded in 1985. In 1987, Melody Green presented President Reagan with the AAA Petition for Life, signed by almost three million people! And in 1989 she took the petition to the Supreme Court. We continue to provide tracts, videos, and other educational tools for those concerned about life.

Another key ministry of LDM is The Intensive Christian Training School (ICT). Since 1982 we've equipped over 1,000 believers for further ministry at home and abroad. ICT was designed to be a powerful time of learning about the character of God and to help Christians enter into a more intimate relationship with the Lord.

Well, that was a quick whirl around Last Days. We hope it gives you some idea of what we're all about! All in all, we are grateful for God's faithfulness. He has helped us every step of the way, and we look to Him as we look towards the future. If there's any further information you'd like, or any way we can serve you, don't hesitate to write us at the address at the end of the next section. We love you in the Lord!

Your Brothers and Sisters at Last Days

WE'D LIKE TO HEAR FROM YOU!!

All of us at Last Days would like to serve you in any way we can. If Keith's story has challenged you to a deeper Christian walk, or inspired you to find out more about being a Christian, please write and let us know. We'd love to hear from you!

Get Four Free issues of the Last Days Magazine!

We'd like to send you four gift issues to get acquainted! After that, if you like it you can continue to receive it by subscribing. But if you can't afford the small subscription price, we'll send it to you for "whatever you can afford."

Would you like to know more about being a Christian?

We have some information we'd like to send you. There's no charge or obligation—and we won't come knocking on your door either! Just ask for the free packet, "Walking With Jesus."

Keith Green's Music and The Keith Green Memorial Concert in the Free LDM Ministry Materials Catalog all for "whatever you can afford!"

If you haven't heard Keith's music, you need to! His musical genius and love for God will move you in a deep way. Our catalog has all of Keith's music as well as dozens of dynamic audio and video teachings by many of the people you've read about in this book—and many others! We also have powerful pro-life teachings and T-shirts, scores of challenging tracts, and music by several different artists. All of our ministry materials are available for "whatever you can afford" so those who cannot afford the suggested price can still receive ministry. Request the free LDM Ministry Materials Catalog. Updated twice a year!

Free Sample Packs of Tracts Including Articles by Keith Green and Melody Green

If you would like a free packet of some of our most ordered tracts just request a "Free Sample Pack" or a "Free Pro-Life Pack" or both!

Intensive Christian Training School

A life changing 10 weeks set aside to learn more about personal holiness and intimacy with the Lord. Write for information or application.

You may also request a list of Mission Opportunities

Address *all* requests to:
Last Days Ministries P.O. Box 40
Lindale, Texas 75771 214-963-8671

THE KEITH GREEN DISCOGRAPHY

FOR HIM WHO HAS EARS TO HEAR
Produced by Bill Maxwell and Keith Green
Released May 20, 1977
Available on record and cassette (Sparrow Records)

NO COMPROMISE
Produced by Bill Maxwell and Keith Green
Released November 9, 1978
Available on record and cassette (Sparrow Records)

SO YOU WANNA GO BACK TO EGYPT
Produced by Bill Maxwell and Keith Green
Released May 7, 1980
Available on record and cassette (Pretty Good Records)

THE KEITH GREEN COLLECTION
Produced by Bill Maxwell
Released August 11, 1981
Available on record and cassette (Sparrow Records)

SONGS FOR THE SHEPHERD
Produced by Bill Maxwell and Keith Green
Released April 12, 1982
Available on record and cassette (Pretty Good Records)

I ONLY WANT TO SEE YOU THERE
Produced by Bill Maxwell
Released March 21, 1983
Available on cassette (Sparrow Records)

THE PRODIGAL SON
Produced by Bill Maxwell and Melody Green
Released August 15, 1983
Available on record and cassette (Pretty Good Records)

JESUS COMMANDS US TO GO
Produced by Bill Maxwell
Released July 20, 1984
Available on record and cassette (Pretty Good Records)

THE MINISTRY YEARS
1977-1979
Volume 1
Produced by Bill Maxwell
Released October 23, 1987
Available on 2 double length cassettes and 2 compact discs with commemorative booklet (Sparrow Records)

THE MINISTRY YEARS
1980-1982
Volume 2
Produced by Bill Maxwell
Released October 18, 1988
Available on 2 double length cassettes and 2 compact discs with commemorative booklet (Sparrow Records)

Also Available:
THE MINISTRY YEARS 1977-1979
   Volume 1 Songbook
THE MINISTRY YEARS 1980-1982
   Volume 2 Songbook

For more information, write to
   Sparrow Records
   9255 Deering Ave., P.O. Box 2120
   Chatsworth, CA 91311